1991 *Wilton* YEARBOOK
Cake Decorating!

P9-ARW-702

Cakes for Special Occasions

Decorator's Mini Course

Products

Credits

Creative Director .... Richard Tracy
Copy Director .... Marie DeBenedictis
Copywriters .... Linda Skender
                           Marita Seiler
Production Coordinator ..... Mary Stahulak
Photography .... Jeff Carter
                           Thomas Zamiar
Photography Assistant ...... Michelle Asher
Design/Production ....RNB Graphics

Senior Cake Decorator .....Susan Matusiak
Cake Decorators .... Mary Gavenda
                           Nancy Guerine
                           Corky Kagay
                           Sandra Mueller O'Toole
                           Steve Rocco

Birthdays

For ages 1 to 100, you'll find whimsical, witty and wonderful ways to wish special people all the joy in the world!

CLOWN DOLLS

- Mini Gingerbread Boy Pan, p. 189
- Tips 3, 16, 67, p. 134-136
- Golden Yellow, Orange, Christmas Red, Black Icing Colors, p. 126
- Poured Fondant, Buttercream Icing

- Place cakes on a rack over a pan to catch excess. Pour fondant icing on cakes; let set.
- With buttercream, pipe tip 3 dot eyes, cheeks and outline mouths. Add tip 16 pull-out star or rosette hair.
- Edge suits with tip 16 zigzags or tip 67 ruffles. Trim with tip 3 dots or tip 16 star buttons. *Each serves 1-2.*

DANDY CANDY TIERS

- 8 & 12 in. Round Pans, p. 168
- Tips 3, 17, 21, p. 134-135
- Leaf Green, Lemon Yellow, Orange, Pink Icing Colors, p. 126

- 10 in. Round Separator Plates, p. 166
- 3 in. Grecian Pillars, p. 164
- Cake Circles, Fanci-Foil Wrap, p. 132-133
- Dowel Rods, p. 164
- Numeral Candle, p. 140
- Cake Dividing Set, p. 130
- Buttercream Icing
- Candy-coated chocolates, candy sticks, round hard candy, candy-coated mini gum squares, wrapping paper

- Cover pillars with wrapping paper. Prepare 2-layer cakes for pillar construction (see p. 106). Edge separator plate on 12 in. tier with tip 17 scallops. Using Cake Dividing set, dot mark 8 in. sides into 8ths; 12 in. into 12ths. Connect marks with tip 21 white zigzag garlands (skip 2 or more front marks on 8 in. side depending on length of name.) Trim garlands with 4 rows of tip 3 zigzags in coordinating colors.
- Break candy sticks into 2 in. pieces for sides of 8 in. cake. Position sticks between garlands.
- Edge tops with tip 21 zigzag borders; bases with tip 21 rosette borders. Trim rosettes with tip 3 dots. Attach candy trims with dots of icing. (Change candy-trim number to any age.) Position candle. Assemble 8 in. cake on pillars. *Serves 48.*

THE CIRCUS EXPRESS

- Little Train Pan, p. 175
- Tips 3, 16, p. 134-135
- Pink, Lemon Yellow, Orange, Brown, Leaf Green Icing Colors, p. 126
- Buttercream Icing
- Animal cookies, candy-coated chocolates, candy disc

- Ice background areas, cab window, front of engine, cage and message area on car smooth. Position "animals" on car and candy disc face in window.
- Outline smokestack, cab, front of engine, cowcatcher, brake shaft, puff of smoke, wheels, roof, sides and bars on car with tip 3 strings. Pipe tip 3 dot eyes, outline mouth and hair.
- Pipe in headlight, puff of smoke and openings on cowcatcher with tip 3 (smooth with finger dipped in cornstarch). Trim headlight with tip 16 stripe. Fill in edge of cowcatcher with tip 16 zigzags. Cover engine and car (top and sides) with tip 16 stars.
- Print tip 3 message and number. Add candy trim to engine. *Serves 12.*

BIRTHDAYS

Big Top Treats

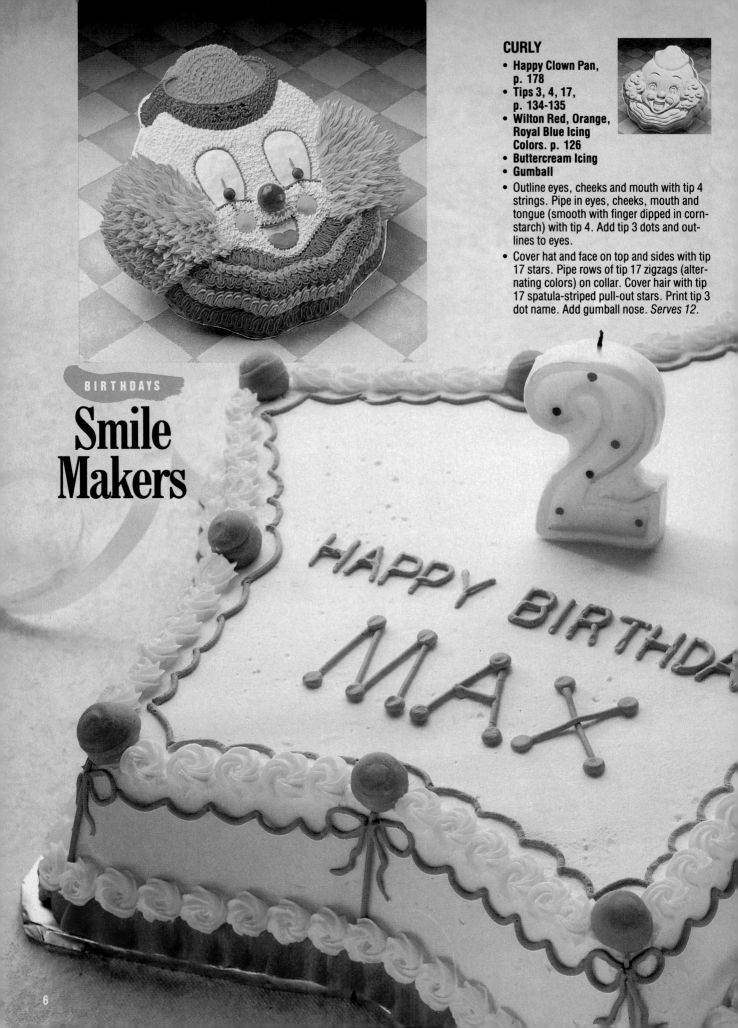

CURLY

- **Happy Clown Pan,** p. 178
- **Tips 3, 4, 17,** p. 134-135
- **Wilton Red, Orange, Royal Blue Icing Colors. p. 126**
- **Buttercream Icing**
- **Gumball**

- Outline eyes, cheeks and mouth with tip 4 strings. Pipe in eyes, cheeks, mouth and tongue (smooth with finger dipped in cornstarch) with tip 4. Add tip 3 dots and outlines to eyes.

- Cover hat and face on top and sides with tip 17 stars. Pipe rows of tip 17 zigzags (alternating colors) on collar. Cover hair with tip 17 spatula-striped pull-out stars. Print tip 3 dot name. Add gumball nose. *Serves 12.*

Smile Makers

STAR SHINE

- **Shining Star Pan, p. 174**
- **Tips 3, 16, 10, 104, p. 134-138**
- **Lemon Yellow, Royal Blue, Wilton Red Icing Colors, p. 126**
- **Number Candle, p. 144**
- **Buttercream Icing**

- Ice cake smooth. Print tip 3 message on top.
- Pipe tip 10 ball balloons and tip 16 rosettes on cake top. Pipe tip 3 outline scallops, balloon strings and bows on sides.
- Edge base with tip 104 ruffle border. Trim ruffle with tip 16 rosettes. Position candle. *Serves 12.*

TEDDY BEAR TWINS

- **11 x 15 in. Sheet Pan, p. 169**
- **Tips 2, 13, 17, 48, 225, 349, p. 134-137**
- **Royal Blue, Lemon Yellow, Wilton Red Icing Colors, p. 126**
- **Teddy Bear Cookie Cutter Set, p. 124**
- **Buttercream Icing**

- Make 50 tip 225 drop flowers with tip 2 dot centers.
- Ice cake smooth. Using running and sitting bear cookie cutters, imprint guidelines (overlap as shown). Outline with tip 2 strings. Pipe in eyes, noses and build up paws with tip 2 (smooth with finger dipped in cornstarch). Add tip 2 dots on bottom of paws. Cover bears and background area with tip 13 stars.
- Print tip 2 message. Position flowers and pipe tip 2 outline vines. Add tip 349 leaves. Cover sides with rows of tip 48 ribbed basketweave. Edge top with tip 17 shell border. *Serves 20.*

BRIGHT SIGHT BEAR

- **Huggable Bear Pan, p. 178**
- **Tips 3, 16, 19, p. 134-135**
- **Wilton Red, Royal Blue, Lemon Yellow Icing Colors, p. 126**
- **Number Cookie Cutter Set, p. 124**
- **Buttercream Icing**

- Ice tummy smooth. With cookie cutter, imprint number on tummy. Outline ears, face, paws, number and tummy with tip 3 strings.
- Pipe in eyes and nose with tip 3 (smooth with finger dipped in cornstarch). Print tip 3 name.
- Cover ears, face, paws and body on top and sides with stars – tip 16 for yellow areas, tip 19 for white stars. Edge base with tip 16 rosette border (alternating colors). Trim with tip 16 stars. *Serves 12.*

BEAT IT!

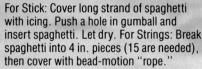

- 8 in. Round Pan, p. 168
- Tips 3, 9, 18, p. 134-135
- Orange, Golden Yellow, Red Red Icing Colors, p. 126
- Meringue Powder, p. 127
- Star Cookie Cutter Set, p. 125
- Message Pattern Press, p. 130
- Cake Dividing Set, p. 130
- Numeral Candle, p. 144
- Buttercream, Royal Icings
- Uncooked spaghetti, large gumball

- For Drum Stick & Strings (see p. 104): Use uncooked spaghetti, royal icing and tip 3.

For Stick: Cover long strand of spaghetti with icing. Push a hole in gumball and insert spaghetti. Let dry. For Strings: Break spaghetti into 4 in. pieces (15 are needed), then cover with bead-motion "rope."

- Ice 2-layer cake smooth. Using Cake Dividing Set, dot mark sides into 12ths. With 2½ in. star cutter, imprint guidelines on sides. With message press, imprint message on cake top.

- Print message with tip 3. Outline stars with tip 3 strings. Fill in with tip 18 stars.

- Edge top and base with tip 18 zigzag borders. Position spaghetti drum strings on sides (ends will meet between each star). Trim ends with tip 9 balls. Position drum stick and candle on cake top. *Serves 12.*

SHAGGY DOG

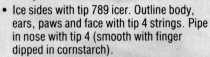

- Puppy Pan, p. 182
- Tips 4, 233, 789, p. 134-139
- Black Icing Color, p. 126
- Buttercream Icing
- Party hat and blower

- Ice sides with tip 789 icer. Outline body, ears, paws and face with tip 4 strings. Pipe in nose with tip 4 (smooth with finger dipped in cornstarch).

- Beginning with paws, cover dog with row upon row of tip 233 pull-out hair (strands should be long for a shaggy effect).

- Edge base with tip 233 pull-out grass border.

- Position hat and party blower. *Serves 12.*

Party Cakes

STRIKE UP
THE BAND

- Long Loaf Pan, p. 172
- Tips 2, 3, 7, p. 134
- Orange, Royal Blue, Lemon Yellow, Leaf Green Icing Colors, p. 126
- '91 Pattern Book (Xylophone Bars Pattern), p. 117
- Color Flow Mix, Meringue Powder, p. 127
- Dowel Rods, p. 165
- Buttercream, Color Flow, Royal Icings
- Black shoestring licorice, large gumball, sugar cubes

- For Bars: With color flow icing and tip 2, outline Xylophone Bar Pattern and flow in with thinned icing (see p. 108). Twelve bars are needed – three of each color (make extras in case of breakage). Let dry. Cut sugar cubes in half and attach to backs of bars with dots of royal icing. Let dry.
- Ice cake smooth. Position licorice string tracks on top (I in. from edge). Print tip 3 dot message on side. Edge base with tip 7 Musical Notes Border, (see p. 104).
- Position bars I in. apart. Pipe tip 7 royal icing dots on ends of bars. Position candles.
- For Hammer: Push a hole in gumball and insert dowel rod. *Serves 12.*

HAPPY BIRTHDAY
CUPCAKES

- Six-Cup Muffin Pan, p. 172
- Tip 2, p. 134
- Orange, Golden Yellow, Leaf Green Icing Colors, p. 126
- Light Cocoa Candy Melts™*, p. 119
- Numbers and Alphabet Molds, p. 121
- Buttercream Icing

- To mold candy: Fill appropriate molds with melted coating. Let set and unmold. (See Candy Making, p. 109).
- Ice cupcakes smooth. Place letters and number on cupcakes. Trim candy with tip 2 icing beads.

*brand confectionery coating

BLOOMING BEAUTY

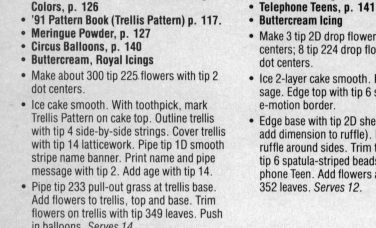

- 10 in. Square Pans, p. 169
- Tips 1D, 2, 4, 14, 225, 233, 349, p. 134-137
- Pink, Lemon Yellow, Leaf Green Icing Colors, p. 126
- '91 Pattern Book (Trellis Pattern) p. 117.
- Meringue Powder, p. 127
- Circus Balloons, p. 140
- Buttercream, Royal Icings

- Make about 300 tip 225 flowers with tip 2 dot centers.
- Ice cake smooth. With toothpick, mark Trellis Pattern on cake top. Outline trellis with tip 4 side-by-side strings. Cover trellis with tip 14 latticework. Pipe tip 1D smooth stripe name banner. Print name and pipe message with tip 2. Add age with tip 14.
- Pipe tip 233 pull-out grass at trellis base. Add flowers to trellis, top and base. Trim flowers on trellis with tip 349 leaves. Push in balloons. *Serves 14.*

FRILLY DILLY

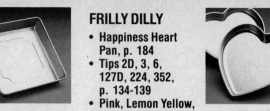

- Happiness Heart Pan, p. 184
- Tips 2D, 3, 6, 127D, 224, 352, p. 134-139
- Pink, Lemon Yellow, Leaf Green Icing Colors, p. 126
- Telephone Teens, p. 141
- Buttercream Icing

- Make 3 tip 2D drop flowers with tip 6 dot centers; 8 tip 224 drop flowers with tip 3 dot centers.
- Ice 2-layer cake smooth. Print tip 3 message. Edge top with tip 6 spatula-striped e-motion border.
- Edge base with tip 2D shells (piped first to add dimension to ruffle). Pipe tip 127D ruffle around sides. Trim top of ruffle with tip 6 spatula-striped beads. Position Telephone Teen. Add flowers and trim with tip 352 leaves. *Serves 12.*

ENCHANTED CASTLE

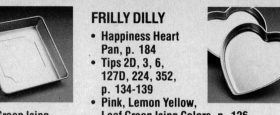

- Angel Food Pan, p. 173
- Tips 1, 5, 55, 104, p. 134-138
- Pink Icing Color, p. 126
- '91 Pattern Book (Castle Windows), p. 117
- Tree Formers, p. 128
- Fanci-Foil Wrap, p. 132
- Buttercream Icing
- Sugar cubes, toothpicks

- For spire: Cover tree former with Fanci-Foil. Cut flag out of foil. Tape to toothpick and glue onto spire. Add tip 5 dot on top of flag pole. Make four spires. For windows: Using Castle Window Pattern, cut 4 to 6 windows out of Fanci-Foil.
- Ice cake smooth. Edge center circle and top edge with tip 5 bead border. Place sugar cubes around bead borders.
- Press Fanci-Foil windows onto cake sides. Outline sides and top of window with tip 1 strings. With tip 1 pipe lattice trim on windows. Add tip 1 bead window "sills"
- Write message with tip 55. Trim capital letters with tip 1 beadwork. Edge base with tip 104 sweet pea border. *Serves 12.*

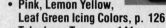

BIRTHDAYS

Pretty in Pink

Yo Ho Ho!

TREASURED CHEST

- 7 x 11 in. Sheet Pan, p. 169
- Tips 3, 16, p. 134-135
- Golden Yellow, Brown Icing Colors, p. 126
- Decorating Comb, p. 130
- '91 Pattern Book (Treasure Chest Patterns), p. 117
- Meringue Powder, p. 127
- Cake Boards, Fanci-Foil Wrap, p. 132-133
  - Birthday Candles, p. 144
  - Buttercream, Royal Icings
  - Candy coins, mini chocolate bars

- Ice 3-layer cake smooth (top yellow, sides brown). Use Decorating Comb to make ribbed effect on chest sides.
- *To make chest lid:* Cut cake board into 11 x 13 in. shape. Cover with Fanci-Foil. With royal icing, ice "open" lid area of board. With toothpick, mark Lettering Pattern. Print tip 3 letters. Edge lid with tip 16 star border and corner C-scrolls. Push lid against back of cake (if necessary, add more buttercream icing to cake until lid is secure). *To make chest lining:* Cut cake board 9 x 5 in. and cover with Fanci-Foil Wrap.
- With toothpick, mark Lock Pattern on front; Handle Pattern on each side. Outline keyhole and lock with tip 3 string. Pipe in keyhole (smooth with finger dipped in cornstarch). Fill in lock with tip 16 stars. Pipe tip 16 scrolls on each corner and handle brackets. Use tip 10 for handle pulls and rim on chest.
- Position "lining" and candies on chest. Pipe tip 16 star candle holders on cake and push in candles. *Serves 30.*

WHERE IT'S AT!

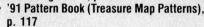

- 11 x 15 in. Sheet Pan, p. 169
- Tips 4, 8, 21, 352, p. 134-136
- Brown, Ivory, Black, Kelly Green, Sky Blue Icing Colors, p. 126
- '91 Pattern Book (Treasure Map Patterns), p. 117
- Meringue Powder, p. 127
- Gone Fishin' Sign Board, p. 142
- Piping Gel, p. 127
- Buttercream & Royal or Snow-White Buttercream Icings
- Granulated light brown sugar, gold foiled chocolates or gum, pretzel sticks, graham crackers

- With royal or snow-white buttercream icing, figure pipe Skull Pattern on waxed paper with tip 8 (see p. 105). Pipe tip 4 patch, dot eye, nose and outline mouth.
- *For ship:* Cut corners from one end of two graham cracker rectangles. With royal or snow-white buttercream icing, generously ice one side and sandwich crackers together. Ice top of crackers and cover sides with tip 21 stripes. Push in pretzel stick sail posts and cannons. Cut Sail Patterns from '91 Pattern Book and attach to pretzels with dots of icing.
- *For map cake:* Ice cake smooth – top ivory, sides brown. With toothpick, mark Map Pattern on cake top. Outline water with tip 4 strings. Fill in water with tip 4 blue tinted piping gel. Sprinkle "land" with brown sugar. Edge top with tip 4 bead border. Pipe tip 21 zigzag border at base.
- Print tip 4 message on signboard. Position ships, skull, sign and candy coins on top and sides. For trees: Pipe tip 352 royal icing leaf clusters on pretzel sticks. Push randomly into top. *Serves 20.*

SHIP AHOY MATE

- Jolly Santa Pan, p. 189
- Tips 3, 6, 16, 18, 21, p. 134-135
- Royal Blue, Copper, Black, Brown Icing Colors, p. 126
- '91 Pattern Book (Pirate Pattern), p. 117
- Buttercream Icing

- Ice face smooth. With toothpick, mark Pirate Pattern on face. Outline eye, patch and cap with tip 3 strings.
- Pipe in eye with tip 3 (smooth with finger dipped in cornstarch). Add tip 3 dot pupil in eye. Pipe tip 6 ball nose and outline lip.
- Cover patch and cap with tip 16 stars. With spatula- striped icing, pipe tip 21 elongated shell eyebrows and pull-out stripe mustache; tip 18 reverse shell beard. Cover pompon with tip 16 pull-out stars. *Serves 12.*

Go ahead, make their day! Your kid will be the star of the class when you bake and decorate these clever treats for them to pass.

FAST FOODS
- 10½ x 15½ in. Jelly Roll Pan, p. 172
- Tips 1A, 3, 12, 104, p. 134-138
- Brown, Golden Yellow, Leaf Green, Wilton Red* Icing Colors, p. 126
- Round Cookie Cutters, p. 125
- Buttercream Icing
- Tinted coconut
- Pour half the batter from one 2-layer cake mix into greased jelly roll pan. Bake for approximately 10 minutes. Remove from pan. Repeat procedure with remaining batter. When cakes are cooled, cut into 2½ in. circles with round cutter. If not decorating immediately, wrap cake in plastic to hold in freshness. After decorating allow icing to set, then wrap securely.

*Be sure to use Wilton red. It has no aftertaste!

Hamburger
- You'll need 2 yellow and 1 chocolate circles of cake. Pipe tip 104 ruffle "lettuce" (even with edge of cake). Position chocolate cake "meat." Pipe tip 12 red outline "ketchup." Top with yellow cake "bun."

Hot dog
- Slice yellow cake round in half. Pipe tip red 12 hot dog. Trim with tip 3 yellow zigzag "mustard."

Tostada
- Pipe icing on top of cake round with tip 12 (flatten with finger dipped in cornstarch). Pat with green and yellow tinted coconut.

Taco
- Slice yellow cake round in half. Pipe tip 12 brown "meat." Sprinkle with green and yellow tinted coconut.

MONSTER SANDWICHES
- 10½ x 15½ in. Jelly Roll Pan, p. 172
- Tips 1A, 3, p. 134
- Buttercream Icing
- Cut circles of chocolate and yellow cake as per Fast Food directions.
- Pipe icing filling with tip 1A. Add tip 1A dot white eyeballs and tip 3 red dot pupils.

BIG TOP CLOWNS
- Mini Ball Pan, p. 180
- Pink, Lemon Yellow Icing Colors, p. 126
- Derby Clowns, p. 140
- Buttercream Icing
- Tinted Coconut
- Ice "bodies" pink or desired color. Pat with coconut. Push a Derby Clown into each cake.

HAPPY FACES
- Mini Ball Pan, p. 180
- Pink, Golden Yellow, Brown Icing Colors, p. 126
- Candy-coated chocolates, shoestring licorice, coconut
- Ice cakes pink, yellow or brown. Tint coconut for hair. Add candy-coated chocolate eyes and nose; shoestring licorice mouth; coconut hair.

BITE-SIZE MICE
- Egg Mini-Cake Pan, p. 186
- Light Cocoa Candy Melts™*, p. 119
- Candy-coated chewy candies, shoestring licorice
- Place cakes on a rack over a drip pan. Pour Candy Melts over cakes. Push wafers of Candy Melts into cake for ears. Attach dot facial features, shoestring licorice whiskers and tail with dots of melted candy.

TERRIFIC TURTLES
- Egg Mini-Cake Pan, p. 186
- Light Cocoa Candy Melts, p. 119
- Tip 3, p. 134
- Buttercream Icing
- Attach marshmallows (large for head, mini for feet and tail) with buttercream icing. Place cakes on a rack over a drip pan. Pour Candy Melts over cake. Let set. With a cut bag and melted candy, pipe outlines on shell. Pipe tip 3 icing facial features.

LITTLE LADYBUGS
- Egg Mini-Cake Pan, p. 186
- Pink Candy Melts™*, Candy Colors Kit, p. 119
- Chocolate chips, shoestring licorice
- Tint Candy Melts red. Pour over 3/4 of cake. Score candy with a spatula. Add chocolate chip spots and licorice antennae. Let set.

FUZZY BEE
- Egg Mini-Cake Pan, p. 186
- Tip 233, p. 134
- Golden Yellow, Brown Icing Colors, p. 126
- Buttercream Icing
- Cinnamon candy, shoestring licorice, vanilla wafer cookies
- Cover cake with tip 233 pull-out hair. Add candy eyes; licorice mouth and stinger; cookie wings (cut about 1/3 off).

*brand confectionery coating

Little Darlings

THRILLS 'N GILLS

- **First 'n Ten Football Pan, p. 181**
- **Tips 2, 6, 21, p. 134**
- **Orange, Black Icing Colors, p. 126**
- **'91 Pattern Book (Fish Patterns), p. 117**
- **Color Flow Mix, p. 127**
- **Birthday Candles, p. 144**
- **Buttercream Icing, Color Flow**

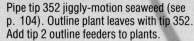

- **For Fins & Tail:** Using color flow icing, outline Fish Patterns with tip 2. Flow in using a cut bag and thinned icing. (See p. 108 for Color Flow.) Let dry.
- With toothpick, mark remaining Fish Patterns on cake (ice areas for easier marking). Outline eye and mouth with tip 6 strings. Pipe in eye (smooth with finger dipped in cornstarch) and add dot pupil with tip 6. Add tip 6 bead heart tongue (flatten with finger dipped in cornstarch).
- Cover cake with tip 21 stars. Write tip 2 name. Pipe tip 6 dot spots.
- Just before serving time, gently push color flow fins and tail in cake. Push in candles. *Serves 12.*

"TANKS" FOR THE MEMORIES

- **11 x 15 in. Sheet Pan, p. 169**
- **Tips 2, 2B, 3, 13, 47, 233, 352, 363, p. 134-139**
- **Black, Kelly Green, Orange, Sky Blue, Ivory Icing Colors, p. 126**
- **Decorator's Brush, p. 130**
- **Piping Gel, p. 127**
- **Sea Friends Cookie Cutter Set, p. 124**
- **Message Pattern Press Set, p. 130**
- **Buttercream Icing**

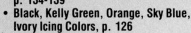

- Ice bottom side of tank black, water area on cake top and sides blue, aquarium stones on cake top green. With fish cutter, mark 3 goldfish on water. Outline with tip 3. Cover with tip 13 stars. Pipe in eyes, trim tail with dots and add outline lashes. Imprint message with message press. Print tip 3 message.
- Outline top with smooth stripes – sides and top with tip 47, bottom with tip 2B. Edge base around sides and top with tip 47. With toothpick, mark seaweed and plants.
- Pipe tip 352 jiggly-motion seaweed (see p. 104). Outline plant leaves with tip 352. Add tip 2 outline feeders to plants.
- For seashells: Spatula-stripe ivory icing with orange. Pipe 5 tip 13 pull-out stars to form starfish. With tip 363, pipe shells randomly. Add tip 363 e-motion snail shells. For sea urchins: Pipe tip 233 pull-out spikes. Trim fish with tip 2 piping gel dot bubbles. *Serves 20.*

GIGGLEPUS

- **Sports Ball Pan, p. 181**
- **12 in. Round Pans, p. 168**
- **Tips 1, 2A, 3, 6, 16, 18, p. 134-135**
- **Sky Blue, Orange, Kelly Green Icing Colors, p. 126**
- **'91 Pattern Book (Octopus Pattern), p. 117**
- **Message Pattern Press Set, p. 130**
- **Piping Gel, p. 127**
- **Birthday Candles, p. 144**
- **Dowel Rods, p. 165**
- **Cake Circles, Fanci-Foil Wrap, p. 132-133**
- **Buttercream Icing**

- Ice 2-layer round cake smooth. Cut and position 3 dowel rods where ball cake will go. With knife, slice off rounded side on one half of ball cake so it sits level and place on a cake circle cut to fit. Position atop round and ice top smooth. Add other half of ball. Push a sharpened dowel rod down through both cakes.
- Lightly ice face area on ball. With toothpick, mark Octopus Face Pattern. Outline mouth with tip 3. Cover ball cake with tip 16 stars. Pipe in tip 6 whites of eyes, dot pupils, nose, cheeks and tongue (shaped and flatten with finger dipped in cornstarch). Add tip 3 dot irises to eyes. Pipe tip 6 elongated bead brows. Mark 8 legs on top of round cake. Figure pipe with tip 2A. Trim with tip 3 dots.

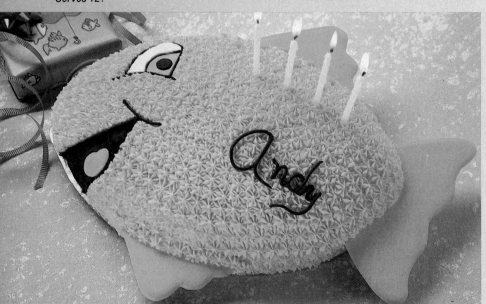

- Imprint message on side with message pattern press. Cover message with tip 3 dots. Outline number and name with tip 6.
- Mark seaweed randomly on sides. Outline with tip 3 strings. For fish bodies: Pipe tip 6 beads randomly on sides. Trim with tip 1 dot eyes and tip 3 outline tails. Add tip 3 tinted piping gel dot bubbles.
- With tip 18 and spatula-striped icing, edge top of round cake with reverse shell borders; base with swirled shells. Push candles into legs. *Serves 48.*

Waves Of Fun

PARTY PALS

- Candy Melts™ *–White, Light Cocoa, p. 119
- Variety of Lollipop II Mold, p. 120
- Tips 1, 3, 4, 13, p. 134-135
- Wilton Red, Royal Blue, Golden Yellow, Kelly Green, Black, Brown Icing Colors, p. 126
- Lollipop Sticks, p. 118
- Royal Icing

- Mold lollipops (see p. 109). Let set.
- Place lollipops on waxed paper to decorate. With royal icing, figure pipe (see p. 105) heads with tip 4, body, arms, legs and shoes with tip 3, hair with tip 13. Use tip 1 to add facial features, fingers, trims on clothes and hair, print names and edge with outline borders.

*brand confectionery coating

JUNGLE SAFARI

- Horseshoe Pan, p. 182
- Tips 1, 2A, 3, 7, 12, 13, 70, 104, 224, 223, p. 134-138
- Kelly Green, Black, Golden Yellow, Christmas Red, Brown Icing Colors, p. 126
- Piping Gel, p. 127
- Cake Board, Fanci-Foil Wrap, p. 132-133
- Buttercream & Royal Icings
- Pretzel rods

- Figure pipe animals with royal icing (see p. 105). Use tips 1, 3, 12, 233 for gorilla; tips 1, 3, 12, 13 for pair of lions; tips 1, 2A, 3, 12, 104 for elephants. Let dry.
- Make 40 tip 224 drop flowers with tip 3 dot centers.
- Ice cake (pat with spatula for a natural effect) on foil-covered cake board. Ice board

in the center with tinted piping gel. Pipe tip 70 upright, elongated leaves on sides. For palm trees (use stiffened buttercream or royal): Starting approximately ¼th of the way from top of pretzel, pipe a row of tip 70 leaves. Add tip 3 bunch of bananas (see p. 105). Continue piping rows of overlapping leaves. Push into cake.

- Edge base with tip 233 pul-out grass. Pipe tip 12 spatula-striped ball rocks randomly around top and sides. Add drop flowers. Write tip 3 message. Position animals. *Serves 12.*

ALL ABOARD FOR BIRTHDAY FUN*

- 12 in. Round Pans, p. 168
- Tips 3, 5, 13, 16, 102, 224, 233, p. 134-138
- Orange, Lemon Yellow, Kelly Green, Pink, Brown Icing Colors, p. 126
- Meringue Powder, p. 127
- '91 Pattern Book (Circus Tent & Easel Patterns), p. 117
- Cake Dividing Set, p. 130
- Comical Clowns & Circus Train Cookie Cutter Sets, p. 124
- Birthday Candles, p. 144
- Roll-out Cookie Dough Recipe, p. 108
- Royal, Buttercream Icings

- Cut out 5 clowns and circus train from cookie dough. Using Easel Pattern, cut 4 easels to support train cookies. Bake and cool. Using royal icing, outline cookies with tip 3 strings. Pipe in small areas with tip 3,

large areas with tip 5 (smooth with finger dipped in cornstarch). Cover remaining area with tip 13 stars. Add tip 16 zigzag "smoke" to circus engine. Let dry. When dry, attach easels and candles to backs of train cookies with royal icing.

- Make 10 drop flowers with tip 224. Add tip 3 dot to flowers.
- Ice 2-layer cake smooth. Using Cake Dividing Set, dot mark sides into 10ths. Using Circus Tent Pattern, with toothpick, mark 5 tents on sides. Mark tracks on cake top.
- Outline tents with tip 3 strings. Pipe in flags with tip 3 (smooth with finger dipped in cornstarch). Fill in tents with tip 13 stars. Add tip 102 ruffles.
- Outline railroad ties with tip 5, rails with tip 16. With tip 13, print message in stars write name. Edge cake top and base with tip 16 rosette borders. Trim top border with tip 16 stars.
- Pipe clumps of tip 233 pull-out grass alongside tracks. Add drop flowers. Push clown cookies onto sides. Position cookie train on cake top. *Serves 36.*

*This is our cover cake.

BIRTHDAYS

Happy Times

19

Our Famous
Character
Cookie Cutters
are on page 125.

JEFF'S
7TH
HAPPY
BIRTHDAY

20

HEY DUDES! IT'S A PIZZA CAKE!

- 12 in. Round Pan, p. 168
- Tips 1A, 6, 102, p. 134-138
- Leaf Green, Red-Red, Ivory, Brown Icing Colors, p. 126
- Birthday Candles, p. 140
- Buttercream Icing & Powdered Sugar Glaze

- Ice cake top red. Pipe tip 1A "crust" around edge.
- Pipe tip 6 clover-shaped green peppers. For mushrooms, pipe a crescent shape with tip 6, then add straight line for stem (flatten with finger dipped in cornstarch). Add tip 102 ribbon onion circles.
- Prepare powdered sugar glaze (see p. 94) and drizzle over cake top. *Serves 18.*

LET'S EAT!

- Teenage Mutant Ninja Turtles® Pan, p.191
- Tips 2, 4, 8, 10, 16, 17, 21, 47, 233, p. 134-139
- Lemon Yellow*, Brown*, Kelly Green, Violet, Wilton Red Icing Colors, p. 126
- Round Cookie Cutter Set, p. 124

- Meringue Powder, 127
- Birthday Candles, p. 140
- Roll-Out Cookie Dough, p. 108
- Buttercream, Royal Icings

*mix colors together for shade shown

- For "pizza": With 4" round cookie cutter, cut pizza cookie "crust" circles (make extra in case of breakage) With royal icing, ice smooth. Pipe tip 233 pull-out strands of "shredded cheese." Add tip 8 dot pepperoni (to be used as a base for candles). Pipe tip 47 ribbon-stripe "green pepper" pieces; tip 2 outline onions. Edge cookie with tip 10. Position candles.
- Ice cake sides and message area smooth. Outline details with tip 4 strings. Pipe eyes with tip 4, mouth with tip 8 (smooth both with finger dipped in cornstarch).
- Cover face, bandanna, body, shell, bandolier, arms and legs with tip 17 stars.
- Print tip 2 message. Edge base with tip 21 shell border.
- Position "pizza" Outline hand again with tip 4 so that it overlaps "pizza." Overpipe with tip 17 stars. *Serves 12.*

® & ©1990 Mirage Studios, U.S.A. Exclusively licensed by Surge Licensing, Inc.

IT'S NO JOKE... IT'S BATMAN*!

- Batman Pan, p. 191
- Tips 2B, 3, 5, 16, 21, p. 134-135
- Black*, Golden Yellow, Pink or Copper, Violet* Icing Colors, p. 126
- Buttercream Icing

*mix violet and black for suit color

- Ice background area on top and sides smooth. For buildings: Pipe tip 2B smooth stripes side-by-side. Outline buildings and batman with tip 3. Pipe face, eyes, emblem and belt with tips 3 and 5 (larger area)—then smooth with finger dipped in cornstarch.
- Outline mouth, belt buckle and windows with tip 3 strings. Print tip 3 message.
- Cover hood, suit and gloves with tip 16 stars. Add tip 21 elongated shell "fringe" to gloves. Edge base with tip 21 shell border. *Serves 12.*

© DC Comics Inc. 1989

BIRTHDAYS

Famous Friends

BIRTHDAY BASHER

- **12 in. Square Pans,** p. 168
- **Teddy Bear Stand-Up Pan, p. 179**
- **Tips 1D, 2B, 2, 3, 6, 12, 16, 18, p. 134-139**
- **Brown, Red-Red, Golden Yellow, Black, Copper Icing Colors, p. 126**
- **Cake Boards, 8 in. Circles, Fanci-Foil Wrap, p. 132-133**
- **Dowel Rods, p. 165**
- **Buttercream Icing**
- Ice 2-layer square smooth for ring. Cut and position dowel rods where wrestler will go. Edge sides at base with tip 1D smooth stripes. With toothpick, mark "rope" lines on sides, 1 in. apart.
- Cover marks with tip 6 strings. Figure pipe tip 12 posts (to red band) on corners. Finish bottoms of posts with tip 18 zigzags. Pipe tip 12 balls on top of posts.
- For wrestler: Position bear cake on an 8 in. cake circle. Cut off ears and tail. Outline eyes, hands, feet and suit with tip 3

strings. Pipe in whites of eyes and add dot pupils with tip 3 (smooth with finger dipped in cornstarch). Highlight pupils with tip 2 dots. Outline ears and build up nose with tip 3. Position wrestler on cake top. Pipe tip 2B smooth stripe headband and ribbed stripe armbands. Cover wrestler with tip 16 stars. Add tip 16 zigzag mustache and trim ends with pull-out stars. Pipe tip 16 pull-out star hair on chest and head. Add tip 16 shell eyebrows.
- Print tip 2 message on "ring" cake. *Serves 55.*

SCUBA DO

- **Little Ducky Pan,** p. 186
- **Tips 4, 5, 17, 18, p. 134-135**
- **Brown, Golden Yellow, Teal, Orange, Copper, Black, Sky Blue Icing Colors, p. 126**
- **'91 Pattern Book (Diver Pattern), p. 117**
- **Piping Gel, p. 127**
- **Buttercream Icing**
- **Jelly candy sharks**

- Ice background areas on top and sides smooth. With toothpick, mark Diver Pattern (for easier marking, lightly ice areas). Position candy sharks in hands. Outline eyes, nose, mouth, mask, body, hands, suit, legs and fins with tip 4 strings.
- Pipe in eyes, mouth, mask strap; build up nose and hands with tip 4 (smooth with finger dipped in cornstarch). Outline suit again with tip 5 strings. Cover face, body, suit, hands, legs and fins with tip 17 stars.
- Pipe tip 18 pull-out stripe strands of hair and eyebrows. Add tip 4 outline eyelashes. Trim suit with tip 5 zigzags. Pipe tip 5 dots randomly on background to resemble bubbles. Flow in mask with tip 4 tinted piping gel. Edge base with tip 18 spatula-striped C-scrolls. *Serves 12.*

SPORTY TREATS

- **Sports Cookie Cutters, p. 124**
- **Tips 3, 16, p. 134-135**
- **Brown, Terra Cotta, Lemon Yellow, Sky Blue Icing Colors, p. 126**
- **Royal Icing**
- Outline cookie with tip 3 strings. Cover with tip 16 stars. Let dry.

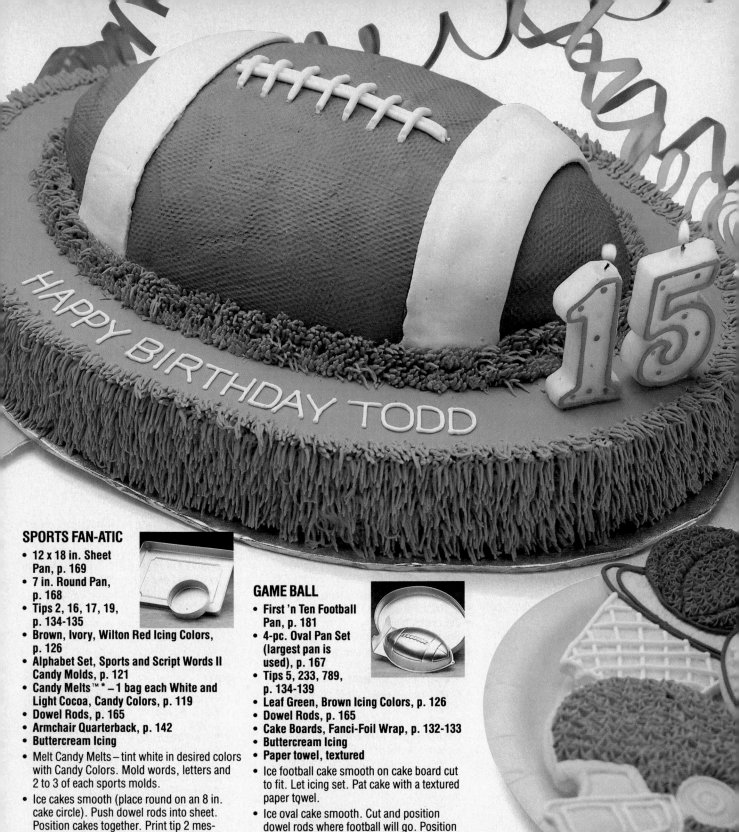

SPORTS FAN-ATIC

- 12 x 18 in. Sheet Pan, p. 169
- 7 in. Round Pan, p. 168
- Tips 2, 16, 17, 19, p. 134-135
- Brown, Ivory, Wilton Red Icing Colors, p. 126
- Alphabet Set, Sports and Script Words II Candy Molds, p. 121
- Candy Melts™ * – 1 bag each White and Light Cocoa, Candy Colors, p. 119
- Dowel Rods, p. 165
- Armchair Quarterback, p. 142
- Buttercream Icing

- Melt Candy Melts – tint white in desired colors with Candy Colors. Mold words, letters and 2 to 3 of each sports molds.
- Ice cakes smooth (place round on an 8 in. cake circle). Push dowel rods into sheet. Position cakes together. Print tip 2 message on round cake.
- Edge cake tops with tip 17 rope borders. Pipe rosette borders at bases – tip 17 on 7 in.; tip 19 on sheet. Trim centers of rosettes with tip 16 stars.
- On Armchair Quarterback, figure pipe cap (smooth and shape with finger dipped in cornstarch), pipe stripes and number on shirt with tip 2.
- Position Armchair Quarterback, sports, words and letter candies. *Serves 35.*

*brand confectionery coating

GAME BALL

- First 'n Ten Football Pan, p. 181
- 4-pc. Oval Pan Set (largest pan is used), p. 167
- Tips 5, 233, 789, p. 134-139
- Leaf Green, Brown Icing Colors, p. 126
- Dowel Rods, p. 165
- Cake Boards, Fanci-Foil Wrap, p. 132-133
- Buttercream Icing
- Paper towel, textured

- Ice football cake smooth on cake board cut to fit. Let icing set. Pat cake with a textured paper towel.
- Ice oval cake smooth. Cut and position dowel rods where football will go. Position football cake.
- Pipe tip 789 smooth stripe bands. Outline seam and stitches with tip 5 strings. Print tip 5 message.
- Cover base of football and sides of oval with tip 233 pull-out grass. *Serves 34.*

Sports Ideas

Favorite Pastimes

COAL TRAIN
- Little Train Pan, p. 175
- Tips 3, 16, p. 134
- Golden Yellow, Black, Wilton Red Icing Colors, p. 126
- Buttercream icing
- Black licorice

- Ice message and age area and top of coal car smooth.
- Outline engine, car, wheels, windows and smokestack with tip 3 strings. Print tip 3 message and age. Pipe in cow catcher.
- Cover bands on smokestack, wheels and brake with tip 16 zigzags. Cover engine, car window and smokestack with tip 16 stars. Cut licorice into bite-size pieces and fill car. *Serves 12.*

SPECIAL DELIVERY
- 9 x 13 in. Sheet Pan, p. 169
- Tips 3, 5, 7, 15, 21, p. 134-135
- Lemon Yellow, Ivory, Pink, Orange, Kelly Green, Teal, Black Icing Colors, p. 126
- '91 Pattern Book (Stamp Pattern), p. 117
- Birthday Candles, p. 144
- Buttercream Icing
- Granulated light brown sugar,
- Ice top and sides smooth. With toothpick, mark Stamp Pattern on top. Outline border with tip 3 strings; overpipe with tip 7.
- Print large letters with tip 5; small letters with tip 3.
- Outline "slice" with tip 7. Pipe in "icing" on slice with tip 7 (smooth with finger dipped in cornstarch). Pat granulated sugar on slice. Pipe tip 3 drop strings and tip 15 shells on slice. Add tip 5 dots.
- Randomly pipe tip 5 scalloped and e-motion streamers and dots on cake top. Push wick end of candle into tip 15 and pull-out flame (if you don't plan to light candle). Push into slice. Edge base with tip 21 shell border. *Serves 18.*

PRETTY TRICKY
- T-Shirt Pan, p. 177
- Tips 1A, 2, 3, 12, 16, p. 134-139
- Black*, Pink Icing Colors, p. 126
- '91 Pattern Book (Black Hat Pattern), p. 117

- Dowel Rods, p. 165
- Buttercream Icing
- Mini marshmallows

*Alternate idea: Substitute chocolate icing for black.

- Position Black Hat Pattern on cake and trim to fit. Generously ice top portion. With toothpick, mark hat opening. Spatula out icing a little from opening for a dimensional effect.
- Edge hat, opening and remainder of cake with tip 16 stars. Print tip 3 message.
- For magic wand: Fit a bag with tip 12. Push dowel rod into tip, pull through and remove from open end of bag. Position rod on cake. Attach marshmallows to end with dots of icing.
- Figure pipe bunny (see p. 105) with tips 1A, 2 and 12. *Serves 12.*

A WHOPPER OF A DAY!
- Guitar Pan, p. 176
- Tips 3, 8, 233, p. 134
- Brown, Black, Kelly Green Icing Colors, p. 126
- End of the Dock Fisherman, p. 142
- Birthday Numbers Set, p. 141
- Piping Gel, p. 127
- Granulated light brown sugar
- Buttercream Icing
- Ice cake smooth—water area white, remainder tan. Using tip 3, fill in pond with blue-tinted piping gel. Pat ground area with brown sugar.
- Figure pipe tip 8 rocks randomly on top and sides. Add tip 233 pull-out clumps of grass. Print tip 3 message.
- Push numbers into cake top. Position End of Dock Fisherman. Loop line loosely through "age numbers." *Serves 12.*

USA **Happy Birthday**

STEVE

TO OUR STAMP COLLECTOR 25 Yrs.

HAVE A MAGICAL BIRTHDAY
CARRIE

39

2546

GREAT AGE TO CATCH
BRIAN

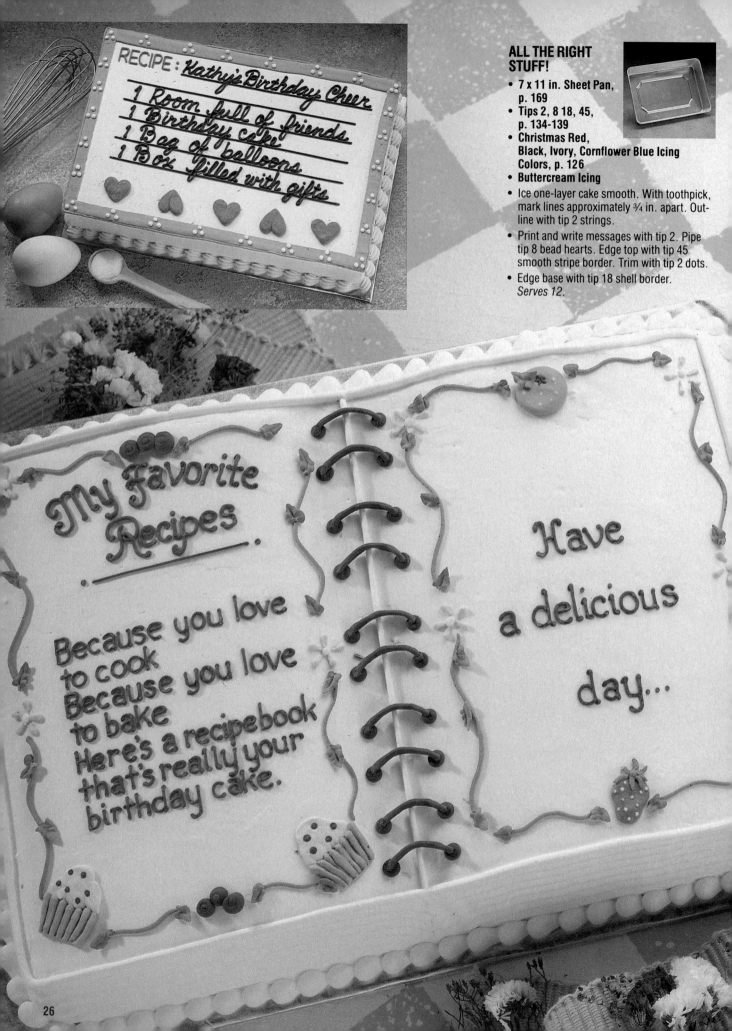

RECIPE: *Kathy's Birthday Cheer*

1 Room full of friends
1 Birthday cake
1 Bag of balloons
1 Box filled with gifts

ALL THE RIGHT STUFF!

- 7 x 11 in. Sheet Pan, p. 169
- Tips 2, 8 18, 45, p. 134-139
- Christmas Red, Black, Ivory, Cornflower Blue Icing Colors, p. 126
- Buttercream Icing

- Ice one-layer cake smooth. With toothpick, mark lines approximately ¾ in. apart. Outline with tip 2 strings.
- Print and write messages with tip 2. Pipe tip 8 bead hearts. Edge top with tip 45 smooth stripe border. Trim with tip 2 dots.
- Edge base with tip 18 shell border. *Serves 12.*

My Favorite Recipes

Because you love to cook
Because you love to bake
Here's a recipebook that's really your birthday cake.

Have a delicious day...

SOMETHING'S COOKIN'!

- Book Pan, p. 177
- Tips 1, 2, 3, 4, 10, 57, 349, p. 134-136
- Royal Blue, Violet, Orange, Christmas Red, Black, Brown, Leaf Green, Golden Yellow Icing Colors, p. 126
- Decorating Comb, p. 130
- Buttercream Icing

- Ice cake smooth. Add ribbed effect to sides with decorating comb.

- With a toothpick, mark vines, headings, rings, cupcakes, strawberry and orange. Print larger letters with tip 2; smaller letters with tip 1.

- Figure pipe icing on cupcakes, orange and strawberry with tip 4 (shape and flatten with finger dipped in cornstarch). Pipe tip 4 dot blueberries. Trim orange with tip 1 dots and outline core. Add tip 349 leaf.

- On cupcakes, pipe tip 57 pull-out stripe muffin cups. Trim "icing" with tip 3 dots. Add tip 2 bead and dot flowers. Pipe tip 3 outline vines and trim with tip 349 leaves.

- With tip 4, edge pages and center with tip 4 strings; pipe dot holes and outline binder rings.

- Edge base with tip 10 bulb border.
Serves 12.

IT'S "FORE" HER!

- Golf Bag Pan, p. 180
- Tips 3, 4, 16, 233, p. 134-135
- Peach, Ivory, Brown Icing Colors, p. 126
- Buttercream Icing

- Ice message area and base of bag smooth. Outline clubs and bag with tip 4 strings. Pipe in club and club poles with tip 4 (smooth with finger dipped in cornstarch).

- Cover bag with tip 16 spatula-striped stars.

- With tip 233 make pull-out "fur" covers for clubs using spatula-striped icing.

- Cover background area around clubs and between handle tip 13 zigzags.

- Pipe tip 3 outline "zippers" on pockets, seam on handle and "topstitching" at top of bag. Add tip 4 dot buttons and pipe zipper pulls (smooth with finger dipped in cornstarch). Write tip 3 message. Edge base with tip 16 shell border.
Serves 12.

ROSE SAMPLER

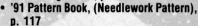

- 10 in. Round Pan, p. 168
- Tips 1, 1D, 2, 47, 127D, p. 134-139
- Leaf Green, Pink, Violet, Ivory, Brown, Black Icing Colors, p. 126
- '91 Pattern Book, (Needlework Pattern), p. 117
- Buttercream Icing

- Ice one-layer cake smooth. With toothpick, mark Needlework Pattern on cake top.

- Outline one bud with tip 1 beads. Fill in letters, petals, leaves and stems with tip 2 side-by-side lines. Edge fill-in with tip 2 beads. Outline loose thread and needle with tip 2 strings.

- On sides, 1 in. from cake top, pipe tip 127D ruffles. Pipe "hoop" with smooth stripes – tip 1D on sides; tip 47 around top.
Serves 12.

BIRTHDAYS

Favorite Pastimes

STAR ATTRACTION

- **Shining Star Pan,** p. 174
- **Tips 2, 3, 5, 14, 17, 101, 352,** p. 134-138
- **Flower Nail No. 9,** p. 132
- **Pink, Leaf Green Icing Colors,** p. 126
- **Heart Cookie Cutter Set,** p. 125
- **Buttercream Icing**

- Make tips 5 and 101 roses. Ice cake smooth. With 2½ in. heart cutter, imprint heart guidelines ¾ in. from edge. Cover hearts with tip 3 latticework. Edge with tip 14 shells. Write tip 3 message.

BIRTHDAYS

Star for a Day

- With toothpick, dot mark sides into 4ths. Pipe tip 2 double-triple drop strings. Trim with tip 2 bead hearts.
- Edge top and base with tip 17 shell border. Add roses and trim with tip 352 leaves. *Serves 12.*

SHOPPER'S PARADISE

- **Shooting Star Pan,** p. 174
- **Tips 2, 14, 16, 70, 233,** p. 134-136
- **Kelly Green, Black, Golden Yellow Icing Colors,** p. 126
- **Small Doll Picks,** p. 174
- **Gone Fishin' Signboard,** p. 142
- **Buttercream Icing**
- **Pretzel rods, car, presents**

- Ice star area yellow, sides green. With toothpick, mark road on cake top (for easier marking, lightly ice area).
- Outline road and star with tip 16 stripes. Cover road with tip 16 stars. Pipe tip 233 pull-out grass on cake top. Print tip 2 messages on cake and signboard.
- Edge base with tip 16 stars. Trim stars with

tip 14 zigzags. For palm trees: Pipe tip 70 leaves (work upwards in rows) on pretzel rods. Push each tree into cake as you decorate it. Add signboard. Cover bodice of doll pick with tip 16 stars. Place her in car and position on cake (to keep car clean, place plastic wrap on cake). Attach presents with dots of icing. *Serves 12.*

LEADING LADY

- **9 x 13 in. Sheet Pan,** p. 169
- **Tips 3, 4, 5, 7, 21, 45, 47,** p. 134-139
- **Royal Blue, Wilton Red, Black Icing Colors,** p. 126
- **'91 Pattern Book (Marquee Pattern),** p. 117
- **Buttercream Icing**

- Ice cake top smooth. With toothpick, mark Marquee Pattern on cake top. Outline marquee lines with tip 3 strings.
- Print blue message with tip 5, black message with tip 4, red letters with tip 47 smooth stripes.
- Edge marquee with tip 45 stripe border. Trim with tip 3 dots. Cover remaining area of cake top and sides with tip 21 stars. *Serves 14.*

Beverly Hills

Nancy's
Birthday
Shopping
Spree

HAPPY BIRTHDAY THEATRE
RETURN ENGAGEMENT
"MARIE IS 30
...AGAIN!"

On A Grand Scale

UTTERLY FLUTTERY

- **10" Ring Mold/Pan,** p. 173
- **16 in. Round Pans,** p. 168
- **Tips 2, 5, 8, 14, 18, 67, 103,** p. 134-138
- **Lemon Yellow, Violet, Kelly Green Icing Colors,** p. 126
- **Flower Nail No. 7,** p. 132
- **'91 Pattern Book (Scallop Design and Butterfly Body Patterns),** p. 117
- **Meringue Powder,** p. 127
- **Flower Formers, Florist Wire,** p. 126
- **Yellow Stamens,** p. 128
- **Tall Tier Stand 12 in. and 18 in. Footed Base Plates, 7¾ in. Column, Top and Bottom Cap Nut, Cake Corer,** p. 162
- **12 & 16 in. Cake Circles,** p. 133

- **Floral Scroll Base,** p. 158
- **Scrolls,** p. 160
- **Royal, Buttercream Icings**
- **Tulle trim, craft block, white floral tape**
- Using royal icing, make 75 daisies with tips 5, 103 (15 of each color – make extra for breakage). Let dry on flower formers. Pipe about 25 calyxes on wires with tip 8; let dry, then attach daisies. Pipe tip 2 and 67 leaves on wires; let dry. Figure pipe 9 butterflies (pipe one on a wire) with tip 8, using Butterfly Body Pattern. Push in Scroll wings and flower stamen antennae. Let dry on concaved flower former. Make tulle puffs and secure with wires. See p. 102 for flower wiring instructions.
- Cut 2 in. circle in center of 16 in. and 11 in. (trim 12 in. size to 11 in.) cake circles. Position ring and 2-layer round on circles and ice smooth. Place round on footed

plate and core out center.
- With toothpick, mark Scallop Design Pattern on top of round. Insert column and secure with bottom bolt. Cover top of ring and fill in design on round with tip 2 cornelli lace. Edge cornelli with tip 14 shell borders.
- Edge top and sides of round (base of ring will be decorated after assembly) with tip 18 "fleur-v-lis" (no center shell). Trim with tip 2 drop strings.
- Secure 12 in. plate to column with top cap nut. Position ring cake and pipe base border. To hold flowers, use the top of Floral Scroll Base (inverted). Secure craft block inside with dots of icing. Push in wired flowers, leaves, butterfly and tulle. Position in ring cake. Attach daisies and butterflies to round with dots of icing. Trim daisies with tip 67 leaves. *Serves 50.*

TOTALLY MASCULINE

- 8 & 12 in. x 3 in. Deep Round Pans, p. 168
- Bevel Pan Set, p. 167
- Tips 4, 14, 32, p. 134-135
- Brown*, Ivory Icing Colors, p. 126
- Cake Dividing Set, p. 130
- Oval Cookie Cutter Set, p. 125
- Meringue Powder, p. 127
- Light Cocoa Candy Melts™*, p. 119
- 8, 12, 18 in. Cake Circles, Fanci-Foil Wrap, p. 132-133
- 10 in. Round Separator Plate, p. 166
- 7 in. Grecian Spiked Pillars, p. 164
- Dowel Rods, p. 165
- Buttercream, Royal or Snow-white Buttercream Icings

- Pour melted candy into 5 in. oval cutter for plaques and 3½ in. cutter for easel backs (see p. 111). Remove cutters when set. With royal icing, write tip 4 messages. Edge with tip 14 C-motion shells. Let dry. With a warm knife, cut remaining oval in half. Straighten one curved side by holding warm knife against it to melt candy. Immediately place side next to back of plaque. Repeat procedure for other plaque. Let set. Place separator plate and pillar on a rack over a pan. Cover with melted candy. Let set.

- Position round cakes on cake circles; beveled base on foil-covered cake circle. Cut and position dowel rods in beveled base. Position bevels and rounds together. Place 8 in. round on candy-covered plate. Ice cakes smooth.

- With toothpick, mark 8 in. round into 8ths (use Cake Dividing Set). On 12 in. round top, indent ½ in., then mark 1¼ in. intervals. On 16 in. bevel, mark 1¼ in. intervals, 1½ ins. up from base.

- On 8 in. cake, connect marks with tip 32 zigzag garlands. Trim with tip 4 drop strings. Edge top with tip 4 bead border. Pipe tip 32 upright shells on bevel. Trim with tip 14 rosettes. Edge base with tip 32 shells, outlined with tip 4 strings.

- Push pillars into 12 in. cake. Edge pillars, seam between cakes and base with tip 4 bead border. Pipe tip 32 shells at marks. Edge top shells with tip 14 zigzags. Trim bevel's shells with tip 4 zigzags and strings. Pipe tip 4 Overlapping Double Drop Strings (see p. 104) on 12 in. sides.

- To assemble: Place plaque on 12 in. top. Position top tier on pillars and add plaque. *Serves 57.*

*substitute chocolate icing
**brand confectionery coating

Milestones

CRASHING BLOW

- **Question Mark Pan, p. 177**
- **Tips 2, 3, 5, 233, p. 134**
- **Golden Yellow, Kelly Green, Black, Brown Icing Colors, p. 126**
- **Meringue Powder, p. 127**
- **Fanci-Foil Wrap, Cake Boards, p. 132-133**
- **Buttercream, Snow-white Buttercream or Royal Icings**
- **Large jelly candies, black dot candy**

- For sign: Cut a 3 x 5 in. rectangle and 2 x 2 in. triangle out of cake board. Cover rectangle with Fanci-Foil Wrap. Ice front with snow-white buttercream or royal. Let dry. Print tip 3 words and tip 5 numbers. Edge with tip 5 bead border. When dry, attach triangle piece to back with icing.

- For car: Trim piece of candy to resemble windshield and windows. Attach top of car to whole piece of candy and candy wheels with icing.

- Ice cake smooth. With toothpick, mark road. Outline with tip 5. Print tip 2 message. Pipe skid marks with tip 2 strings.
- Cover top and sides with tip 233 pull-out grass. Position "car" and sign on cake top. *Serves 12.*

IT ALL FITS TOGETHER!

- **12 x 18 in. Sheet Pan, p. 169**
- **Tips 3, 16, 18, 80, p. 134-139**
- **Terra Cotta, Golden Yellow, Black Icing Colors, p. 126**
- **'91 Pattern Book (Puzzle Pattern), p. 117**
- **Buttercream Icing**

- Ice cake smooth. With toothpick, mark Puzzle Pattern (number can easily be changed). Pipe outer edges of missing pieces and all inside edges with tip 3 strings. Outline outer edges of "filled in" pieces with tip 80.
- Fill in appropriate pieces with tip 16 stars. Print tip 3 message. Edge base with tip 18 star borders. *Serves 30.*

GOING TO PIECES

- **Sports Ball Pan, p. 180**
- **Tips 3, 16, p. 134-135**
- **Brown Icing Color, p. 126**
- **'91 Pattern Book (Numbers Pattern), p. 117**
- **Light Cocoa Candy Melts™*, p. 119**
- **Birthday Candles, p. 144**
- **Buttercream Icing**
- **Marshmallow, posterboard**

- Push candle into marshmallow. Dip marshmallow into melted candy and let set.

- Slice a small piece off rounded side of one half of ball so cake stands level. Fill and ice halves together.

- With toothpick, mark Numbers Pattern on side. Outline with tip 3. Fill in number and cover cake with tip 16 stars.

- Position marshmallow on cake top. Write message on card with tip 3. Place next to cake. *Serves 12.*

*brand confectionery coating

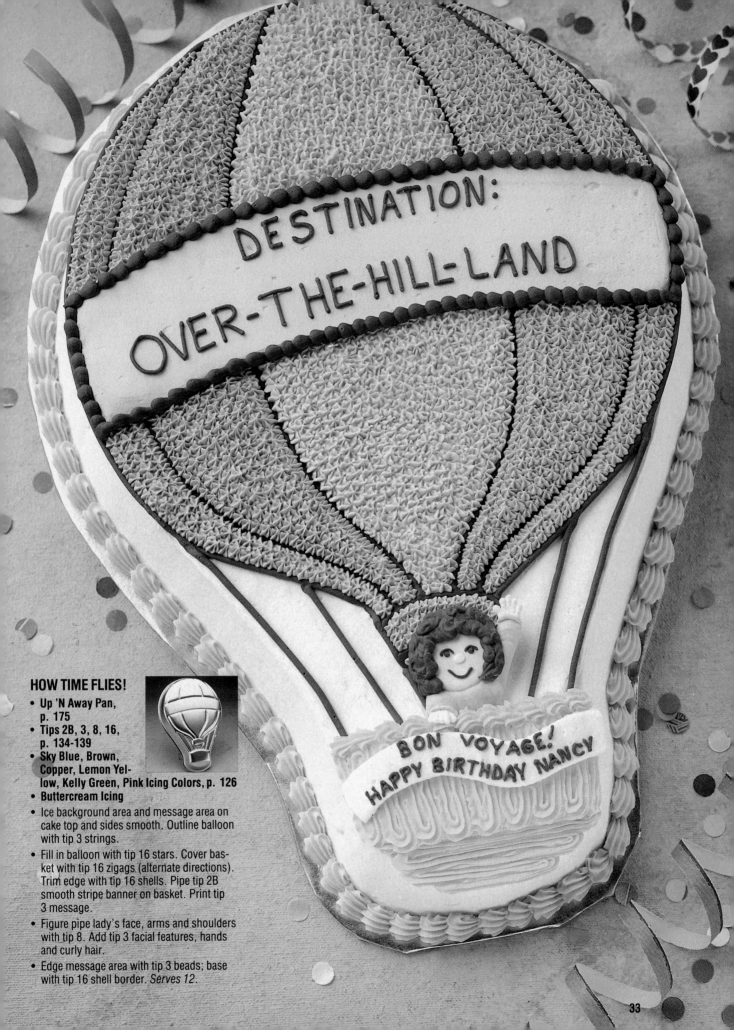

DESTINATION: OVER-THE-HILL-LAND

BON VOYAGE! HAPPY BIRTHDAY NANCY

HOW TIME FLIES!

- Up 'N Away Pan, p. 175
- Tips 2B, 3, 8, 16, p. 134-139
- Sky Blue, Brown, Copper, Lemon Yellow, Kelly Green, Pink Icing Colors, p. 126
- Buttercream Icing
- Ice background area and message area on cake top and sides smooth. Outline balloon with tip 3 strings.
- Fill in balloon with tip 16 stars. Cover basket with tip 16 zigags (alternate directions). Trim edge with tip 16 shells. Pipe tip 2B smooth stripe banner on basket. Print tip 3 message.
- Figure pipe lady's face, arms and shoulders with tip 8. Add tip 3 facial features, hands and curly hair.
- Edge message area with tip 3 beads; base with tip 16 shell border. *Serves 12.*

33

PETAL PERFECTION

- **12 in. Petal Pans,** p. 172
- **Tips 1, 2, 4, 6,** p. 134
- **Violet, Kelly Green, Golden Yellow Icing Colors,** p. 126
- **'91 Pattern Book (Lacework Pattern),** p. 117
- **Gum Paste Flowers Kit, Glucose, Flower Formers,** p. 128
- **Candy Melts™ – White, Yellow,** p. 119
- **Meringue Powder,** p. 127
- **Buttercream & Royal Icings**
- **Modeling Candy Recipe,** p. 110
- Using royal icing, outline Lacework Pattern with tip 1. You'll need 63 (make extras in case of breakage). Let dry (see p. 104).

HAPPY ONE HUNDREDTH

Mary Catheri

- Out of modeling candy, make 13 daffodils, 23 leaves and 25 violets (see p. 110). With royal icing, edge daffodils with tip 2 strings.
- Ice 2-layer cake smooth. Arrange flower spray with leaves on cake top. Write tip 2 message.
- With toothpick, mark drop strings on sides — 2 in. wide, 1½ in. deep on outer curves; 2 inner strings should be 1 in. wide, ¾ in. deep. Pipe drop strings with tip 2.
- Edge top with tip 4 bead border. Carefully position lacework pieces around edge. Pipe tip 6 bead border at base. Add flowers and leaves to base. *Serves 28.*

*brand confectionery coating

IT'S BEEN A CENTURY!

- **12 x 18 in. Sheet Pan, p. 169**
- **Ring Mold & Loaf Pans, p. 170-171**
- **Tips 4, 18, 22, p. 134-135**
- **Leaf Green, Pink, Golden Yellow Icing Colors, p. 126**
- **8 in. Cake Circles, Cake Boards, Fanci-Foil Wrap, p. 132-133**
- **Dowel Rods, p. 165**
- **Buttercream Icing**
- Ice two 12 x 18 in. sheets and position side-by-side. Position dowel rods where "number" cakes will go. Ice rings on 9 in. cake circles and loaf on a 9¾ x 5½ in. cake board. Ice tops in colors; sides white.
- Cover sides of all cakes with tip 4 dots.
- Edge cake tops with reverse shell borders — tip 18 on "numbers;" tip 22 on sheet. Edge bases with shell borders using the same tips. Position "numbers" atop sheet. Print and write tip 4 message. *Serves 100.*

FOREVER SHINING

- **14 in. Square Pans, p. 169**
- **Tips 2D, 3, 10, 16, 21, 86 or 87, 129, 352, p. 134-139**
- **Royal Blue, Lemon Yellow, Leaf Green Icing Colors, p. 126**
- **'91 Pattern Book (Diamonds & Number Pattern), p. 117**
- **Color Flow Mix, p. 127**
- **Buttercream & Color Flow Icings**
- With dark blue color flow icing, outline Diamonds (20 are needed) and Number Patterns with tip 3. When outlines set, flow in designs with lighter shades of blue. Let set. See p. 108 for Color Flow instructions. Alternate idea: Mark designs on cake. Outline and pipe in with tip 3.
- Make 32 drop flowers — 16 with tip 129 and 16 with tip 2D. Add tip 3 dot centers.
- Ice 2-layer cake smooth. Write tip 3 message. Pipe tip 16 stripe vines on cake top. Edge top with tip 21 swirled shell border.
- With toothpick, dot sides into 4ths. Edge base with tip 10 bead border. Pipe tip 86 or 87 ruffle garlands. Overpipe with tip 3 drop strings. Trim points with tip 16 rosettes.
- Attach larger diamonds & number on cake top and small diamonds to sides with dots of icing. Position large drop flowers on top and smaller on sizes. Trim with tip 352 leaves. *Serves 54.*

BIRTHDAYS

Very Special

RTHDAY

All Occasions

*Whatever goes…birthdays to dinner parties –
love, marriage or even a baby carriage, the ideas
ahead are so right to delight!*

HEART WREATH

- **9 in. Heart Pans,** p. 185
- **Tips 1, 3, 5, 16, 59s/ 59°, 104, 125, 301,** p. 134-138
- **Flower Nail No. 7,** p. 132
- **Brown, Lemon Yellow, Golden Yellow, Violet, Royal Blue, Moss Green Icing Colors,** p. 126
- **Decorator's Brush,** p. 130
- **Flower Formers,** p. 128
- **Buttercream, Royal Icings**

- With royal icing, make 10 pansies with tips 1 and 104; 3 daffodils with tips 1, 3 and 104; 15 violets with tips 1 and 59s/59°; 10 tip 104 violet leaves. Dry on flower formers.

- Ice 2-layer cake smooth. Print tip 301 message. Mark wreath approximately 2 in. from edge. Cover area with tip 16 curved stripe grapevines (overpipe randomly to build dimension). Add tip 16 pull-out stripe twigs.

- Edge base with tip 16 shell border to add dimension to ruffles. Pipe tip 125 rows of ruffles. Edge top ruffle with tip 5 beads.

- Arrange flowers and leaves on cake top and at base. *Serves 16.*

Best Wishes

Get Well Soon Bridget

Cookie Cutter Ideas

ROSE CAMEO

- Oval Pan Set (10¾ x 7⅞ in. size used), p. 167
- Tips 3, 12, 14, 103, 352, p. 134-138
- Flower Nail No. 7, p. 132
- Pink, Kelly Green Icing Colors, p. 126
- Oval Cookie Cutter Set, p. 125
- Tuk 'n Ruffle, Fanci-Foil Wrap, Cake Boards, p. 132-133
- Buttercream Icing

- Make 4 roses with tips 12 and 103 and 16 rosebuds with tip 103.

- On Tuk 'n Ruffle-trimmed cake board, ice 2-layer cake smooth. Using largest oval cutter, imprint oval on top. On sides, imprint outer oval using 4⅛ in. cutter. Using 2¾ in. cutter, imprint inner oval (½ in. from outer) guidelines.

- Outline top oval and inner ovals with tip 14 stars. Edge base with tip 103 ruffle border. Cover background area on sides with tip 14 stars.

- Pipe tip 3 outline stems on sides. Position roses and rosebuds. Add tip 3 calyxes and sepals to buds. Trim flowers with tip 352 leaves. *Serves 22.*

IT SAYS IT ALL

- 9 x 13 in. Sheet Pan, p. 169
- Tips 3, 14, 17, p. 134-135
- Pink Icing Color, p. 126
- Meringue Powder, p. 127
- Alphabet Cookie Cutters, p. 125
- Decorating Comb, p. 130
- Roll-Out Cookie Dough Recipe, p. 109
- Buttercream, Royal Icings

- Cut letters out of cookie dough. Bake and cool. Using royal icing, outline letters with tip 3 and fill with tip 14 stars. Let dry.

- Ice cake smooth top white; sides pink. Use Decorating Comb to make ribbed effect on sides.

- Edge cake top with tip 17 shells. Edge base with tip 17 rosettes. Place letters on cake top. *Serves 14.*

CLUB NIGHT

- 10 in. Round Pans, p. 168
- Tips 16, 32, p. 135
- Wilton Red, Black Icing Colors, p. 126
- Playing Card Cookie Cutter Set, p. 124
- Buttercream Icing

- Ice 2-layer cake smooth. Use Playing Card Cutters to imprint designs on cake top. Fill in designs with tip 16 stars.

- Edge top with tip 32 upright shell border. Trim with tip 16 stars. Edge base with tip 32 shell border. *Serves 24.*

CANDY KITTIES
- Cute Kitties Cookie Cutter Set, p. 124
- Candy Melts™* – Dark Cocoa, White, p. 119
- Candy Colors Kit, p. 119
- Prepare Candy Melts for molding, see p. 110. Using Cute Kitties Cookie Cutters as molds. So cutters sit level place atop a rack.

For a multi-color effect, follow directions on p. 111.

- Fill cutters with melted candy. Place in freezer to until set (approximately 4 to 5 minutes). Check often. Unmold.

*Brand confectionery coating

45

Holidays & Events

From jingle bells to wedding bells…it takes all kinds of ideas to greet the seasons and all the special reasons!

Christmas Cheer

REAL CHARMERS

- Mini Gingerbread Boy Pan, p. 189
- Tips 3, 16, p. 134-135
- Wilton Red, Kelly Green Icing Colors, p. 126
- Buttercream Icing
- Trim gingerbread cakes with tip 16 outlines, tip 3 dots and strings. *Each serves 1.*

THE STOCKINGS WERE HUNG...

- Holiday House Kit, p.188
- Tips 3, 4, 8, 13, 17, 47, 352, p. 134-139
- Christmas Red, Kelly Green, Golden Yellow, Brown, Ivory, Black Icing Colors, p. 126
- '9l Pattern Book (Fireplace Pattern), p. 117.
- Buttercream Icing
- Ice sides and top smooth—peak, brown; bricks white; opening, black. Using

Fireplace Pattern, mark tree and fireplace.
- Edge peak on top and sides with tip 47 ribbed stripes. Cover mantel with two rows of tip 8 strings. Outline tree and opening with tip 4 strings. Pipe in tree stand with tip 3 (smooth with finger dipped in cornstarch). Trim stand with tip 3 strings. Working from bottom to top, cover tree with tip 352 leaves. Add tip 3 dot ornaments. Outline candles and holders with tip 3 strings. Add tip 13 spatula-striped flames.
- Pipe tip 17 stripe logs. Outline andirons with tip 4 strings. Trim with tip 3 dot knobs. Pipe tip 13 spatula-striped pull-out star flames.
- Cover fireplace with tip 3 outline mortar and tip 47 ribbed stripe bricks (see p. 104). Pipe tip 4 dot stocking hangers. Outline stockings with tip 3 and pipe-in (smooth with finger dipped in cornstarch). Cover mantel with tip 352 leaf garland. Trim with tip 3 dots. *Serves 12.*

FESTIVE, FANCY, FROSTY

- Snowman Pan, p. 188
- Tip 4, p. 133
- Orange, Brown, Kelly Green, Christmas Red Icing Color, p. 126
- '91 Pattern Book (Snowman Attire Patterns), p. 117
- White Candy Melts™*, p. 119
- Dowel Rods, p. 165
- Modeling Candy Recipe, p. 110
- Buttercream Icing
- To make hat, holly, eyes, nose, teeth, scarf, buttons and broom out of modeling candy, see p. 110.
- Ice cake smooth. Position modeling candy hat on cake; smooth down. Add hatband, and holly. Outline holly veins with tip 4. Position modeling candy berries.
- Lay scarf piece on cake. With tip 4, outline edge and add zigzag borders. Position eyes, nose, mouth, buttons and broom. *Serves 12.*

*brand confectionery coating

49

"HOLLYDAY" CHEER

- 11 x 15 in. Sheet Pan, p. 169
- Tips 3, 5, 12, 55, p. 134-135
- Kelly Green, Wilton Red Icing Colors, p. 126
- Christmas Treats Cookie Cutter Set, p. 122
- Decorating Comb, p. 130
- Buttercream Icing

- Ice cake smooth. Using Decorating Comb, add wavy effect to sides. Using Holly Cookie Cutter, imprint guidelines on cake top. Using Decorating Comb, add wavy effect to sides.
- Write message with tip 55. Outline holly with tip 3 strings. Pipe tip 12 ball berries.
- Edge top with tip 5 curved bead border and trim with tip 3 dots. Edge base with tip 12 bulb border. *Serves 20.*

"BERRY" EASY TO TRIM

- Treeliteful Pan, p. 188
- Christmas Red, Leaf Green Icing Colors, p. 126
- Decorator's Brush, p. 130
- Boiled Icing Recipe, p. 94
- Grapes, granulated sugar, light corn syrup

- Lightly brush grapes with light corn syrup. Let set approximately 5 minutes. Tint sugar red and green with icing color. Roll grapes in sugar.
- Ice cake generously and fluff boughs with a spatula.
- Arrange grapes on boughs trunk. *Serves 12.*

A FUN-FILLED FOREST

- Mini Christmas Tree Pan, p. 188
- Tip 4, p. 134
- Kelly Green Icing Color, p. 126
- Quick-Pour Fondant and Buttercream Icing
- Cinnamon dot candy

- Lightly ice trees with buttercream icing. Place cakes on a rack over a pan or plate to catch excess icing. Cover with green fondant and let set.
- Drizzle thinned buttercream garlands with tip 4. Add cinnamon dot candies. *Each serves 1.*

BY GOLLY, HE'S JOLLY!

- 16 in. Round Pans, p. 168
- Jolly Santa Pan, p. 189
- Tips 3, 4, 101, 104, 352, p. 134-138
- Ivory, Red-Red, Kelly Green Icing Colors, p. 126
- Candy Melts™* – 1 bag each White, & Christmas Mix, p. 119
- Cake Dividing Set, p. 130
- Dowel Rods, p. 165
- Buttercream Icing

- Make Santa plaque out of melted Candy Melts (see p. 109). For pink candy, mix white and red together until desired shade is reached (or use pink Candy Melts).
- Ice 2-layer round smooth. Cut and position dowel rods in cake top where Santa plaque will go. Position Santa plaque on cake top. Using Cake Dividing Set, dot mark sides into 12ths. Also mark Merry Christmas on cake top. Edge cake top with tip 4 bead border.
- Using tip 352 and a shell-motion, edge candy plaque, pipe side garlands and print cap letters. Print remaining letters with tip 3 and trim leaves with tip 3 dots. Add tip 101 ribbon bows. Edge base with tip 352 shell-motion border. *Serves 60.*

*brand confectionery coating

HOLIDAYS & EVENTS

Festive!

Christmas House Walk

All of these enchanting gingerbread houses were constructed using the patterns included in our **Gingerbread House Centerpiece Kit**, p. 123.

For any of the houses shown, cut front, back, side walls and roof pieces from gingerbread. For Candy Cane Lane, cut windows and door the sizes specified.

Some building hints to know: From mortaring to decorating, whatever you do to your house will be done with royal icing. Add 1 Tbsp. of piping gel or corn syrup to each cup of icing for a shiny, snow-like effect.

For "painted" walls: Place gingerbread pieces to be covered on racks over a "drip" pan to catch excess icing. Thin royal icing to a pourable consistency with water. Pour evenly over each panel. Let dry.

To assemble your house: On either a styrofoam or cake board base, ice bottom edge and sides of each piece. Place front, side walls and back together on base. Hold each piece in place a few minutes so icing sets a little. Position a heavy jar or can on each side for support until completely dry. Don't worry about icing squeezing through seams. It will be covered with decorations later.

Please refer to the Gingerbread House Instructions for gingerbread and icing recipes, baking, building and decorating basics.

TEDDY BEAR HIDE-AWAY

- **Tips 3, 6, 48, p. 134-139**
- **Brown Icing Color, p. 126**
- **Christmas Mix & White Candy Melts™ * (1 bag each), p. 119**
- **Edible Glitter, p. 128**
- **Piping Gel, Meringue Powder, p. 127**
- **Cake Boards, p. 133**
- **Graham cracker teddy bear cookies, vanilla wafer, graham crackers, wafer sandwich cookies, cinnamon dot candies, gumdrops, spearmint leaves, round hard candies**

- "Paint" gingerbread pieces. Let dry completely. Construct house on cake board base.
- For chimney: Cut two gingerbread crackers 2½ in. long. Sandwich together with icing. Outline walls, wooden trim, door and chimney with tip 48 ribbed stripes.
- Attach Candy Melt wafers to roof (work from bottom upward, overlapping slightly). Attach graham cracker and vanilla cookie windows to sides.
- With tip 6 or a spatula, edge roof, cover chimney top and generously ice base board with drifting snow. Pat with edible glitter.
- Pipe tip 3 drop strings on paws of five bear cookies. Attach candy-coated chocolates. Attach bear cookies and candies to roof and sides of houses.
- Cut eight Candy Melts in half. Attach halves together with icing and edge pathway. For "fir tree:" Starting at base, stack spearmint leaf candies. Attach leaf candies around door and sides of house. Trim with cinnamon dots.

CANDY CANE LANE

- **Tips 16, 21, 73, p. 134-136**
- **Leaf Green Icing Color, p. 126**
- **Meringue Powder, p. 127**
- **Small candy canes, cinnamon dots, peppermint disks, dragees, waxed paper, 12 x 16 craft block, ribbon, electric nightlight socket, 15 watt bulb, assorted wrapped candies**

- Before baking, cut 3½ x 2 in. doorway, trim ¼ in. off door. Cut 2 in. square window in front wall, 2 x 4½ in. side windows. After baking, attach waxed paper to windows. Outline windowpanes with tip 3 strings. Construct house per kit instructions booklet. Ice base.
- Cover roof with tip 16 latticework (space stripes about 1¼ in. apart). Edge roof, windows and door with tip 16 stripes. Position door.
- Pipe tip 16 pull-out star trees on walls. Trim with tip 3 dots. Pipe tip 21 stars on roof; tip 16 stars on side walls. Trim stars, roof, windows, door, corners of house and base with candy. Attach ribbon and bow to base.

SNOWFLAKE COTTAGE

- **Tips 3, 5, 15, 16, 301, p. 134-135**
- **Pink Icing Color, p. 126**
- **Meringue Powder, Piping Gel, p. 127**
- **Round Cutter Set, p. 125**
- **Cake Boards, Fanci Foil Wrap, p. 132-133**
- **Small candy canes, wafer sandwich cookies, sugar jelly drops, candy disks, candy-coated gum square (regular and mini sizes)**

- In addition to house pieces, cut out Santa using cutter included in kit. "Paint" wall panels white; roof pink. Let dry. With straight pin, mark 2 x 3 in. windows, 2 in. circle (use round cutter as a guide) for wreath and name plaque. Construct house. Ice base.
- Outline windows with tip 5, plaque and wreath with tip 3. Attach mini gum squares to wreath. Trim with tip 3 dots and tip 301 ribbon bow. Fill in plaque with tip 3 and thinned icing (add more corn syrup). When dry, write tip 3 name.
- Print tip 3 message on roof. Add tip 3 outline and dot snowflakes. Pipe a line of icing on seam of roof with tip 16. Push in large gum squares. Edge gum with tip 16 scallop border.
- On front wall: Edge roof line with two rows of tip 16 side-by-side stripes; edge corners with three rows. Pipe pull-out icicles and edge roof with tip 5.
- Attach cookies and candy canes to house; candies and cookies to base. Trim cookie fence with tip 3 side-by- side strings. Add tip 3 dot top knobs.
- For Santa: Outline face, suit, mittens and boots with tip 3. Add tip 3 dot facial features. Pipe in suit, mittens and boots with tip 3. Pipe tip 15 reverse shell beard, shell mustache, and zigzag trim on suit with tip 15. Outline bag and pipe in (smooth with finger dipped in cornstarch) with tip 3. Attach mini gum squares with dots of icing. Outline bag again with tip 3.

Away We Go!

"DEERLIGHTFUL" TREAT

- Rudy Reindeer Pan, p. 189
- Candy Melts™ * White, Light Cocoa, Christmas Mix, (one bag of each), p. 119
- Crispy rice cereal, black shoestring licorice

- Lightly grease inside of pan with vegetable oil. Melt ½ bag of white Candy Melts. Stir in 1¾ cup of rice cereal. Pack mixture into antler, eye and inside of ear indentations.
- Melt ½ bag red Candy Melts. Add 1¾ cup cereal. Pack into nose and bow areas.
- Melt ½ bag green Candy Melts. Add 1¾ cup cereal. Fill in background area.
- Reserve 1 piece of cocoa candy for eye. Melt remaining cocoa candy melts. Stir in 3¼ cup cereal. Pack into face. Chill pan in refrigerator for 1 hour. Unmold.
- Add licorice string eyelashes and mouth. Position candy wafer for eye.

*brand confectionery coating

DASH AWAY ALL!

- Santa Sleigh & Reindeer Cookie & Gingerbread Kit, p. 123
- Red-Red, Kelly Green, Brown Icing Color, p. 126
- Meringue Powder, p. 127
- Gingerbread Cookie Dough
- Royal Icing
- Dragees

- Cut out and bake gingerbread pieces following kit instructions.
- For sleigh: Outline lower portion of side with tip 3 zigzags. Flow in sides and runner with tip 3 thinned royal icing (add water until pourable consistency is reached). Let set. Add band of tip 16 zigzags, then a band of tip 3 zigzags. Trim runner with tip 16 stars. Trim with dragees. Pipe wreath with tip 16. Add tip 3 dot berries and bow.
- For Santa: Outline with tip 3 strings. Pipe tip 3 dot eyes, nose and outline mouth. Fill in "fur" trim and beard with tip 3 zigzags. Cover cap, scarf, mittens and suit with tip 16 stars. Add tip 3 bead mustache.
- Reindeer: Outline with tip 3 strings. Fill in ears and hooves with tip 3 zigzags and cover tail with pull-out strings. Pipe tip 16 zigzag bridle and outline wreath. Trim with tip 3 dots and bow.
- When icing dries, assemble per kit instructions.

CHRISTMAS CHEER TWINS

- Gingerbread Boy Pan, p. 189
- Tips 3, 4, 8, 16, 18, 21, 104, p. 134-137
- Kelly Green, Christmas Red, Ivory, Black, Brown, Lemon Yellow Icing Colors, p. 126
- '91 Pattern Book (Christmas Twins Pattern), p. 117
- Buttercream Icing
- Candy canes

- Ice cakes smooth. With toothpick, mark Christmas Twins Patterns on each cake. Outline with tip 4 strings. Pipe in eyes, bow tie, belts and shoes with tip 8 (smooth with finger dipped in cornstarch).
- Pipe tip 4 dots in eyes; tip 8 dot noses and cheeks (flatten with finger dipped in cornstarch). Outline belt buckles with tip 4.
- Cover hats, faces, outfits, mittens, legs and feet with tip 18 stars. Add tip 16 pull-out star pompons on caps. Pipe tip 18 pull-out stripe hair. On girl, add tip 18 rope braids. Trim ends with tip 3 pull-out strings.
- Trim girl's blouse with tip 104 ruffles. Pipe tip 3 string eyelashes. Overpipe trees on vests--outline and pipe in with tip 3. Edge bases with tip 21 rosette border. Trim with tip 3 dots. Add candy canes. *Each serves 12.*

55

FOND OF YOU HEART

- **Heart Ring Mold, p. 184**
- **Tips 2, 5, 129, 349, p. 134-137**
- **Pink, Lemon Yellow Icing Colors, p. 126**
- **Buttercream, Poured Fondant Icings**
- With stiffened buttercream, make 55 drop flowers with tip 129. Add tip 2 dot centers.
- Lightly ice cake with buttercream icing. Place cake on a rack over a shallow pan. Pour fondant on cake. Let set.
- With buttercream icing, pipe tip 2 pinwheel vine designs on top (space approximately 2 in. apart). With tip 2, pipe dots around vines and in triangle designs on sides.
- Edge top and base (inside opening, too) with tip 5 bead borders. Attach flowers with dots of icing. Trim with tip 349 leaves. *Serves 12.*

BLOOMIN' ROMANTIC

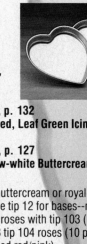

- **Happiness Heart Pan, p. 184**
- **Tips 6, 12, 48, 67, 103, 104, 364, p. 134-139**
- **Flower Nail No. 7, p. 132**
- **Pink, Christmas Red, Leaf Green Icing Colors, p. 126**
- **Meringue Powder, p. 127**
- **Buttercream, Snow-white Buttercream or Royal Icings**
- With snow-white buttercream or royal, make 30 roses. Use tip 12 for bases--make 17 spatula-striped roses with tip 103 (light pink/dark pink); 13 tip 104 roses (10 pink and 3 spatula-striped red/pink).
- Ice cake smooth. Cover sides with tips 6 and 48 basketweave. Edge top and base with tip 364 rope borders.
- Position roses and trim with tip 67 leaves. *Serves 12.*

ALL-HEART WREATH

- **Heart Cookie Cutter Set, p. 125**
- **Cookie Sheets or Pans, p. 125, 172**
- **Red-Red, Pink Icing Colors, p. 126**
- **Meringue Powder, p. 127**
- **Roll-Out Cookie Recipe, p. 109**

- **Royal Icing**
- **Ribbon, lollipops**
- Cut 16 hearts with 4⅛ in. cutter and 10 with 1¼ in. cutter. Bake and cool.
- Place cookies on a wire rack over a cookie pan. Pour icing over cookies. Let icing set.
- Attach small cookies to 10 large hearts with dots of icing. Arrange cookies in a heart shape on pretty platter. Add ribbon and lollipops (homemade or store-bought).

CANDY HEARTS

- **Heart Mini-Cake Pan, p. 185**
- **White Candy Melts™*, p. 119**
- **Cake Boards, p. 133**
- **Doilies, nonpareils, chewy heart candy**

- Place cakes on a rack over a pan to catch excess. Pour melted candy over cakes. Immediately pat nonpareils onto sides. Let set partially, then add heart candy. Serve on doilie-covered cake boards (cut to fit). *Each serves 1.*

Valentine

FLOWERY 'N FRILLY

- **6 & 12 in. Heart Pans, p. 185**
- **Tips 3, 12, 14, 16, 18, 103, 104, 352, p. 134-138**
- **Flower Nail No. 7, p. 132**
- **Pink, Leaf Green Icing Colors, p. 126**
- **'91 Pattern Book (Open Heart Pattern), p. 117**
- **8 in. Heart Separator Plate, p. 166**
- **5 in. Grecian Spiked Pillars, p. 164**
- **White Candy Melts™*, p. 119**
- **Lollipop Sticks, p. 118**
- **Piping Gel, p. 127**
- **Buttercream Icing**

- For candy hearts: Pour melted candy into 6 in. heart pan (¼ in. deep). Mold per instructions on p. 109.

- Make heart collar using Open Heart Pattern. When pieces are set, cut 6 in. heart in half with a warm knife. With cut bag, edge candy hearts with scallops and bead borders using melted candy. Let set.

- With stiffened buttercream or royal icing, make 15 spatula-striped roses. Use tip 12 for bases; make 9 with tip 103; 6 with tip 104.

- Ice one-layer cakes smooth and prepare for push-in leg construction, see p. 106. Edge cake tops with swirled shell borders – tip 16 on top tier, tip 18 on 12 in. heart. Edge bases with tip 18 zigzag puffs trimmed with tip 14 zigzags. Pipe tip 3 bead hearts on sides.

- Arrange roses and candy hearts (use lollipop sticks to prop up sides of 6 in. heart) on cake tops. Trim roses with tip 352 leaves. Push in pillars and assemble top tier. *Serves 38.*

*brand confectionery coating

STRAWBERRIES & CREAM

- **Heart Ring Mold, p. 184**
- **Tip 21, p. 134**
- **Pink Icing Color, p. 127**
- **Cream Cheese Icing or Stabilized Whipped Cream Recipes**
- **Strawberries, mint leaves**

- Tint cream cheese icing or stabilized whipped cream pink. Pipe tip 21 zigzags on top. Edge base with tip 21 rosette border.

- Trim top and base with sliced strawberries. Add leaves to top border. Fill center with whole strawberries. *Serves 12.*

LOVE LOCKET

- **Heart Flan Pan,** p. 185
- **Tips 2, 5, 8, p. 133**
- **Meringue Powder, Piping Gel, p. 127**
- **Heart Cookie Cutter Set, p. 122**
- **Cake & Pastry Filling, p. 127**
- **Royal & Buttercream Icings**

- To make lace collar: Lightly grease the inside bottom of heart pan with vegetable shortening. Center the largest cookie cutter on bottom to make a guideline. Add 1 tsp. piping gel to each cup of royal icing. Outline center and outer edge of collar with tip 2. Fill in area with tip 2 sotas (see p. 104). Cover edges with tip 5 bead borders. Let dry overnight.

- Ice cake top with filling. Carefully lift collar out of pan and position on cake. With buttercream, pipe tip 5 bead hearts on sides. Edge base with tip 8 bead border. *Serves 12.*

CROWN JEWELS

- **Heart Quartet Pan, p. 184**
- **Tips 2, 3, 8, p. 134**
- **Meringue Powder, Piping Gel, p. 127**
- **Cake & Pastry Filling, p. 127**
- **Buttercream, Royal Icings**

- To make lace bands: Follow procedure for making lace collar on Love Locket cake. When piping sotas, just cover the the raised sides on each heart.

- Fill hearts on cake with filling. Position heart collars on cake top. Edge top and base with C-motion borders – tip 3 on top, tip 8 at base. *Serves 12.*

SWEET "TWEETS"

- **Double Tier Heart Pan, p. 184**
- **Tips 2, 6, 16, 125, p. 134**
- **Lemon Yellow, Red-Red, Pink, Brown Icing Colors, p. 126**
- **'91 Pattern Book (Dove Pattern), p. 117**
- **Color Flow Mix, p. 127**
- **Edible Glitter, p. 128**
- **Buttercream, Color Flow Icings**
- **Sugar cubes**

- With color flow icing, outline Dove Pattern with tip 2. Flow in design with a cut bag. Sprinkle with edible glitter. Let dry.

- Ice cake smooth. Cover side of top heart with tip 16 zigzags. Pipe tip 6 bead hearts on cake top. Write tip 2 message. Pipe tip 2 scrolls, wavy lines and dots on top.

- Edge base with tip 16 shell border. Add tip 16 rosette at point. Pipe tip 125 ruffle garlands (approximately 2 in. wide) on sides. Edge top with tip 16 zigzags.

- Position sugar cubes on cake top. Attach color flow piece to sugar cubes with dots of icing. *Serves 12.*

SWEET-FACE

- **Gentle Lamb Pan,** p. 187
- **Tips 4, 16, 18, 789,** p. 134-139
- **Kelly Green Icing Color,** p. 126
- **White Candy Melts™*,** p. 119
- **Candy Color Kit,** p. 119
- **Buttercream Icing**

- Tint melted Candy Melts with candy color. Mold candy plaques of face/bow, inside of ears and hooves (see p. 109). Let set.
- Lightly ice areas where candy goes and position candy on cake. Ice sides smooth with tip 789. Outline lamb with tip 4 strings.

- Cover legs with tip 16 stars. Pipe tip 18 reverse shell "wool" on rest of cake. Edge base with tip 18 reverse shell border. *Serves 12.*

*brand confectionery coating

HARE WITH FLAIR

- **Cottontail Bunny Pan,** p. 186
- **Tips 2, 3, 4, 8, 17, 233,** p. 134-135
- **Lemon Yellow, Black, Sky Blue, Pink Icing Colors,** p. 126

- **'91 Pattern Book (Tuxedo Bunny Patterns),** p. 117
- **Buttercream Icing**
- **Uncooked spaghetti, jelly bean**

- Ice smooth – bunny's ears, face and shirt white, background areas and sides yellow. With toothpick, mark Tuxedo Bunny Patterns. Add dimension to eye by building up with tip 4.
- Outline hat, bunny and eggs with tip 4 strings. Pipe in hat, tie, collar and eggs with tip 8 (smooth with finger dipped in cornstarch). Pipe tip 17 stars on snout, inside of ears, jacket and paw.
- Trim tie and shirt with tip 3 dots. Add tip 3 eyelashes and brow.
- Pipe tip 2 dot and string designs on eggs. Pipe tip 17 reverse shell tail.
- Break spaghetti into 4 in. pieces and cover with icing (see p. 105). Push into cake for whiskers. Add jelly bean nose.
- Edge "ground" with tip 233 pull-out grass. Pipe tip 17 zigzag puff border at base. *Serves 12.*

CUTE LITTLE QUACKER

- **Little Ducky Pan,** p. 186
- **Tips 3, 16, 233,** p. 134-135
- **Orange, Lemon Yellow, Brown, Kelly Green, Violet Icing Colors,** p. 126
- **Buttercream Icing**

- On top and sides, ice eggshell, background areas and feet smooth. With toothpick, mark eggshells. Outline eggshells and duckling with tip 3. Print tip 3 message and overpipe with dots.
- Pipe in eyes and beak with tip 3 (smooth with finger dipped in cornstarch). Add tip 3 dot pupils.
- Cover face with tip 16 stars. Pipe tip 16 pull-out stars on wings. Outline eyebrows and lines on wings with tip 3 strings.
- Edge base with tip 233 pull-out grass. *Serves 12.*

HOLIDAYS & EVENTS

Easter

LILIES OF LIGHT

- Cross Pan, p. 187
- Tips 3, 5, 14, 68, 352, p. 134-139
- Green Icing Color, p. 126
- Dark Cocoa Candy Melts™ *, p. 119
- Lily Nail Set, p. 132
- '91 Pattern Book (Joy Pattern), p. 117
- Scrolls, p. 160
- Ganache Glaze Recipe, p. 109
- Buttercream, Royal Icings

- With royal icing, using 1⅝ in. lily nail, pipe tips 14 and 68 lilies . Let dry. Four lilies are needed (make extras to allow for breakage).
- Place cake on rack over a pan to catch excess glaze. Pour ganache glaze over cross. Let set.
- Using Joy Pattern as a guide, write tip 3 script message.
- With buttercream icing, edge base with tip 5 bead borders. Attach lilies and Scrolls with dots of icing. Pipe tip 352 leaves. *Serves 12.*

*brand confectionery coating

BUNNY TOT

- Sunny Bunny Pan, p. 187
- Tips 3, 16, 21, p. 134-135
- Pink, Lemon Yellow, Violet Icing Colors, p. 126
- Buttercream Icing

- Ice background areas, bottom of feet and sides smooth. Outline ears, facial features, head, bow, suit, hands and feet with tip 3 strings.
- Pipe in eyes; add dot irises and highlights with tip 3 (flatten with finger dipped in cornstarch). Pipe tip 3 beads and dots on bottom of feet (flatten with cornstarch). Fill in inside of ears with tip 3 zigzags.
- Cover remaining cake with tip 16 stars. Outline eyelashes and brows with tip 3 strings. Pipe tip 3 dot nose. Edge base with tip 21 shell border. Trim with tip 3 dots. *Serves 12.*

FLEECE AS WHITE AS SNOW

- Little Lamb Pan, p. 186
- Tips 3, 6, 8, 16, 47, p. 133-134
- Pink, Leaf Green, Lemon Yellow Icing Colors, p. 126
- Buttercream Icing

- Ice face, inside of ears and basket area smooth. Pipe tip 6 dot eyes and nose (flatten with finger dipped in cornstarch). Outline mouth and eyelashes with tip 3 strings.
- Cover basket with tips 6 and 47 basketweave. Horizontal ribbed stripes are spatula-striped.
- Fill in lamb's wool with tip 16 stars. Edge basket with tip 8 rope borders. *Serves 12.*

"HARE-RAISING EGGSEMBLY" LINE

- Egg Pan Set, Egg Mini-Cake Pan, p. 186
- Tips 2, 3, 16, 47, 233, p. 134-139
- Violet, Pink, Lemon Yellow, Kelly Green Icing Colors, p. 126
- Candy Melts™* – White, Yellow, Dark Cocoa, p. 119
- Meringue Powder, p. 127
- Playful Bunnies Candy Mold, Easter Treats, Easter Variety Set, Alphabet Set Candy Mold, p. 121
- Cake Boards or Circles, Fanci-Foil Wrap, p. 132-133
- Buttercream, Royal or Snow-white Buttercream Icings
- Open-centered candies, small jelly beans, candy sticks, malted milk eggs
- Melt Candy Melts. Mold at least 12 bunnies (one for cake should be half the depth of mold) and letters. Let set. With royal or snow-white icing, trim letters with tip 2 strings and dots. Pipe in eyes and carrots on bunnies with tip 2.

- For cars: Position mini egg cakes on foil-covered cake boards. Push bunnies into cakes. Cover cakes with tip 16 stars. Pipe tip 233 pull-out grass in back of bunnies. Where wheels go, pipe small circles with tip 16 and position candy wheels. Pipe in holes with tip 2. Add candy steering wheel and jelly bean eggs. Pipe in hubcaps on wheels with tip 3.

- For basket: Slice a small piece off curved side of egg so cake sits level. Cover sides with tip 47 ribbed stripe basketweave. Mound icing on top, position bunny and add jelly beans. Pipe tip 233 pull-out grass.

- For egg factory: Slice off curved side on one half of egg so cake sits level. Fill and position halves together. Ice front side and ends smooth. With toothpick, mark windows on front and ends. Cover remaining cake with tip 16 stars. Edge windows with tip 16 zigzags. Push bunny onto cake. Pipe tip 233 pull-out grass on front window. Position letters and add candy trims. For egg shoots: Attach 2 candy sticks together with dots of icing, then attach jelly bean eggs. Arrange egg factory, shoots, basket and cars together. Serves 20 (large egg cake serves 12, a mini egg cake serves 1).

*brand confectionery coating

Easter Greetings

Happy Haunting!

Trick or Treat

HAPPY HALLOWEEN

64

GOOD WISH WITCH

- Wicked Witch Pan, p. 183
- Tips 3, 14, 16, p. 134-135
- Black, Lemon Yellow, Orange, Royal Blue, Pink Icing Colors, p. 126
- '91 Pattern Book (Witch Pattern), p. 117
- Buttercream Icing

- Ice background area on top and sides smooth. Ice hat band and under brim smooth. With toothpick, mark Witch Pattern (for easier marking, lightly ice area).
- Outline hat and facial features with tip 3 strings. Pipe in eyes, mouth and tongue with tip 3 (flatten with finger dipped in cornstarch). Add tip 3 blue and black dots to eyes (flatten with finger dipped in cornstarch). Print tip 3 "wavy" message.
- Cover hat, face, neck and dress with tip 16 stars. Fill in buckle on hat with tip 14 stars.
- Pipe tip 16 side-by-side swirled stripe strands of hair. Trim hat and dress randomly with tip 16 orange stars. Add tip 3 outline eyelashes. *Serves 12.*

GHOST RIDERS

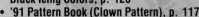

- Up 'N Away Balloon Pan, p. 175
- Tips 1, 4, 9, 16, 47, p. 134-139
- Orange, Cornflower Blue, Golden Yellow, Brown, Black, White, Icing Colors, p. 126
- '91 Pattern Book (Pumpkin Face Pattern), p. 117
- Buttercream Icing

- Ice sides smooth. With toothpick, mark Pumpkin Face Pattern on balloon (for easier marking, lightly ice area). Outline facial features, balloon, basket and ropes with tip 4 strings.
- Pipe in eyes, nose and mouth with tip 4 (flatten with finger dipped in cornstarch).
- Cover pumpkin balloon and sky with tip 16 stars. Cover basket with tip 47 smooth stripes. Edge top of basket with tip 16 shells. lengths for a wooden effect).
- Pipe tip 47 smooth stripe banner on basket. Allow icing to crust slightly, then print tip 1 message. Figure pipe tip 9 ghost (see p. 105). Add tip 1 dot eyes and outline mouths. Edge base with tip tip 16 shell border. *Serves 12.*

GUESS WHO?

- Scarecrow Pan, p. 183
- Tips 2, 4, 16, 17, 18, p. 134-135
- Golden Yellow, Orange, Brown Black Icing Colors, p. 126
- '91 Pattern Book (Clown Pattern), p. 117
- Buttercream Icing
- Gumball

- Ice background area white, bag area tan. With toothpick, mark clown patterns. Cover marks with tip 4.
- Outline face, suit and bag with tip 4. Pipe in mask, mouth, eyes, hands with tip 4 (smooth with finger). Outline smile; add tip 4 dots to eyes.
- Cover face with tip 16 stars, suit and hat with tip 17 stars. Pipe tip 18 spatula-striped pull-out star hair. Edge hat and fill in ruffles with tip 18 zigzags. Add tip 18 pull-out star pompon and stars to hat. Print tip 2 message. Add gumball nose. *Serves 12.*

FUNNY BONES

- Boo Ghost Pan, p. 183
- Tips 4, 16, 47, p. 134-139
- Violet, Orange, Black Icing Colors, p. 126
- '91 Pattern Book (Skeleton Pattern), p. 117
- Buttercream Icing

- Ice ghost and center of letters black. With toothpick, mark Skeleton Pattern. Outline skull with tip 4 strings. Cover with tip 16 stars.
- Outline letters with tip 16 stars. Fill in letters and edge base with tip 16 stars.
- Pipe tip 47 ribbed stripe fingers, ribs and spine. Add tip 16 shell finger tips. *Serves 12.*

SPOOKY FACES

- Mini Pumpkin Pan, p. 183
- Tip 4, p. 134
- Black Icing Color, p. 126

- Ice cakes smooth. With toothpick, mark facial features.
- Pipe in eyes with tip 4 (flatten with finger), add tip 4 dot highlights. Pipe tip 4 bead nostrils and zigzag mouth. *Each serves 1.*

Halloween

COUNTRY BUMPKIN

- **Scarecrow Pan, p. 183**
- **Tips 4, 16, 21, 67, 233, p. 134-136**
- **Orange, Moss Green, Golden Yellow, Ivory, Brown, Burgundy Icing Colors, p. 126**
- **Buttercream Icing**

- Ice sides smooth. With toothpick, mark face (lightly ice area for easier marking). Outline hat, face, shirt, overalls, patches and cuffs with tip 4 strings. Pipe in facial features and patches with tip 4 (smooth with finger dipped in cornstarch).
- Cover hat, face, shirt and overalls with tip 16 stars. Cover cuffs of overalls with tip 16 zigzags.
- Pipe tip 233 pull-out straw hair, hands, feet and border at base. Trim neck and sleeves with tip 67 ruffles. Add tip 21 star buttons to overalls. *Serves 12.*

SEEDY MEANIE

- **Jack-O-Lantern Pan, p. 183**
- **14 in. Square Pans, p. 169**
- **Tips 4, 8, 17, 21, 67, 199, p. 134-136**
- **Moss Green, Ivory, Golden Yellow, Orange Icing Colors, p. 126**
- **'91 Pattern Book (Eyes & Smile Pattern), p. 117**
- **Buttercream Icing**

- Ice square cake smooth. Position jack-o-lantern cake atop square. With toothpick, mark Eyes & Smile Pattern on jack-o-lantern (for easier marking, lightly ice area). Outline pumpkin and facial features with tip 4 strings. Pipe in small triangles in eyes with tip 4.
- Cover jack-o-lantern with stars – tip 17 on facial features, tip 21 on rest of top and sides. Pipe tip 199 side-by-side stripes and rosette on stem. Add tip 21 elongated shell eyebrows.
- Edge top of square with tip 8 bead border. In corners, pipe tip 199 star puff pumpkins. Trim with tip 4 pull-out dot stems.

Pipe tip 4 outline vines on cake top. Add tip 67 leaves on vines and elongated leaves on sides. *Serves 54.*

LOADS OF FUN FOR FALL

- **18-Wheeler Pan, p. 175**
- **Tips 3, 4, 7, 16, 48, 233, p. 134-139**
- **Brown, Moss Green, Golden Yellow, Orange Icing Colors, p. 126**
- **Buttercream Icing**
- **Chocolate sandwich cookies**

- Ice wheel area, window, light, fender and trailer hitch on top and sides smooth. Outline cab and door with tip 4 strings. Fill in cab and door with tip 16 stars.
- Cover side and tailgate of truck with tip 48 ribbed stripes. Figure pipe tip 7 pumpkins (see p. 105). Add tip 4 outline stems. Pipe tip 233 pull-out straw.
- Write tip 3 message. Position cookies and add tip 7 dot hubcaps (flatten with finger dipped in cornstarch). Edge base with tip 7 bead border. *Serves 12.*

HOLIDAYS & EVENTS

Halloween

GOBBLIN' GOODY BOXES

- **Cookie Sheets, p. 172; Cookie Pans, p. 125**
- **Mini Loaf Pan, p. 173**
- **Tips 2, 233, p. 134**
- **Orange, Kelly Green, Black, Icing Colors, p. 126**
- **Candy Melts™ *–Fall Mix, p. 119**
- **Halloween Variety Candy Mold Set, p. 121**
- **Halloween Cookie Cutter Set, p. 122**
- **Meringue Powder, p. 127**
- **Roll-Out Cookie Dough Recipe, p. 108**
- **Royal Icing**

- Divide cookie dough into 3rds. Tint ⅓ orange with icing color. Roll dough out to ⅜ths thickness. Cut out pumpkins and ghost (3 of each cookie needed for each basket). Thin approximately ⅛ cup of dough with water. Add a ½ teaspooon of water until piping consistency is reached. Tint a small amount green; remainder black. Outline ghosts and pipe in details on pumpkins with tip 2. Bake and cool.

- For bases of baskets: Roll out dough to same thickness. Using bottom of mini loaf pans as a guide, cut rectangle shapes, ½ in. larger than pan size. Press into bottom of pans and bring up sides. Bake per recipe directions.

- Attach cookies to base with icing. Pipe tip 233 pull-out blades of grass around base. Let dry. Recipe yields enough to make 4 baskets.

- Using melted Candy Melts, mold an assortment of candy delights. Fill baskets.
*brand confectionery coating

LUCKY LADY!

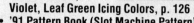

- 18-Wheeler Truck Pan, p. 175
- Tips 1, 3, 10, 16, 47, 67, p. 134-139
- Red-Red, Black, Lemon Yellow, Violet, Leaf Green Icing Colors, p. 126
- '91 Pattern Book (Slot Machine Pattern), p. 117
- Buttercream Icing
- Foil-covered candy coins, candy stick
- Ice cake smooth – background areas grey, machine red and white. With toothpick, mark Slot Machine Patterns. Outline message area with tip 47 smooth stripes.
- Outline windows, message bars, star designs, coin drop and sides with tip 3; coin tray with tip 10. Pipe in star designs, 25 button and coin slot with tip 3 (smooth with finger dipped in cornstarch).
- Position coin on coin drop. Outline top edge with tip 3. Print tip 1 messages on windows and button. Figure pipe tip 3 lemons, plums and cherries. Outline stems with tip 3 strings. Add tip 67 leaves.
- Cover coin slot and body of machine with tip 16 stars. Edge base with tip 16 star border. Position candy stick handle and an assortment of candy coins. *Serves 12.*

JUST HANGIN' AROUND!

- Horseshoe Pan, p. 182
- Tips 3, 18, 74, 102, 104, 233, p. 134-138
- Brown, Ivory, Golden Yellow, Kelly Green Icing Colors, p. 126
- Flower Nail No. 7, p. 132
- Flower Formers, Edible Glitter, p. 128
- Meringue Powder, p. 127
- Lazy Bones, p. 144
- Buttercream, Royal Icings
- With royal icing, make 15 daisies – 5 with tip 102, 10 with tip 104. Add tip 3 dot centers. Pat centers with edible glitter and dry on flower formers.
- Ice cake smooth. With toothpick, mark 3 in. intervals on sides. Connect marks with tip 74 garlands. Edge top with tip 74 C-shell border. Pipe tip 18 shell border at base.
- Print tip 3 message. Pipe tip 233 pull-out grass on cake top. Position Lazy Bones and daisies. *Serves 12.*

TIME TO BE A SWINGER

- USA Pan, p. 181
- Tips 2, 3, 11, 233, p. 134
- Kelly Green, Royal Blue Icing Colors, p. 126
- Golf Set, p. 141
- Buttercream Icing
- Granulated light brown sugar
- Ice cake smooth – green areas green, sand traps and sides white.

Retirement

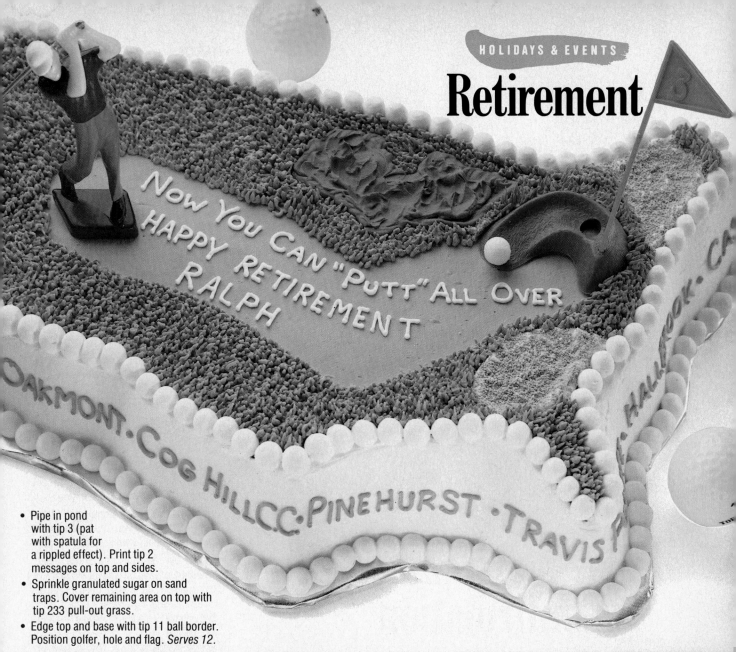

Now You Can "Putt" All Over
Happy Retirement
Ralph

Oakmont•Cog Hill C.C.•Pinehurst•Travis P
Hallbrook•Ca

- Pipe in pond with tip 3 (pat with spatula for a rippled effect). Print tip 2 messages on top and sides.

- Sprinkle granulated sugar on sand traps. Cover remaining area on top with tip 233 pull-out grass.

- Edge top and base with tip 11 ball border. Position golfer, hole and flag. *Serves 12.*

QUITE A SEND-OFF!

- **Congratulations Pan, p. 181**
- **Oval Pan Set (largest size is used), p. 165**
- **Tips 3, 16, 21, 23, 24, 129, 352, p. 134-137**
- **Pink, Leaf Green Icing Colors, p. 126**
- **Tuk 'N Ruffle, Cake Boards, Fanci-Foil Wrap, p. 132-133**
- **Buttercream Icing**

- Make 90 drop flowers – 15 with tip 129, 45 with tip 24 and 30 with tip 23. Use tip 3 for dot centers.

- Ice "2-layer" (one-layer oval and congratulations) cakes smooth.

- Cover top with tip 16 stars. Cover letters with tip 21. Print name with tip 16 or 21 depending on length of name.

- Edge base of congratulations cake and top of oval with tip 16 shell borders. Edge bases with tip 21 C-scroll borders.

- Position flowers on congratulations cake and trim with tip 352 leaves. *Serves 34.*

HOLIDAYS & EVENTS

Bar & Bat Mitzvah, Confirmation

STAR OF THE TEMPLE

- **16 in. Round Pans,** p. 168
- **9 & 12 in. Hexagon Pans,** p. 167
- **Sports Ball Pan,** p. 180
- **Tips 1, 2, 3, 16, 18, 21, 101, 224,** p. 134-138
- **Royal Blue, Golden Yellow, Black Icing Colors,** p. 126
- **'91 Pattern Book (Star & Alphabet Patterns),** p. 117
- **7 in. Crystal-Clear Separator Plates,** p. 163
- **5 in. Crystal-Clear Pillars,** p. 163
- **Groomsman,** p. 157
- **Color Flow Mix, Meringue Powder, Piping Gel,** p. 127
- **Cake Dividing Set,** p. 130
- **Dowel Rods,** p. 165
- **Cake Circles, Fanci-Foil Wrap,** p. 132-133
- **Buttercream, Royal, Color Flow Icings**
- **Yellow paper**

- Using Star (7 are needed) and Alphabet Patterns (make extras in case of breakage) with color flow icing, outline with tip 1 and flow in. Let dry. Attach a star to a toothpick with dots of royal icing.

- Make 50 tip 224 drop flowers with tip 2 dot centers with royal or stiffened buttercream.

- With royal icing, cover groomsman's head with tip 3 dot yarmulke. Outline scarf with tip 101. Trim with tip 1 string stripes and stars.

- Ice one-layer hexagons and 2-layer round cakes smooth and prepare for stacked construction (see p. 106). Position half ball on 6 in. cake board atop 7 in. plate. Cover ball with tip 16 stars. Using Cake Dividing Set, divide half ball into 8ths. Dot mark Stairstep Garland (see p. 104) on sides of 16 in. cake. Divide side of 9 in. hexagon in half for garlands.

- Edge tops and bases with shell borders—tip 16 at base of ball and tops of hexagons; tip 18 at bases of hexagons and top of round; tip 21 at base of round.

- Pipe tip 18 e-motion garlands. Trim with tip 3 drop strings on ball, 9 in. hexagon and 16 in. round. Pipe tip 18 fleur-de-lis on sides of 12 in. hexagon.

- Cover separator plate with yellow paper with holes cut for pillars. Position atop 9 in. cake.

- To serve: Assemble ball on pillars. Position figure. Push color flow* star into ball. Attach remaining stars and letters to sides with dots of royal icing. *Serves 85.*

*Note: Since buttercream icing breaks down color flow, attach pieces shortly before serving.

BEAUTIFUL HONORS BESTOWED

- **12 in. Round Pans,** p. 168
- **Bevel Pan Set (12 in. top, 16 in. base are used),** p. 167
- **Tips 2, 3, 5, 14, 352, 362, 364,** p. 134-136
- **Pink, Brown Icing Colors,** p. 126
- **Meringue Powder,** p. 127
- **White Candy Melts™* (2 pkgs.),** p. 119
- **Dowel Rods,** p. 165
- **Decorator Pattern Press Set, Cake Dividing Set, Decorator's Brushes,** p. 130
- **Modeling Candy Recipe,** p. 110
- **Buttercream, Royal or Snow-white Buttercream Icings**

- Using modeling candy (see p. 110), make 17 roses–14 three-petal, 2 five-petal and 1 seven-petal and Torah ornament. Allow candy pieces to dry several days. Paint rose leaf with melted candy. Let set. Make 10 candy leaves.

- Cut and position dowel rods in bevel base. Add one-layer round and bevel top. Ice smooth. Using cake dividing set, dot mark sides of round into 12ths. Using C-scroll pattern press, imprint back-to-back (approximately 1 in. apart) scrolls on bevel base.

- Stringwork and scrolls will be overpiped to create a dimensional effect. For stringwork on round, use tips 2, 3 and 5. For scrolls on bevel, use tips 2, 5 and 14. Directions on p. 104.

- Edge tops and bases with shell borders–tip 364 on bevel top and round, tip 362 on bevel base.

- Trim stringwork with tip 362 inverted fleur-de-v's. Add tip 5 large dots and tip 3 small dots between each.

- Position candy Torah, roses and leaves on cake top. To decorate Torah: With royal icing, pipe tip 2 message; outline vines and scrolls. Trim vines with tip 352 leaves, scrolls with tip 2 dots. Position remaining roses at base and trim with tip 352 leaves. *Serves 51.*

*brand confectionery coating

INSPIRING SPIRIT

- **Dessert Shell Pan,** p. 182
- **Tips 4, 16, 17,** p. 134-135
- **Golden Yellow, Red-Red Icing Colors,** p. 126
- **'91 Pattern Book (Dove Pattern),** p. 117
- **Buttercream Icing**

- Lightly ice cake top smooth. With toothpick, mark Dove Pattern. Cover marks and outline rays with tip 4 strings.

- Cover Dove with tip 17 stars. Fill in rays and background area with tip 16 stars. Print tip 4 message. *Serves 12.*

THE WINGS OF LOVE

- **Half Round Pan,** p. 170
- **Tips 2, 3, 10,** p. 134
- **Ivory, Red-Red, Teal Icing Colors,** p. 126
- **'91 Pattern Book (Communion Spirit & Fancy Script Patterns),** p. 117
- **Color Flow Mix,** p. 127
- **Buttercream Icing**

- Using Communion Spirit Patterns and color flow icing, outline dove and water with tip 3 and flow in (see Color Flow, p. 108).

- Ice one-layer cake smooth with buttercream. Print name and message using Fancy Script Pattern as a guide with tip 2. Optional: Overpipe capital letters.

- Edge top and base with tip 10 bulb borders. Position color flow pieces*. *Serves 18.*

*Note: Since buttercream icing will break down color flow, position on a piece of plastic wrap cut to fit, sugar cubes or mini marshmallows.

Christening & Communion

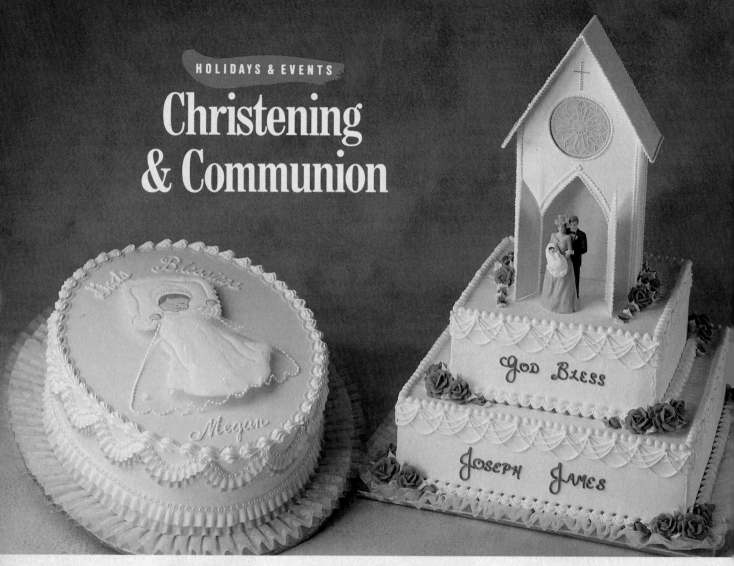

A JOY TO BEHOLD!

- Oval Pan Set, (largest size is used), p. 167
- Tips 2, 16, 104, 125, p. 134-138
- Pink, Brown Icing Colors, p. 126
- '91 Pattern Book (Baby Pattern), p. 117
- Color Flow Mix, p. 127
- Large (6mm) Pearl Beads, p. 159
- Cake Boards, Fanci-Foil Wrap, Tuk 'N Ruffle, p. 132-133
- Buttercream, Color Flow Icings
- Tulle trim (9 ins. long), sugar cubes

- Using Baby Pattern and color flow icing, outline baby with tip 2 and flow in (see Color Flow, p. 108). Let dry. For skirt: With needle and thread, gather one edge of tulle up to 1¾ ins. wide. Cut scallops in other edge. Using regular strength color flow, pipe tip 2 string over gathered edge of tulle at yoke. Let dry. Edge tulle with tip 2 beads. Randomly trim tulle with tip 2 bead and dot flowers.

- Ice 2-layer cake smooth—top pink, sides white on foil-covered, Tuk 'N Ruffle trimmed board. With toothpick, mark garlands on sides—1 in. from top, 2¾ in. wide and 1¼ in. deep. Connect marks with tip 104 double ruffles.

- Edge top and base with tip 16 shell borders. Above base border, pipe two rows of tip 125 ruffles. Trim shell on top with tip 2 zigzags. Attach Pearl Beads to sides with dots of icing. Write tip 2 message.
- Place sugar cubes where baby will go and position color flow. *Serves 44.*

CHRISTENING DAY

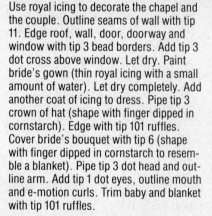

- 10 & 14 in. Square Pans, p. 169
- Tips 1, 3, 6, 11, 12, 101, 103, 104, 352, p. 134-138
- Flower Nail No. 7, p. 132
- Royal Blue, Copper, Brown Icing Colors, p. 126
- '91 Pattern Book (Script Letters Pattern), p. 117
- Meringue Powder, Piping Gel, p. 127
- Cathedral Cake Kit, p. 162
- Decorator's Brush, p. 130
- Cake Boards, Fanci-Foil Wrap, Tuk 'N Ruffle, p. 132-133
- Dowel Rods, p. 165
- Side-by-Side Couple, p. 157
- Buttercream, Royal Icings

- Assemble chapel from Cathedral Kit. Tape a piece of Fanci-Foil Wrap behind window.

Use royal icing to decorate the chapel and the couple. Outline seams of wall with tip 11. Edge roof, wall, door, doorway and window with tip 3 bead borders. Add tip 3 dot cross above window. Let dry. Paint bride's gown (thin royal icing with a small amount of water). Let dry completely. Add another coat of icing to dress. Pipe tip 3 crown of hat (shape with finger dipped in cornstarch). Edge with tip 101 ruffles. Cover bride's bouquet with tip 6 (shape with finger dipped in cornstarch to resemble a blanket). Pipe tip 3 dot head and outline arm. Add tip 1 dot eyes, outline mouth and e-motion curls. Trim baby and blanket with tip 101 ruffles.

- Using tip 12 for base, make 30 roses—10 with tip 104, 20 with tip 103.
- Ice 2-layer cakes smooth. Prepare cakes for stacked tiers construction (see p. 106).
- Pipe tip 3 double/triple drop string borders on sides of tiers. Edge tops with bead borders—tip 6 on top tier, tip 11 on bottom. Edge bases with ball borders using the same tips as above. Between balls, pipe tip 3 dots.
- Write tip 3 message on sides (use Script Letters Pattern as a guide). Add roses and trim with tip 352 leaves. Position chapel and godparents on top. *Serves 55.*

FAITHFUL DAY

- **Two-Mix Book Pan,** p. 176
- **Mini-Bell Pan,** p. 176
- **Tips 3, 6, 12, 16, 55, 104, 224, 349,** p. 134-138
- **Golden Yellow, Sky Blue, Leaf Green Icing Colors,** p. 126
- **Decorating Comb,** p. 130
- **Buttercream Icing**
- **Wafer paper or parchment**

- Make 50 tip 224 drop flowers with tip 3 dot centers.

- Ice book cake smooth—top white, sides yellow. Use Decorating Comb on sides to resemble pages.

- For chalice: Ice wide ends of two mini bells. Position atop book with narrow ends together. Outline circle design (approximately 1½ in. diameter) and sides of chalice with tip 3 strings. Pipe in circle with tip 3 (smooth with finger dipped in cornstarch). Pipe tip 3 cross in circle. Cover chalice with tip 16 stars, building up stars where cakes meet. Edge top, center and base with 2 rows of tip 3 strings.

- Pipe tip 104 spatula-striped scallops on cake top. Edge top and base with bulb borders—tip 6 at top, tip 12 at base.

- Cut a circle from wafer or parchment paper to resemble host. Print tip 55 letters on host and message on cake. Position host in chalice. Add flowers to top and base. Trim with tip 349 leaves. *Serves 26.*

BLESSINGS ON HER

- **Petal Pan Set (9 & 15 in. pans used),** p. 167
- **Petite Doll Pan,** p. 174
- **Tips 2, 12, 16, 18, 55, 102, 103, 104, 352,** p. 133-138
- **Flower Nail No. 7,** p. 132
- **Pink, Leaf Green Icing Colors,** p. 126
- **Freckle-Faced Little Girl Pick, Shining Cross,** p. 141
- **Florist Wire,** p. 128
- **Dowel Rods,** p. 165
- **Tuk 'N Ruffle, Cake Boards, Fanci-Foil Wrap,** p. 132-133
- **Buttercream Icing**

- Using tip 12 for base, make 16 roses—6 with tip 103, 10 with tip 102.

- Ice one-layer cakes smooth and prepare for stacked construction (p. 106). Print tip 2 message on cake top.

- For girl: Ice petite doll cake smooth on a cake board cut to fit. Attach a piece of Tuk 'N Ruffle to doll's head with pins or glue. Push doll into cake. Build up waist with icing. Cut a 6 in. piece of florist wire. Form a loop for rosary, twist around to hold hands together and bring end around to front. Pipe tip 2 beads on wire (use stiffened buttercream). Position atop tiered cakes. Cover bodice with tip 16 stars. Pipe collar and cuffs with tip 55. Edge skirt with tip 102 rows of ruffles.

- Edge tops with C-Scrolls—tip 16 on 9 in., tip 18 on 15 in. Edge bases with shell borders using the same tips as above. Pipe tip 104 ruffles at bases—one row on 9 in., two rows on 15 in. Attach Shining Cross to cake side with dots of icing. Position roses and trim with tip 352 leaves. *Serves 26.*

TO CAP IT OFF!
- **Jumbo Muffin Pan, p. 172**
- **Tips 2, 4, p. 134**
- **Royal Blue, Golden Yellow Icing Colors, p. 126**
- **Cake Boards, p. 133**
- **Glad Graduate, p. 143**

- **Meringue Powder, p. 127**
- **Roll-Out Cookie Dough Recipe, p. 108**
- **Buttercream, Royal Icings**
- For tops of mortarboards: Cut 4 in. squares out of cookie dough. Bake and cool. Ice smooth with royal icing. Let dry. Alternate idea: Cut squares out of cake board and ice.
- Trim crowns; invert large cup cakes (bottoms

up) and ice with buttercream. Attach tops to muffins with dabs of icing.
- With royal icing, pipe tip 2 outline cord on each. Overpipe with tip 2 e-motion. Add tip 2 pull-out strings tassel. Trim tassel with tip 2 dot; cord end with tip 4 dot (flatten dots with finger dipped in cornstarch). Pipe tip 2 date on tassel. Position Glad Graduate on serving plate. *Each serves 1.*

THE SKY'S THE LIMIT!
- **Shooting Star Pan, p. 174**
- **Tips 3, 17, p. 134-135**
- **Wilton Red, Golden Yellow Icing Colors, p. 126**
- **Star Cookie Cutter Set, p. 125**
- **Glowing Grad, p. 143**
- **Color Flow Mix, p. 127**
- **Buttercream & Color Flow Icings**
- Make four color flow stars, using 2 of the smallest star cookie cutters from the set as a pattern. Outline stars with tip 3 and flow in icing. Allow icing to set.
- Ice star area, top and sides, smooth. Outline star with tip 3. Write tip 3 message.
- Cover rainbow with tip 17 stars. Edge base around star with tip 17 star border. Position color flow stars and Glowing Grad. *Serves 12.*

Note: Since buttercream icing will break down color flow, either position pieces on cake shortly before serving or place a piece of plastic wrap cut to fit on area first.

Graduation

IT'S ALL LOCKED UP!

- Long Loaf Pans, p. 170
- Tips 1D, 2, 9, 44, 47, p. 134-139
- Red-Red, Black, Golden Yellow, Royal Blue, Ivory Icing Colors, p. 126
- '91 Pattern Book (Locker Stuff Patterns), p. 117
- Cake Boards, Fanci-Foil Wrap, p. 132-133
- Parchment Triangles, p. 129
- Buttercream Icing
- Edible confetti trims

- Ice each loaf cake on a cake board cut to fit. Position cakes together on serving board. With toothpick, mark louvers, pendants, shoes and note paper.

- Outline pendants, shoes and note paper with tip 2. Pipe in with tip 9 (smooth and shape with finger dipped in cornstarch). Make holes in paper with point of knife. Cover toes, soles of shoes and add tape to papers with tip 44. Pipe tip 2 outline streamers and poles on pendants, laces on shoes, lines on note paper.

- Pipe tip 47 smooth stripe louvers, message banner and handles. Edge tops amd bases with tip 44 stripes. Print messages on banner and papers with tip 2.

- Cut a 2½ x 12 in. strip from parchment triangle for large banner. Write tip 2 message. Position on cake: Add candy "confetti." Serves 54.

Anniversary

BELLS & SPANGLES

- 6 in. Round Pan, p. 168
- 4-pc. Hexagon Pan Set (15 in. used), p. 167
- Mini Bell Pan, p. 176
- Tips 3, 12, 16, 18, 21, 103, 104, p. 134-138
- Flower Nail No. 7, p. 132
- Golden Yellow Icing Color, p. 126
- Meringue Powder, p. 127
- Cake Dividing Set, Decorator's Brush, p. 130
- 7 in. Round Separator Plate, p. 166
- 9 in. Spiked Pillars, p. 164
- Small Gold Artificial Leaves, p. 156
- Small Gold Rings, Flower Spikes, p. 158
- Anniversary Couple, p. 157
- Scrolls, p. 160
- Petite Anniversary, p. 154
- Florist Wire, p. 128
- Cake Boards, Fanci-Foil Wrap, Tuk 'N Ruffle, p. 132-133
- Buttercream, Royal Icings
- Craft Block

- With royal or stiffened buttercream, make 15 roses using tip 12 for bases—10 with tip 103, 5 with tip 104. Make 48 tip 104 sweet peas. For spray: Cut 25 pieces of florist wire—one 6½ ins., 8 of each length—3½, 4½ and 5½ ins. Pipe tip 3 beads every ½ in. Push into a craft block to dry. Twist ends of stems together. With thinned royal, paint 12 Scrolls and let dry.

- Ice 6 mini bells on cake boards cut to fit. With toothpick, mark 1 in. wide scallops. Cover marks with tip 3 zigzags. Trim with tip 3 drop strings and dots. Attach pairs of rings with dots of icing and add tip 103 ribbon bows.

- Ice 2-layer tiers smooth and prepare for push-in pillar construction (see p. 106).

- Using Cake Dividing Set, with toothpick, mark round into 6ths. Mark 3 in. wide garlands on hexagon. Position bells atop hexagon. Edge bell bases with tip 3 bead borders.

- Edge tops and bases with shell borders—tip 16 at top, tip 21 at base of round; tip 18 on top and tip 21 at base of hexagon. Pipe tip 16 zigzag garlands on sides. Trim with tip 3 triple drop strings. Push Scrolls into sides.

- Position Petite Anniversary. Outline birds with tip 3. Push flower spike into round cake behind ornament. Insert flower spray into spike. Add flowers to tops and sides. Trim with artificial leaves.

- To serve: Position couple on hexagon. Assemble tier on pillars. *Serves 48.*

STILL CHIMIN' TOGETHER

- **Double Bell Pan, p. 176**
- **Tips 3, 12, 16, 18, p. 134-135**
- **Brown, Pink Icing Colors, p. 126**
- **Buttercream Icing**

- Ice message areas smooth. Outline bells and bow with tip 3 strings. Print tip 3 message.

- Edge rims of bells with tip 18 zigzags. Cover bow and bells with tip 16 stars.

- Figure pipe tip 12 faces (shape and flatten with finger dipped in cornstarch). Add tip 3 outline facial features, dot eyes and noses, bead ears. Pipe tip 3 e-motion hair (overpipe to add dimension).

- Edge base with tip 18 shell border. *Serves 12.*

ROSY HEARTS

- **Heart Mini Tier, p. 184**
- **Tips 1, 18, 103, 352, p. 134-138**
- **Creamy Peach, Ivory, Moss Green Icing Colors, p. 126**
- **Flower Nail No. 7, p. 132**
- **Cake Boards, p. 133**
- **Meringue Powder, p. 127**
- **Buttercream, Royal Icings**
- **Ribbon banner**

- Using royal icing, make 60 tip 103 wild roses (20 in each shade) with tip 1 pull-out dot centers.

- Prepare one-layer cakes for push-in pillar construction (see p. 106). Ice cakes smooth.

- Edge top and bases with tip 18 shell borders. Add tip 18 rosettes to sides at points.

- Position flowers on top and sides. Trim with tip 352 leaves.

- To serve: Assemble tiers. Write names on ribbon and place on cake. *Serves 12.*

STILL UP IN THE AIR!

- Country Goose Pan, p. 182
- Tips 3, 6, 16, 199, p. 134-135
- Sky Blue, Golden Yellow, Pink Icing Colors, p. 126
- '91 Pattern Book (Stork & Baby Patterns), p. 117
- Roll-Out Cookie Recipe, p. 108
- Buttercream Icing

- Out of cookie dough, using Stork & Baby Patterns, cut out hat, beak, tie and face. Bake and cool. Timesaving idea: Cut pieces out of cake board. Using royal or snow-white buttercream, outline hat, beak and tie with tip 3 strings. Fill in with tip 16 stars. Ice face smooth. Add tip 3 dot eyes, outline ears and mouth; tip 16 rosette curl. Let dry.

- Ice background area on top and side smooth. Outline stork's head, neck and wing with tip 3. Fill in face, neck and body with tip 16 stars. Add tip 16 pull-out star feathers on wing. Pipe tip 6 dot eye.

- Position baby's face. Pipe tip 199 star blanket. Edge base with tip 6 bead border. Attach hat, beak and tie to cake with icing. *Serves 12.*

FEEDING TIME

- 12 in. Round Pans, p. 168
- Tips 3, 6, 9, 11, 18, 20, p. 134-135
- Lemon Yellow, Sky Blue, Pink Icing Colors, p. 126
- '91 Pattern Book (Clock Face Pattern), p. 117
- Baby Bracelets (3 pkgs. needed), p. 141
- 3 A.M. Feeding, p. 141
- Cake Dividing Set, p. 130
- Buttercream Icing

- Ice 2-layer cake smooth. Mark Clock Face Pattern on cake top with a toothpick. Cover hands with tip 9, numbers with tip 6. Print tip 3 message.

- Using cake dividing set, divide sides into 12ths. Connect marks with tip 18 zigzag garlands. Bend Baby Bracelets to fit garlands. Position and pipe tip 11 balls at each end.

- Edge top and base with shell borders—tip 18 at top, tip 20 at base. Position 3 A.M. Feeding. *Serves 36.*

PATTY CAKE

- Dessert Shell Pan, p. 182
- Tips 3, 6, 16, 45, 47, 104, 127D, p. 134-139
- Lemon Yellow, Pink, Brown Icing Colors, p. 126
- '91 Pattern Book (Baby Face Pattern), p. 117
- Buttercream Icing
- Open-center candy

Baby Shower

- Ice cake smooth—face area pink, remainder yellow. With toothpick, mark Baby Face Pattern. Outline eyes, lashes, nose and mouth with tip 3 strings. Pipe in whites of eyes with tip 6 (smooth with finger dipped in cornstarch). Pipe tip 6 dot cheeks, pacifier and pupils of eyes (flatten with finger tip). Add tip 3 elongated bead eyebrows.

- Edge top and base with tip 16 shell borders. Pipe tip 127D ruffle bonnet (do outer row first).

- Edge ruffles with tip 45 smooth stripe. Overpipe with tip 47 ribbed stripes. Trim stripes and outline bow with tip 3 beads. Fill in inside of bow with tip 3 zigzags. Cover bow with tip 16 stars. Pipe tip 16 pull-out stripe hair.

- Edge base with tip 104 ruffle. Trim edge with tip 3 beads. Attach candy to pacifier with dots of icing. *Serves 12.*

BRIDAL TOAST

- Heart Pan Set, (15½ in. is used), p. 185
- Tips 3, 14, 16, 21, 104, 352, p. 134-138
- Creamy Peach, Lemon Yellow, Leaf Green Icing Colors, p. 126
- 1⅝ in. Lily Nail, p. 132
- Pearl Stamens, p. 128

- Small (4mm) Pearl Beads, p. 159
- Meringue Powder, p. 127
- Bride & Groom Champagne Glasses, p. 154
- Dowel Rods, p. 165
- 7 in. Round Crystal-Clear Separator Plate (optional), p. 163
- Cake Boards, Tuk 'N Ruffle, Fanci- Foil Wrap. p. 132-133
- Buttercream, Royal Icings
- Gift wrap filler

- Using royal icing, make petunias with tips 14 and 104. 7 are needed (make extras in case of breakage). Add artificial stamens.

- Ice 2-layer cake smooth on Tuk 'n Ruffle-trimmed cake board. Dowel rod cake top where glasses will go. Optional: Position Crystal-Clear Plate over dowel rods (projections down) for added support.

- With toothpick, dot mark 3 in. wide intervals on sides. Connect marks with tip 16 double drop strings. Pipe tip 16 fleur-de-lis on sides. Overpipe with tip 14 in contrasting shade. Add tip 14 stars to sides.

- Write tip 3 message on top. Add tip 3 bead heart. Edge top with double rows of tip 16 shells. Pipe tip 21 shell border at base. Trim point with tip 21 rosette.

- Cut a strand of small pearl beads, 48 in. long. Place between rows of top shells. Fill glasses with giftwrap filler. Position champagne glasses. Arrange flowers on top and trim with tip 352 leaves. *Serves 46.*

Remove pearl beads before serving.

BOWLED OVER

- 12 in. Square Pans, p. 169
- Sports Ball Pan, p. 180
- Tips 3, 6, 16, 18, 129, 233, 349, p. 134-137
- Leaf Green, Pink, Golden Yellow, Black Icing Colors, p. 126
- Gone Fishin' Signboard, p. 142
- Reluctant Groom Couple, p. 156
- Cake Boards, Fanci-Foil Wrap, Tuk 'n Ruffle, p. 132-133
- Dowel Rods, p. 165
- Buttercream Icing

- Make about 80 tip 129 drop flowers with tip 3 dot centers.

- Ice 2-layer cake smooth on Tuk 'n Ruffle-trimmed cake board. Cut and position dowel rod where ball cake will go.

- Trim curved side off one half of ball so cake sits level and place on a cake circle cut to fit. Cover rounded side with tip 16 stars. Position atop square cake. Ice top of this ball cake smooth. Position other half ball on top to form ball. Push sharpened dowel rod thru ball cake and cake circle to base of square. Cover rest of ball with tip 16 stars.

- Cover areas on cake top with tip 233 pull-out grass. Pipe tip 6 outline chain links.

- Edge top and base with tip 18 shell borders. With toothpick, dot mark sides at 3 in. intervals. Pipe tip 16 zigzag garlands. Trim with tip 3 drop strings.

- Print messages on signboard and cake side. Pipe tip 3 bells and bead hearts on sign and push into cake. Add flowers to top and sides. Trim with tip 349 leaves. Position Reluctant Groom Couple. *Serves 54.*

Bridal Shower

WEDDING BELLES

- **Wonder Mold Kit, Petite Doll Pan,** p. 174
- **14 in. Round Pans,** p. 168
- **Tips 1, 3, 5, 10, 103, 104, 124, 352,** p. 134-138
- **Teal Icing Color,** p. 126
- **Flower Nail No. 7,** 132
- **'91 Pattern Book (Scallop Design Patterns),** p. 117
- **Small Doll Picks,** p. 174
- **Floating Tier Stand,** p. 162
- **8 & 14 in. Cake Circles,** p. 133
- **Floral Puff Accent,** p. 156
- **Buttercream Icing**
- **Tulle trim, ribbon**
- Reminder: Color choices and numbers of bridesmaid cakes needed will vary. Decorate each cake on a cake circle (for bridesmaids, trim circles to fit cakes).

- For bride: Push doll pick into wonder mold cake. Ice bodice and skirt smooth (build up waistline with icing for a natural look). With toothpick, mark skirt 2 in. up from base. Cover bodice, arms, torso and skirt with tip 3 cornelli lace. Edge base with tip 5 bead border. Pipe two rows of ribbon swags (approximately 1 in. wide) on skirt. Trim dress with tip 3 dots. Remove one flower from Floral Puff for bouquet. Wrap around hand. Attach a piece of tulle trim to puff. Position on doll's head.

- For bridesmaids: Push doll picks into petite doll cakes. Ice smooth – bodices and torsos white; skirts teal. Cover skirts with tip 1 cornelli lace. Edge dresses at neck, waist and hem with tip 104 ribbon swags. Add tip 104 ribbon bows to backs.

- Make 8 spatula-striped roses with tips 10 and 103. Ice 2-layer cake smooth. For two-tone effect, ice cakes with white icing and let set until dry to the touch (approximately 15-20 minutes). Make Scallop Design Pattern out of waxed paper and place on coordinating areas. With teal icing, frost exposed areas smooth.

- Fill in areas on top and sides with tip 3 cornelli lace. Pipe tip 5 beads around center and top edge. Edge base with tip 10 bulb border. Pipe tip 124 ribbon swags on top and at base (2 rows). Edge cornelli on sides with tip 3 beads. Pipe rows of tip 3 dots on top and sides. Position roses and trim with tip 352 leaves.

- At shower: Position cakes on Floating Tier Stand. Trim stand with ribbons and tulle. (Round cake is usually the only cake served. Other cakes are given to bride and bridesmaids.) Serves 46.

BLOOMING ROMANTIC

- 7, 9, 12 in. Round Pans, p. 168
- 18 in. Half Round, p. 170
- Tips 3, 67, 102, 103, 199, 362, 363, p. 134-138
- Flower Nail No. 7, p. 132
- Meringue Powder, p. 127
- Cake Dividing Set, 15-pc. Decorator Pattern Press Set, p. 130
- Pearl White Stamens (2 pkgs.), Flower Formers, p. 128
- Crystal-Clear Cake Dividing Set—8 & 14 in. Plates, 1 set each of 7½ & 9 in. Twist Legs, p. 162
- Cake Circles, Tuk 'N Ruffle, Fanci-Foil Wrap, p. 132-133
- Floral Puff Accent, p. 156
- Shimmery Ribbon Tier Top, p. 156
- Rejoice, p. 146
- Buttercream, Royal Icings

- Using royal icing, make 56 wild roses—24 with tip 102, 32 with tip 103. Add tip 3 dot centers. Push in flower stamens. Let flowers dry on concaved flower formers.

- To prepare 2-layer cakes for pillar and stacked construction, see p. 106. Note: 18 in. base tier is made with 4 half rounds. Using Cake Dividing Set, with toothpick, dot mark 7 in. round into 6ths, all the rest into 8ths. Using garland marker (included in Cake Dividing Set), mark 1 in. deep garlands on sides of 7 in. cake.

- Using both sides of scroll pattern press, imprint scrolls on sides of stacked tiers. Imprint fleur-de-lis pattern press on 18 in. top and sides. Cover garlands, scrolls and fleur-de-lis designs with Fancy Overpiped Zigzag Scrolls using tips 3 and 362 (see p. 104). Add tip 3 double drop strings to 7 in. and 18 in. sides.

- Pipe tip 362 fleur-de-lis on top of 9 in. and sides of 12 in. Edge tops and bases with shell borders—tip 362 on top and base of 7 in., top of 9 in.; tip 363 at base of 9 in., top and base of 12 and top of 18 in.; tip 199 base of 18 in.

- Position wild roses (larger size on sides of stacked tiers and center bloom at base of 18 in.). Trim roses at base with tip 67 leaves.

- At reception, position tiers on pillars. Position Rejoice, Floral Puff Accent and Shimmery Ribbon Tier Top on cake tops.
  Serves 214.

REGAL

- 7, 10, 14 in. Round Pans, p. 168
- Tips 2, 3, 16, 18, 20, 101, 102, p. 134-138
- Lily Nail Set, p. 132
- Violet Icing Color, p. 126
- Disposable System—8 in. and 12 in. Plates, 7 and 9 in. Pillar Sets, p. 165
- Meringue Powder, p. 127
- Cake Dividing Set, Decorator's Brush, p. 130
- Contour Filigree (1 pkg. needed), p. 160
- Artificial White Leaves (1 pkg.), Floral Puff Accent, Pearl Tier Top, p. 156
- Pearl Stamens (2 pkgs.), Edible Glitter, p. 128
- Dreams Come True, p. 146
- Buttercream, Royal Icings

- Using royal icing, make 60 (allow extras for breakage) spatula-striped petunias. Make 36 with tip 102 and tip 18 centers, on 1⅝ in. lily nail and 24 with tip 101 and tip 16 centers on 1¼ in. nail. Add stamens. On Contours, with Decorator's Brush, "paint" edges of front sides with thinned royal icing. Cover with Edible Glitter. Let dry. On back sides, pipe tip 3 royal icing latticework between lines. Make 12 and let dry.

- To prepare 2-layer cakes for push-in pillar construction, see p. 106. Using Cake Dividing Set, dot mark 7 in. sides into 4ths and 14 in. into 8ths. Using garland marker, mark 3½ wide, 3 in. high garlands on 10 in. sides. Pipe tip 3 drop string guidelines. Cover area above garlands with tip 3 latticework. Trim lattice with tip 2 dots. Pipe tip 18 zigzag garlands. Add tip 2 triple drop strings. Trim points with tip 18 stars.

- Edge cake tops with tip 18, bases with tip 20 shell borders. Attach leaves (five at each top and base), Contours and petunias with dots of icing.

- At reception, push pillars into cakes and assemble tiers. Position Floral Puff, Pearl Tier Top and Dreams Come True. *Serves 116.*

83

TRILOGY

- 4-pc. Petal Pan Set (9, 12, 15 in. pans used), p. 167
- Tips 3, 16, 17, 18, 32, p. 134-135
- Ivory Icing Color, p. 126
- Floating Tiers Stand, 10 in. Crystal-Clear Cake Divider Set Plate,* p. 162
- Round Cookie Cutter Set, p. 125
- Cake Circles, Fanci-Foil Wrap, Tuk-N-Ruffle, p. 132-133
- Crystal-look Bases (2 needed), p. 158
- Rose Garden, p. 147
- Fresh flower arrangements (bring crystal-look bases to florist—invert for use)

*Substitute 10 inch in place of 8 in. plate included with stand.

- Ice 2-layer cakes on cake circles cut to fit. Position atop plates.
- With toothpick, mark garlands 1½ in. deep on 9 in. sides; 2 ins. deep on 12 and 15 in. sides. Pipe tip 3 drop string guidelines on sides. To mark scallops on 12 and 15 in. tops, use a round cookie cutter to imprint design, 2 in. from edge.
- Using the following . . . tip 16 on 9 in., tip 17 on 12 in. and tip 18 on 15 in., pipe zig-zag garlands on sides, zigzag scallops and borders on tops. Trim garlands with tip 3 drop strings.
- Pipe tip 32 columns on 15 in. sides. With tip 16, trim tops of columns with rosettes, bases of column with zigags. Edge bases with shell borders using the same tips as above, adding pairs of reverse shell on top and center tiers.
- At reception, postion bottom cake with flowers, center tier and flowers, top tier and Rose Garden. *Serves 99.*

ENGAGING

- 6, 8, 12, 16 in. Square Pans, p. 168
- Tips 1, 3, 15, 16, 18, 21, 59, 59,° 101s (left-handers), 125, 349 p. 134-138
- Flower Nail No. 7, p. 132
- Black Icing Color, p. 126
- 9-Pc. Pattern Press Set, p. 130
- Meringue Powder, p. 127
- 13 in. Square Separator Plates, p. 166
- 5 in. Corinthian Pillars, p. 162
- Flower Formers, p. 128
- Dowel Rods, p. 165
- Filigree Bells—1 in. (1 pkg.), 2 in. (1 pkg.), 2¾ in. (2 pkgs.), p. 158
- Cake Boards, Tuk-N-Ruffle, Fanci-Foil Wrap, p. 132-133
- Florist Wire, p. 128
- Pearl Tier Top, p. 156
- Glorious, p. 146
- Buttercream, Royal Icings
- Tulle trim

- Using royal icing, make 120 violets—40 with tip 59 and 80 with tip 59.° Note: Left-handed decorators should use tip 101s. Add tip 1 dot centers to violets. Let dry on flower formers.

- Using royal icing, pipe tip 1 bead borders and dots on bells. Let dry. Attach tulle trim inside of bells with florist wire (make four each in 1 & 2 in. size, and eight 2¾ of the largest). Wire pairs of large bells together, allowing enough excess wire to twist around pillars.

- To prepare 2-layer cakes for stacked and pillar construction, see p. 106. Using "medallion" pattern press, imprint design guidelines on half of 6 in. sides and side-by-side on 12 in. With toothpick, mark sides of 8 in. into 3rds, 16 in. into 4ths.

- Edge medallion designs with tip 15 shells and trim corners on 6 and 12 in. sides. Pipe shell borders at tops and bases—tip 16 on 6 in. top and base, tip 18 on 8 and 12 in. tops and bases, tip 21 top and base. Edge separator plate on 16 in. top with tip 18 scallops.

- Connect dot marks on 8 and 16 in. sides with tip 125 ruffle garlands (double ruffle on 16 in.). Edge ruffles with tip 3 beads. Attach 1 and 2 in. bells to 6 and 8 in. corners with dots of icing. Attach violets to sides and trim with tip 349 leaves.

- At reception: Attach pairs of bells to pillars. Position tiers on pillars. Add Pearl Tier Top and Glorious. *Serves 232.*

MELODY

- 8, 10, 14 in. Round Pans, 18 in. Half Round Pan, p. 170
- Tips 1, 3, 7, 12, 17, 18, 21, 81, 101s, 103, 349, 352, p. 134-138
- Flower Nail No. 7, p. 132
- '91 Pattern Book (Scalloped Panels A & B), p. 117
- Cake Dividing Set, p. 130
- 9, 11 in. Crystal-look Plates (2 of each needed), p. 163
- 5 in. Crystal-look Pillars (2 sets needed), p. 163
- Iridescent Doves (2 pkgs. needed), p. 163
- Large (6 mm) Pearl Beading (2 pkgs. needed), p. 159
- Pearl Leaves & Blossom Tier Tops, p. 156
- Cake Boards, Fanci-Foil Wrap, p. 132-133
- True Love, p. 146
- Buttercream Icing
- 23 in. diameter serving base
- Make 52 roses—24 tips 7 and 101s, 28 tips 12 and 103.
- To prepare 2-layer cakes for pillar and stacked construction, see p. 106. Note: 18 in. base tier is made with 4 half rounds. Using Cake Dividing Set, with toothpick, dot mark 8 in. cake into 8ths, 10 and 14 in. cakes into 4ths, 18 in. into 16ths. Mark Scalloped Panel Patterns—A on 10 in., B on 14 in. Connect garlands and edge scallop panels on sides with tip 17 zigzags. Position pearl beading (see p. 105).
- Pipe tip 3 drop strings beneath garlands on 8 in. On 18 in., add a tip 3 zigzag garland, then a drop string.
- Edge tops and bases with shell borders—tip 17 on 8 in. top, tip 18 on 8 in. base, 10 in. top and base, tip 21 at top and base of 14 & 18 in.
- On base plate, mark 2½ in. invervals, then pipe tip 17 zigzag scallops. Trim with pearl beading.
- On 10 and 14 in. sides, pipe lily of the valley sprays with tips 1, 3, 81 and 352 (see p. 104). Position large roses on sprays, mini at 18 in. base. Trim with tip 349 leaves. Attach doves to 18 in. with dots of icing.
- At reception: Position tiers on pillars. Add Tier Tops and True Love. Remove pearl beading before cutting. *Serves 243.*

LOVELY

- 6, 9, 12 in. Heart Pans, p. 185
- Tips 3, 16, 17, 225, 349, p. 134-137
- Pink, Kelly Green Icing Colors, p. 126
- '91 Pattern Book (Scalloped Ribbons A & B Patterns), p. 117
- 11 in. Heart Separator Plates, p. 166
- 7 in. Corinthian Pillars, p. 162
- Small (4 mm) Pearl Beads (4 pkgs.), p. 165
- Cake Boards, Tuk-N-Ruffle, Fanci-Foil Wrap, p. 132-133
- Meringue Powder (optional), p. 127
- Heart Cookie Cutter Set, p. 125
- Timeless, p. 147
- **Buttercream, Royal Icings**

- With royal (or stiffened buttercream), make 43 tip 225 drop flowers (33 light pink, 10 dark pink). Add tip 3 dot centers.

- To prepare 2-layer cake for pillar and stacked constructions, see p. 106. Note: Tops and sides of cakes are iced in alternating colors. Position separator plate on 12 in. top, then position 6 in. cake (secure to plate with icing). Note: This cake can be decorated (except base border), then position.

- With toothpick, mark Scalloped Ribbons Patterns–A on 6 in. sides; B on 9 & 12 in. Using largest (4⅛ in.) heart cookie cutter, imprint heart on 6 in. top.

- Outline scalloped ribbons and heart on 6 in. with tip 3 strings. Pipe tip 3 scalloped string on separator plate on 12 in. top (as a guide, connect 2 scallops on edge of plate). Attach pearl beading to strings. Edge pearls with tip 3 rows of beads.

- Edge tops and bases with zigzag puffs– tip 16 on 6 in., tip 17 on 9 and 12 in. Also edge separator plate with tip 17 zigzag puffs.

- Attach drop flowers to sides. Pipe tip 3 outline stems and add tip 349 leaves on sides.

- At reception, position tier on pillar. Add Timeless. Remove pearl beading before serving. Note: 6 in. heart is saved. *Serves 72.*

- Oval Pan Set, p. 167
- Tips 16, 18, 104, p. 135
- '91 Pattern Book (Graduated Garlands A,B,C,D), p. 117
- 14½ in. Oval Plates (2 needed), p. 166
- 5 in. Grecian Pillars (1 pkg.), p. 164
- 5 in. Snap-On Filigree (1 pkg.), Filigree Stairways (2 needed), p. 160
- Small (4 mm) Pearl Beading (5 pkgs. for cake; 3* pkgs. for stairway and pillars), p. 159
- Pearl Leaf Puffs (4 needed), Pearl Leaves (6 pkgs. needed), Pearl Leaves Tier Top, p. 156
- Round Cutter Set, p. 125
- Decorating Comb, p. 130
- Tuk 'n Ruffle, Fanci-Foil Wrap, Cake Boards, p. 132-133
- First Kiss Couple, p. 157
- Opulence, p. 148
- Buttercream Icing

- Optional*: Glue pearl beading to sides of Stairways and Snap-On Filigree.
- To prepare 2-layer ovals for pillar and stacked construction, see p. 106. Use smallest and two largest ovals for center tiers; two 10¾ x 7⅞ in. for side cakes. Side and base tier are on Tuk 'N Ruffle-trimmed, foil-covered cake boards.
- Using Graduated Garland Patterns (A on top, B on center, C on bottom tier and D on satellite cakes), with toothpick, mark guidelines. Using Decorating Comb (small teeth), add a ribbed effect to sides beneath garland guidelines. Pipe tip 16 zigzag puff garlands on sides.
- Edge cake tops with tip 18 shell borders. Pipe tip 16 shell border at bases, then add tip 104 ruffles. Edge ruffles with tip 16 shells.

- To use Pearl Beading, see p. 104. Drape and gently push beads into points of each garland. Cut pearls after each row is completed. Overpipe points of garlands with tip 16 rosettes.
- Cut eight strands of pearls 8 in. long. Pipe a mound of icing on top edge of center, base and side cakes with tip 16. Fold 2 strands of pearls in half (creating 4 strands) and push into the icing mound on each tier. Add 3 pearl leaves and one Pearl Leaf Puff to each cake.
- At reception: Add Snap-On Filigree to pillars. Position stacked tiers atop pillars, side cakes and Stairways. Place Opulence, First Kiss Couple and Pearl Leaves Tier Top on cake tops. Before cutting, remove pearl beading. *Serves 174.*

FANCY

- 8, 12, 16 in. Round Pans, p. 168
- Tips 3, 14, 16, 66, p. 134-135
- Creamy Peach, Willow Green Icing Colors, p. 126
- 10 in. Decorator-Preferred Round Separator Plate, p. 166
- 6½ in. Arched Pillars, Dowel Rods, p. 164
- Arched Tier Set, p. 161
- Lacy Hearts, p. 160
- Ready-to-use Icing Roses (7 large, 18 medium, 20 small needed), p. 132
- Kolor-Flo Fountain, Set, Flower Holder Ring, p. 163
- Cake Dividing Set, p. 130
- Cake Circles, p. 133
- Blossom Tier Top, p. 156
- Classique, p. 146
- Buttercream Icing
- Fresh flowers

- To prepare 2-layer rounds for pillar and stacked construction, see p. 106. Using Cake Dividing Set, dot mark 12 in. sides into 6ths. Using Garland Marker, mark 2 in. wide, 1½ in. deep garlands on 8 in.; 3 in. wide, 1¼ in. deep garlands on 16 in. Pipe tip 16 double drop string garlands. Trim garlands with tip 3 bead hearts.

- Edge 10 in. separator plate on top of 12 in. tier with tip 16 curved shells. Pipe shell borders—top of 8 in. with tip 14, top and base of 12 in. and top of 16 in. with tip 16. Edge bases of 8 in. and 16 in. with tip 16 Triple Shell Border (see p. 104).

- Position six Lacy Hearts around 12 in. cake. Edge with tip 3 beads. Attach small and medium roses to hearts with dots of icing. Position large roses on 18 in. cake top. Trim roses with tip 66 leaves.

- At reception, place Flower Holder Ring and Kolor-Flo Fountain on base plate. Arrange flowers in ring. Assemble tiers on pillars. Position Tier Top and Classique. *Serves 156.*

*Serving size is 1-in. wide x 2-in. deep x 4-in. high. By tradition, the top tier is saved for the couple's first wedding anniversary, We do not figure it in with the number of servings.

Wilton's How-To Secrets for Great Cakes

Baking Cakes

Beneath a beautifully decorated cake is a perfectly baked cake. Here's how to achieve baking success. **Note:** *If you're baking with a Wilton shaped pan, follow the instructions included with your pan.*

GREASE	FLOUR	SHAKE	PLACE RACK	REMOVE
			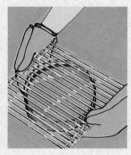	

• Preheat oven to temperature specified in recipe or on packaged mix.

• Thoroughly grease the inside of each pan with solid vegetable shortening or use a vegetable cooking spray. Use a pastry brush to spread the shortening evenly. Be sure sides, corners and all indentations are completely covered.

• Sprinkle flour inside of pan and shake back and forth so the flour covers all the greased surfaces. Tap out excess flour and if any shiny spots remain, touch up with more shortening and flour. This step is essential in preventing your cake from sticking. If you prefer, the bottom of a simple geometric shaped pan (round, square, hexagon, etc.) may be lined with waxed paper after greasing. This eliminates flouring pan. Your cake will unmold easily, but with more crumbs.

• Bake the cake according to temperature and time specifications in recipe or on package instructions. Remove cake from oven and let cool 10 minutes in pan on a cake rack. Larger cakes over 12-in. diameter may need to cool 15 minutes.

• So cake sits level and to prevent cracking, while in pan, cut away the raised center portion with serrated knife. To unmold cake, place cake rack against cake and turn both rack and pan over. Remove pan carefully. If pan will not release, return it to a warm oven (250°) for a few minutes, then repeat procedure. Cool cake completely, at least 1 hour. Brush off loose crumbs and frost.

Baking Hints

• If you like to plan ahead, do so. Your baked cake will stay up to three months wrapped in heavy-duty foil in the freezer. Always thaw cake completely before icing. Your cake will still be fresh and easy to ice because it will be firm.

• Wilton Bake-Even Cake Strips will help prevent crowns from forming on basic shaped cakes as they bake.

• Packaged, two-layer cake mixes usually yield 4 to 6 cups of batter, but formulas change, so always measure. Here's a handy guide: one 2-layer cake mix will make: two 8-in. round layers, one 10-in. round layer, one 9 x 13 x 2-in. sheet, one character cake, one Wonder Mold cake, one mini-tier cake.

• If you're in doubt as to how many cups of batter you need to fill a pan, measure the cups of water it will hold first and use this number as a guide. Then, if you want a cake with high sides, fill the pan ⅔ full of batter. For slightly thinner cake layers, fill ½ full. Never fill cake pans more than ⅔ full. Even if the batter doesn't overflow, the cake will have a heavy texture.

• For 3-in. deep or 3-D pans, we recommend pound or pudding-added cake batters. Fill pan half full only.

• For 3-D cakes: When using the baking core, it's essential to be exact about baking time, as it's very difficult to test 3-D cakes for doneness. Be sure to preheat the oven. If your 3-D cake is to be given away or sold, after baking you can remove the baking core and insert crumpled aluminum foil into the opening for support.

The Serving Base

The Boards

Most of our cake ideas are shown on coordinating foil-covered boards. These surfaces are economical and convenient, especially when your decorated cake is to be given away. Stock up on our strong cake boards (round and rectangle shapes) and Fanci-Foil Wrap.

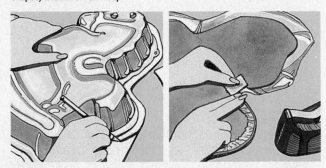

To make: Trace the shaped pan onto a Wilton cake board, ½ to 1 inch larger than inside of pan. Cut out board with an artist's matte knife.

Trace board shape onto foil wrap, making outlines 3 to 4 inches larger than board. Cut out foil cover. Cut deep slits at several points around foil, leaving about a ½ inch uncut so it folds neatly around board. Cover board with foil and tape securely to underside. Note: If the cake is heavy, use 2 or more boards for added serving support.

Show 'N Serve

Show 'N Serve Boards combine the prettiness you love with the function you need.

Tuk 'N Ruffle

Trim your cake boards with elegant Tuk 'n Ruffle. Here's how easy it is to surround your cakes with a frilly band of tulle and "lace." The cake board or plate under your iced cake should extend approximately 2 to 3 inches. Place dots of icing on board and press Tuk 'n Ruffle around cake base. Overlap ends 1 inch and cut.

Placing the cake on a sturdy yet attractive base is essential. Here are several very pretty ways to present your decorated masterpiece. See them all on pages 132 and 133.

Silver Trays

Sized to fit Wilton Doilies, Cake Circles and Boards

16¾″ Round Tray holds 14″ Circles & Doilies
14⅜″ Round Tray holds 12″ Circles & Doilies
12⅛″ Round Tray holds 10″ Circles & Doilies
10⅛″ Round Tray holds 8″ Circles & Doilies
12⅛″ x 16⅛″ Tray holds 10″ x 14″ Boards & Doilies

Beautiful, durable serving trays are specially designed to fit Wilton doilies, cake circles and boards. Inner recessed area holds cakes firm and secure. Also great for hors d'oeuvres, breads, pastries, cookies, candy.

Mirror-finished laminated plastic will not tear with normal use. Trays can be washed or reused and disposed of—whichever suits your needs.

Doilies

Elegant Doilies have wide borders of lace that stand out beautifully around decorated cakes.

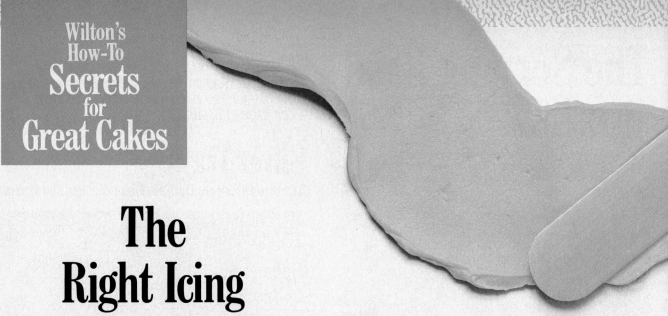

The Right Icing

Since proper consistency is the key to making decorator icing that will shape the petals of a flower, show the details of a border or cover the surface of a cake, it's important that you use the recommended icing and consistency for any technique. As a general rule, flowers require a stiff icing consistency, borders a medium-stiff consistency and writing or leaves a slightly thinned consistency. Icing that can peak to an inch or more is stiff, less than that is medium consistency. Icing that flows easily from a tip without running is a thin consistency. Every Wilton icing recipe is tested for taste and other important qualities. This chart will tell you each recipe's qualities, so you can determine which is the right one for your cake.

Icing	Recommended Uses	Tinting	Flavor & Consistency	Storing Icing	Special Information
Buttercream (Wilton Mix or Homemade)	• Borders, writing • Roses, drop flowers & sweet peas • Figure piping • Icing cakes smooth	• Deep colors • Most colors deepen upon setting	• Sweet, buttery flavor • Thin-to-stiff consistency	• Refrigerate icing in an airtight container for 2 weeks	• Iced cake can be stored at room temperature for 2-3 days • Flowers remain soft enough to be cut with a knife
Snow-White Buttercream	• Borders, writing • Roses, drop flowers & sweet peas • Figure piping • Icing cakes smooth	• Deep colors • Most colors deepen upon setting • Gives true colors	• Sweet, almond flavor • Thin-to-stiff consistency	• Refrigerate icing in an airtight container for 2 weeks	• Iced cake may be stored for 2-3 days • Air-dried flowers have translucent look • Flowers remain soft to be cut with a knife • Good for wedding cakes • Tints true colors due to pure white color
Deluxe Buttercream (Use Wilton Icing Mix)	• Borders, writing • Drop flowers & sweet peas • Figure piping • Icing cakes smooth	• Deep colors	• Rich, creamy flavor • Medium-to-stiff consistency	• Refrigerate icing in an airtight container for 2 weeks	• Texture remains soft on decorated cake • Iced cake may be stored at room temperature one day • All-purpose
Cream Cheese	• Basic borders, writing, stars, shells, drop flowers • Icing cake smooth	• Pastels	• Cream cheese • Thin-to-medium consistency	• Refrigerate icing in an airtight container for 1 week	• Iced cake must be refrigerated • Cream cheese flavor is especially good with spice cakes, carrot cakes, etc • All-purpose
Stabilized Whipped Cream	• Borders, writing • Icing cake smooth	• Pastels only • Paste colors are best to use	• Creamy, delicate sweetness • Light, thin-to-medium consistency	• Use immediately	• Iced cake must be refrigerated • Texture remains soft on decorated cake • Especially good on cakes decorated with fruits
French Buttercream	• Basic borders • Writing • Icing cake smooth	• Pastels only	• Tastes similar to vanilla ice cream • Consistency similar to whipped cream	• Use immediately	• Store iced cake in refrigerator • Texture remains soft on decorated cake • Cooked icing gives a special flavor, similar to vanilla ice cream
Quick-Pour Fondant Icing	• For icing	• Pastels	• Very sweet flavor • Pourable consistency	• Use immediately; excess fondant drippings can be reheated & poured again	• Dries to a shiny, smooth surface to coat cakes, petit fours and cookies • Seals in freshness
Rolled Fondant Icing	• For covering heavy pound or fruit cake • Cutting small decorations and ruffles	• Pastels	• Rich, sweet flavor • Dough-like consistency	• Excess can be refrigerated 3 weeks • Bring to room temperature before kneading	• Gives a perfectly smooth, velvety surface • Seals in freshness and moisture • Always decorate with royal icing • Cake can be stored room temp. 3-4 days
Royal	• Flower-making, figure piping, making flowers on wires • Decorating cookies & gingerbread houses	• Deep colors • Some colors may fade upon sitting in bright light	• Very sweet and hard • Thin-to-stiff consistency	• Store in airtight grease-free container at room temperature for 2 weeks	• Dries candy-hard for lasting decorations • Bowl & utensils must be grease free • Cover icing with damp cloth to prevent crusting
Boiled Icing 100% Fat-free!	• Borders • Figure piping • Writing, stringwork • Icing cakes smooth and fluffy	• Pastel & deep shades	• Marshmallow-like flavor • Very fluffy consistency	• Use immediately	• Serve within 24 hours • Sets quickly! Ice smooth or fluffy, immediately • Ideal for figure piping

Icing Recipes

Buttercream Icing

½ cup solid vegetable shortening
½ cup butter or margarine*
1 tsp. Clear Vanilla Extract
4 cups sifted confectioners sugar
  (approx. 1 lb.)
2 Tbsps. milk**

Cream butter and shortening with electric mixer. Add vanilla. Gradually add sugar, one cup at a time, beating well on medium speed. Scrape sides and bottom of bowl often. When all sugar has been mixed in, icing will appear dry. Add milk and beat at medium speed until light and fluffy. Keep icing covered with a damp cloth until ready to use. For best results, keep icing bowl in refrigerator when not in use. Refrigerated in an airtight container, this icing can be stored 2 weeks. Rewhip before using. YIELD: 3 cups

*Substitute all-vegetable shortening and ½ teaspoon Wilton Butter Extract for pure white icing and stiffer consistency.
**Add 3-4 Tbsps. light corn syrup per recipe to thin for icing cake.

Chocolate Buttercream

Add ¾ cup cocoa or three 1 oz. unsweetened chocolate squares, melted, and an additional 1 to 2 Tbsps. milk to recipe. Mix until well blended.

For a unique change of pace, add Wilton Candy Flavors in Rum, Orange or Cherry, in place of vanilla extract.

Snow-White Buttercream

⅔ cup water
4 Tbsps. Wilton Meringue Powder Mix
12 cups sifted confectioners sugar
  (approximately 3 lbs.)
1¼ cups solid shortening
¾ tsp. salt
½ tsp. almond extract
½ tsp. Clear Vanilla Extract
¼ tsp. Butter Extract

Combine water and meringue powder; whip at high speed until peaks form. Add 4 cups sugar, one cup at a time, beating after each addition at low speed. Alternately add shortening and remainder of sugar. Add salt and flavorings; beat at low speed until smooth.

YIELD: 7 cups

Note: Recipe may be doubled or cut in half. If cut in half, yield is 2 ⅔ cups.

Frozen Non-Dairy Whipped Topping

Non-dairy whipped topping must be thawed in the refrigerator before coloring or using for decorating. Can be used for decorating techniques similar to stabilized whipped cream. Do not allow to set at room temperature, as it becomes too soft for decorating. After decorating, store cake in refrigerator.

French Buttercream

⅔ cup sugar
¼ cup flour
¼ tsp. salt
¾ cup milk
1 cup cold butter; cut in several pieces
1 tsp. Clear Vanilla Extract

Place sugar, flour and salt in sauce pan and mix thoroughly; stir in milk. Cook over medium heat and stir constantly until very thick. Remove from heat and pour into a medium mixing bowl. Cool at room temperature. Add ½ cup butter at a time (cut into several pieces) and beat at medium-high speed until smooth. Add vanilla and beat well. Chill icing for a few minutes before decorating. Iced cake must be refrigerated until serving time.

YIELD: 2 cups

Stabilized Whipped Cream Icing

1 tsp. unflavored gelatin
4 tsps. cold water
1 cup heavy whipping cream (at least 24
  hours old and very cold)
¼ cup confectioners sugar
½ tsp. Clear Vanilla Extract

Combine gelatin and cold water in small saucepan. Let stand until thick. Place over low heat, stirring constantly just until gelatin dissolves. Remove from heat and cool slightly. Whip cream, sugar, and vanilla until slightly thickened. While beating slowly, gradually add gelatin to whipped cream mixture. Whip at high speed until stiff. YIELD: 2 cups. Cakes iced with whipped cream must be stored in the refrigerator.

Cream Cheese Icing

3-8 oz. packages slightly softened
  cream cheese
3 cups sifted confectioners sugar

Beat cream cheese until smooth. Add confectioners sugar and mix thoroughly. Beat at high speed until light and fluffy.

YIELD: 3½ cups

Packaged Topping Mix

Whipped topping mix can be used for decorating similar to stabilized whipped cream. However, use immediately after preparing. Do not allow to set at room temperature as topping becomes too soft for well-defined decorations.

Wilton Creamy White Icing Mix

You'll love its creamy taste, luscious texture and convenience. Ideal for icing smooth and decorating. Just add butter and milk, the shortening's already in the mix. For chocolate icing: Mix icing according to package directions. Stir in 2-oz. melted, unsweetened baking chocolate. If too stiff, add a few drops of milk. For Deluxe Buttercream: Use 6 Tbsps. butter and ¼ cup whipping cream.

No Time to Make Your Own? Try Our Delicious Ready-to-Spread Wilton Decorator's Icing!

Wilton's How-To Secrets for Great Cakes

Specialty Icing Recipes

ROYAL ICING

This smooth, hard-drying icing makes decorations that last. Ideal for making flowers, piping figures, overpiping and decorating cookies. Flowers and decorations made from royal icing will last for months, if stored properly, without softening. Royal icing decorations should be air dried. Allow several hours drying time for large decorations. Make sure bowl and utensils are grease free, since any trace of grease will cause royal icing to break down.

Royal icing dries quickly, so keep icing bowl covered with a damp cloth at all times. Store in air tight container. Rebeat at low speed before using.

Note: Royal icing is edible. Since it dries candy-hard, it is not recommended for icing your cakes. Use only for special effects you want to last.

For piping delicate stringwork, add 1 teaspoon of piping gel or light corn syrup to 1 cup icing.

Royal Meringue Recipe

3 level Tbsps. Wilton Meringue Powder
4 cups sifted confectioners sugar
  (approx. 1 lb)
6 Tbsps. water*

Beat all ingredients at low speed for 7 to 10 minutes (10 to 12 minutes at high speed for portable mixer) until icing forms peaks.
YIELD: 3 cups

*When using large counter top mixer or for stiffer icing, use 1 Tbsp. less water.

QUICK-POUR FONDANT ICING

6 cups confectioners sugar
½ cup water
2 Tbsps. light corn syrup
1 tsp. almond extract
Wilton Icing Colors

Place sugar in a saucepan. Combine water and corn syrup. Add to sugar and stir until well mixed. Place over low heat. Don't allow temperature of fondant to exceed 100°. Remove from heat, stir in flavor and icing color. Optional: Cakes may be covered with a thin coating of buttercream icing or apricot glaze. Allow to set before covering with fondant. To cover, place cake or cookies on wire rack over a drip pan. Pour fondant into center and work towards edges. Touch up bare spots with a spatula. Let set. Excess fondant can be reheated. Even easier...use Wilton Candy Wafer/Fondant Center Mix. Fondant Icing Recipe on label.

Boiled Icing

This fluffy, pleasant-tasting icing is totally fat-free – contains about half the calories of buttercream icing! It's ideal for icing the cake, piping borders and stringwork. Remember that it sets quickly, so smooth or fluff surface of cake immediately!

Boiled Icing Recipe

Meringue:
3 Tbsps. Meringue Powder
½ cup cold water

Syrup:
2 cups granulated sugar
¼ cup corn syrup
½ cup water

Beat meringue powder and cold water until stiff, about 4 minutes. In large microwave-safe measuring cup stir sugar, corn syrup and water. In microwave oven, bring syrup mixture to a boil (approximately 5 minutes). Remove when boiling stops. Slowly add syrup to meringue mixture while beating on low. Beat on HIGH for 4 minutes until stiff and glossy.

Yield: 8 cups

For top of range: Mix sugar, corn syrup and water in 2 quart saucepan. Bring to a boil; cool slightly and follow directions above.

Powder Sugar Glaze

Great to drizzle on dessert cakes, muffins and cookies. Looks just like "cheese" on our pizza cake, p. 20.

1¼ cups powdered sugar
3 Tablepoons milk

Stir milk into sugar.

Try Our Delicious NEW Wilton Fillings...
Order some today!

Torting

By simply cutting a cake into layers, you can enhance its taste and create impact! Classic and novelty shapes are easy to torte especially with our Cake Leveler! It cuts perfectly-even layers on cakes up to 10 in. in diameter and adjusts to desired height.

Slice the cake horizontally into two or four layers. Make layers the same thickness. Follow directions for using our Cake Leveler on the package or use a serrated knife. Hold knife level at desired height and with a gentle sawing motion, rotate the cake against blade of knife.

• For easy handling, slide the sliced layer onto a cake board (for each layer follow this procedure).

• Fill bottom layer as shown on page 96. Slide next layer off board onto filled layer.

Hints For Easier Icing:

• Thinning buttercream icing with light corn syrup makes consistency best for easy spreading.

• When icing small areas or sides of a shaped cake, be sure to ice a little past the area or edge or top to create a neat surface that can be outlined or covered with stars.

• To smooth the icing surface on 3-dimensional cakes such as the ball, egg, bear, lamb or bunny cakes, let buttercream icing crust slightly. Then place plastic wrap over the icing and smooth over the surface gently with your hands. Carefully remove wrap. For a textured surface, follow the same procedure using a cloth or paper towel.

• To make clean-up easier and quicker when decorating with buttercream icing, use a degreaser liquid soap to dissolve icing from tools. It is especially important to have grease-free utensils when using royal or color flow icings.

Coloring Icing Techniques

To Tint

• Start with white icing and add the color a little at a time until you achieve the shade you desire. Use a toothpick to add icing color; (use more depending on amount of icing). Hint: Tint a small amount of icing first, then mix in with remainder of white icing. Colors intensify or darken in buttercream icings 1 to 2 hours after mixing, so keep this in mind when you're tinting icing. You can always add extra color to deepen the icing color, but it's difficult to lighten the color once it's tinted. Use White- White Icing Color to make your buttercream icing the purest snow-white!

• To mix deep or dark color icing (such as red for roses), you may need a larger amount of Wilton Icing Color. The color should still be added gradually, but use a clean small spatula each time to add the color. Wilton Red Color has no after-taste! It's ideal for decorating large areas. Red-Red or Christmas Red Color is still better to use in royal icing and for accent color, as each offers more color intensity. If you plan to use flavorings, make icing stiff consistency, then use enough flavoring to improve taste.

• Always mix enough of any one color icing. If you're going to decorate a cake with pink flowers and borders, color enough icing for both. It's difficult to duplicate an exact shade of any color. As you gain decorating experience, you will learn just how much of any one color icing you will need.

IMPORTANT HINTS

• Royal icing requires more base color than buttercream to achieve the same intensity.

• Use water, not milk, in buttercream icing recipe when using Violet Icing Color, otherwise the icing may turn blue.

• Substitute chocolate icing for dark brown colors. Use just 6 Tablespoons unsweetened cocoa powder, or 2 one-ounce squares, of melted unsweetened baking chocolate. 1 Tablespoon milk, and add to 1½ cups white icing.

• Add color to piping gel, color flow, gum paste, cookie dough, marzipan, cream cheese, sugar molds and even cake batter for striking decorating effects!

• To restore the consistency of Wilton Icing Colors that have dried out, add a few drops of Wilton Glycerin. Mix until proper consistency is reached.

• Use a clean toothpick or spatula to add Wilton Icing Colors each time, until you reach desired shade.

Color brings cake decorations to life; therefore it's essential that you learn how to tint icings to achieve different decorating effects. Wilton Icing Color is concentrated color in a creamy, rich base. It gives icing vivid or deep, rich color without changing icing consistency. See page 126 for a complete selection of quality Wilton Icing Colors. Icing Color Kits are also available.

Color Dramatics

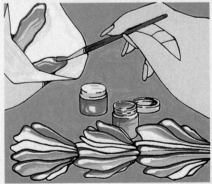

BRUSH STRIPING

Striping is a method used to give multiple or deep color effects to icing. To do this, one or more colors are applied to the inside of the parchment paper bag with a brush. Then the bag is filled with white or pastel-colored icing and, as the icing is squeezed past the color, out comes the striped decorations!

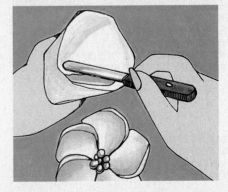

SPATULA STRIPING

Use a spatula to stripe the inside of a decorating bag with Wilton pastel colored icing. Then fill the bag with white icing, or another shade of the same color as the striping, and squeeze out decorations with pastel contrasts. Use the above color techniques when figure piping for exciting results. It's fun to experiment with color! Try to achieve natural-looking flower colors by using the spatula striping method. (Roses look especially beautiful with this effect.)

Wilton's How-To Secrets for Great Cakes

Icing the Cake

To Ice Areas On Shaped Cakes
The sides of shaped cakes are usually the only areas iced smooth. Just place icing on side with your spatula and spread. After sides are covered, run spatula lightly over icing in the same direction. Sometimes small backgound areas or facial features on top are iced smooth. Use a small spatula or decorating tip (3 or 4) and squeeze icing onto area, then smooth with finger dipped in cornstarch.

The Cake Icer Tip Will Save You Time
If you haven't discovered this versatile tip (No. 789) you should! You'll love how quickly and easily you can cover flat-surfaced cakes with wide bands of icing. Just hold tip flat against cake surface, serrated side up, and squeeze out a ribbed band. Holding the smooth side up gives you a smooth band. To cover side, turn cake stand clockwise as you squeeze out a band of icing, wrapping it around the cake. When your cake is completely iced, use a fork to blend ribbed seams; a spatula to join smooth bands together.

Sheet & Other Flat Surfaced Cakes
Use the same icing procedure as shown here for sheet cakes, heart, oval, square and other shaped cakes with flat surfaces.

Think of your cake as the canvas that your beautiful icing decorations will be presented upon. So it's essential that it be smooth and free of crumbs. By following our 5-easy-steps icing method, we feel you'll get the results you want.

1. Leveling
There are two ways to remove the slight crown your baked cake will have. Cool cake for 10 minutes in the pan. Carefully slice off the raised center with a serrated knife. Or after cake is cooled completely as per directions on p. 90, invert so that its brown top crust is uppermost and trim away the crust for a flat surface (see pic. 1). Our Bake-Even Cake Strips will help prevent crowns from forming on basic shaped cakes (see p. 168 for details).

2. Filling Layers
Place one cake layer on a cake board or circle atop a cake stand or plate, top side up. **Hint:** To prevent cake from shifting, place a few strokes of icing on base surface before positioning cake. Fit bag with coupler and fill with icing. Make a dam by squeezing out a band of icing about 3/4-in. high around the edge. With your spatula, spread icing, jam, pudding or other filling in center. Position top layer with bottom side up.

3. Icing The Top
Thin your buttercream icing with light corn syrup (approximately 2 teaspoons for each cup). The consistency is correct when your spatula glides over the icing. With large spatula, place mound of icing in center of top and spread across cake pushing excess down onto sides. Always keep spatula on the the iced surface. Pulling toward the cake surface will mix in crumbs. **Hint:** To keep your serving base free of icing, place 3-in. wide strips of waxed paper under each side of cake.

4. Icing The Sides
Cover the sides with excess icing from the top, adding more icing if necessary. Work from top down, forcing any loose crumbs to the cake base. Again, be sure spatula touches only icing. You'll find that an angled spatula is ideal for icing sides. When you're icing a curved side, hold the spatula upright against the side of the cake and, pressing lightly, turn cake stand slowly around with your free hand without lifting the spatula from the side surface. Return excess icing to bowl and repeat procedure until sides are smooth. For angled sides such as on a cross cake, do each straight side individually; hold spatula firmly to smooth.

5. Smooth Top
Place spatula flat on one edge of cake top and sweep it across to center of cake. Lift off, remove excess icing and repeat, starting from a new point on edge of cake top. Repeat procedure until entire top surface is smooth. To smooth center, apply an even pressure to spatula as you turn cake stand around in a full circle. Lift off spatula and any excess icing.

Hints for cakes-to-go! Use our Cake Pan Cover to protect sheet cakes in our 9 x 13-in. pan (p. 169). The Cake Saver is a great way to take cakes places (p. 168).

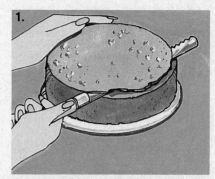

1.

2.

3.

4.

5.

Decorating Guidelines

These easy-to-follow guidelines outline the basic steps in decorating. Our steps are very general because each cake you decorate has special needs. We hope these guidelines will inspire you to design original cakes on your own.

• We suggest that flowers, candy, cookies or any special accent be made ahead of time, perhaps while your cake cools. To allow for breakage, make extras of any fragile addition. Heavy trims that protrude out of cake should be attached to a craft stick or coffee stirrer with royal icing. When using cookie trims, easel backs can be cut out of dough and attached with royal icing.

• Before icing or decorating, place each cake to be decorated on a cake circle or board cut to fit. If a small cake is to be set atop a larger cake, we usually recommend that you decorate both cakes first, then put them together. To transfer, let icing set (a slight crust will form and be more workable), then slip a wide spatula under cake and lift. Position cake and slowly pull spatula out (to prevent sticking, lightly dust spatula with cornstarch). If cake is large, support with free hand and redecorate areas that may get damaged.

• Marking design: Use a toothpick, pattern press or cookie cutter. Patterns for more intricate designs are included in the '91 Pattern Book (contains easy pattern transfer instructions). Often geometric shaped cakes are divided into 6ths, 8ths, 12ths, etc. You'll find dividing a round cake is quick 'n easy when you use our Cake Dividing Set (instructions included).

Decorating Hints

• Tips from the same basic group that are close in size may be substituted for one another. The effect will be a slightly smaller or larger decoration.

• Use tip 20, 21 or the super fast Triple-Star Tip, when you're covering a large area with stars. You can also use zigzags or side-by-side stripes to fill in large areas.

• When using parchment bags, you can place a tip with a smaller opening over the tip you're using and tape it in place. This saves time changing bags and tips when you're using the same color icing.

• Stock up on the bags and tips in the sizes you use the most. Your decorating will go faster if several are filled and ready to use. Close tips securely with convenient Tip Covers.

• Overpiping: Outlining a piped decoration with the same technique will add dimension and make it stand out. Overpiping with a different technique in a contrasting color creates an eye-catching effect.

Decorating Step-by-Step

Basic Shapes
• Outline design.
• Pipe in small areas. Fill in areas with stars, zigzags, etc.
• Add top and bottom borders.
• Add message.
• Ruffles and "overpiped" decorations.
• Attach trims such as flowers, cookies, color flow and candy.
Note: If a decoration doesn't seem secure enough, just add a few dots of icing.
• Pipe leaves on flowers.
• Position Wilton cake tops or wedding ornaments.

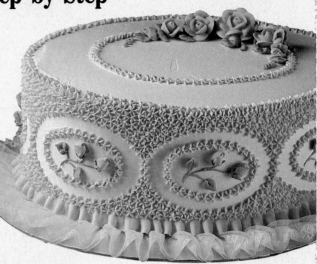

Novelty Shapes

When decorating a cake that's basically covered with stars, here are the easy steps involved.

1. Ice sides and others areas per instructions smooth.

2. Outline details.

3. Pipe in facial features, small details, windows, doors, etc.

4. Cover areas with stars, stripes, zigzags or hair.

5. Add message.

6. Edge top and base with borders. Attach flowers or trims.

3 Essentials of Bag and Tip Decorating

1. Icing Consistency
Remember, if the consistency of your decorating icing isn't exactly right, your decorations won't be either. Follow the general guidelines on p. 92.

2. Bag Position
To hold the decorating bag correctly, grip the bag near the top with the twisted or folded end locked between your thumb and fingers. Guide the bag with your free hand.

Generally, there are two basic positions for the decorating bag—the 90° angle with the bag straight up, perpendicular to the surface. And the 45° angle with the bag half-way between vertical and horizontal.

Pointing the back end of your decorating bag in the right direction is also important. Sometimes instructions will tell you to hold the back end of bag pointing to the right or towards you.

Left-handed decorators do things differently. Hold the decorating bag in your left hand and guide the decorating tip with the fingers of your right hand. If the instructions say to hold the decorating bag over to the right, you should hold your decorating bag over to the left. A right-handed person will always decorate from left to right. A left-handed person

should always decorate from right to left. The only exception to this rule is when you are writing or printing. When decorating a cake on a turntable, rotate the stand counterclockwise. For flower making on a flower nail, turn nail clockwise in right hand as you pipe petals using left hand.

3. Pressure Control
The size and uniformity of your icing design are directly affected by the amount of pressure you apply to the decorating bag and the steadiness of the pressure— how you squeeze and relax your grip on the decorating bag. Strive to apply pressure so consistently that you can move the bag in a free and easy glide while just the right amount of icing flows from the tip. Practice to achieve this control.

The Techniques

PLAIN OR ROUND TIPS

Use to outline details, filling and piping in areas, printing and writing messages, figure piping, stringwork, beads, dots, balls, stems, vines, flower centers, lattice, cornelli lace. These tips are smooth and round—small plain tips include numbers 1,2,3,4; medium, 5,6,7,8,9,10,11,12; large, 1A, 2A. For fine stringwork, use 1S, 1L, 2L, 0L, 00L,000. For Philippine method flower making, oval tips 55 and 57. Writing tip 301 pipes fine, flat lines.

Printing & Writing

Use a small round tip and thin icing consistency.
Hint: With a toothpick or Message Pattern Presses draw guidelines to follow. With practice, you'll achieve control and soon be piping out messages free-handed.

To Print: Hold bag at 45° angle with tip resting lightly on surface with back of to the right for horizontal lines, toward you for vertical. With a steady, even pressure, squeeze out a straight line, lifting tip off surface to let icing string drop. Be sure to stop squeezing before you lift the tip to end the line so a tail doesn't form.

To Write: You must move your whole arm to write effectively with icing. Hold bag at a 45° angle with back of bag to the right. The tip should lightly touch the cake as you write.

To Outline:
Use thin icing consistency and bag at a 45° angle and touch tip (usually 3 or 4) to surface. Now raise the tip slightly and continue to squeeze. The icing will flow out of the tip while you direct it along the surface. To end an outline, stop squeezing, touch tip to surface and pull away.

To Pipe In: After area is outlined, squeeze out tip 3 or 4 zigzag motion strings to fill area. Immediately smooth over strings with finger tip or spatula dipped in cornstarch.

To Fill In: Follow same procedure as Pipe In, but thin icing before piping.

Dots

Use medium icing consistency. Hold bag at a 90° angle with tip slightly above surface. Squeeze and keep point of the tip in icing until dot is the size you want. Stop pressure, pull away; use tip to clean point away or smooth with finger dipped in cornstarch. To make large dots or balls, lift tip as you squeeze to allow greater icing build-up.

Beads

Use medium icing consistency. Hold bag at 45° angle with tip slightly above surface and end of bag pointing to the right. Squeeze and lift tip slightly so icing fans out into base. Relax pressure as you draw tip down and bring bead to point. Ideal for borders or piped in side-by-side rows to cover large areas.

For Hearts: Pipe two beads side by side and smooth together with finger dipped in cornstarch.

For Shamrocks: Pipe 3 bead hearts so points meet. Add tip 3 outline stem.

Cornelli Lace

With thin icing, use a 90° angle with tip slightly above surface. Pipe a continuous string of icing, curve it up, down and around until area is covered. Stop pressure; pull tip away. Make sure strings never touch or cross.

Drop Strings

Use stiff consistency icing that has been thinned with corn syrup. Icing is the right consistency if you can pick up a loop of icing from your finger. With toothpick, mark horizontal intervals in desired widths. Hold bag at 45° angle to surface so that end of bag points slightly to the right. Touch tip to first marks and squeeze, holding bag in place momentarily so that icing sticks to surface.

Then pull tip straight out away from surface, allowing icing to drop into an arc. Stop pressure as you touch tip to second mark to end string.

Repeat procedure, attaching string to third mark and so on, forming row of drop strings. It's very important to let the string, not your hand, drop to form an arc. Try to keep your drop strings uniform in length and width.

For Double Drop Strings: Start at first mark again, squeeze bag. Let icing drop into a slightly shorter arc than arc in first row. Join end of string to end of corresponding string in first row and repeat procedure.

Always pipe longest drop strings first and add shorter ones. This technique is ideal for cake sides. Practice is important in making drop strings uniform.

Dropped Lattice Garlands: With stiff royal icing, connect garland marks with drop string guidelines. Cover strings with three rows of tip 16 zigzags (overpipe rows). Ease pressure at ends so icing doesn't build up too high. Drop a string guideline directly on top of zigzags. From cake to edge of zigzags, pipe tip 3 diagonal lines across area. From the opposite side, work strings in the other direction. Cover edges of lattice with tip 3 strings.

STAR TIPS

The star-shaped openings create the most popular decorations... stars, zigzags, shells, rosettes and more. The most often used star tips are numbers 13 through 22. Star tips range in size from small to extra large. For deep ribbed decorations, try tips 23-31, 132, 133 and 195. Large star tips include numbers 32, 96, 4B, 6B and 8B. Fine cut star tips are numbers 362, 363, 364, 172 and 199. For these techniques use medium icing consistency.

Stars

Hold bag at 90° angle with tip slightly above surface. Squeeze bag to form a star, then stop pressure and pull tip away. Increase or decrease pressure to change star size. An entire cake or just one area can be covered with stars made very close together so that no cake shows between stars. Use the triple-star or use large star tips to save time.

For Pull-Out Stars: Hold bag at 45° angle to surface. As you squeeze out icing, pull tip up and away from cake. When strand is long enough, stop pressure and pull tip away. Work from bottom to top of area to be covered with pull-out stars.

For Star Puffs: Use a large tip and hold tip in place to allow icing to build up.

For Star Flowers: Squeeze and keep tip in icing until star petals are formed. Stop pressure and pull tip away. Add tip 2 or 3 dot centers.

Ropes

Hold bag at 45° angle to surface with end of bag pointing over right shoulder. Touch tip to surface and squeezing bag, move tip down, up and around to the right forming a slight "s" curve. Stop pressure, pull tip away. Tuck tip under bottom arch of first "s" and repeat procedure. Continue joining "s" curves to form rope.

The size and shape of the opening on a decorative tip identifies the basic group to which the tip belongs and determines the type of decorations the tip will produce.

Zigzags
Hold bag at 45° angle to surface, so that end of bag points out to the right and fingers on the bag are facing you. Allow the tip to touch the surface lightly. Steadily squeeze and move hand in a tight side-to-side motion. To end, stop pressure and pull tip away. **Elongated Zigzags:** Follow procedure but keep an even pressure as you move hand in the desired length. Very large areas can be covered in this manner. **Relaxed Zigzags:** Simply relax pressure as you move bag along.

Zigzag Garlands
Hold bag as for basic zigzag procedure. Allow tip to touch the surface lightly and use light-to-heavy-to-light pressure to form curves of garland. To end, stop pressure, pull tip away. Practice for rhythmic pressure control so garlands are uniform.

Puffs
Hold bag at 45° angle to surface, finger tips on bag facing you. Touch tip to surface and use a light-to-heavy-to-light pressure and zigzag motion to form puff. Repeat procedure again and again as you move tip in a straight line to form row of puffs. To end row, stop pressure, pull tip away.

C, E & S-Motion (only "E" motion shown)
Hold bag at 45° angle to surface, finger tips on bag facing you. As you squeeze out icing, move tip down, up to the right and around as if writing the letter "c, e or s." Use a steady, even pressure as you repeat procedure. To end, stop pressure, pull tip away.

Shells
Hold bag at 45° angle with tip slightly above surface and end of bag pointing to the right. Squeeze with heavy pressure and slightly lift tip as icing builds and fans out into a full base. Relax pressure as you pull bag down to the right as you make the tail. Stop pressure completely, pull tip away. When you make the shells, always work to the right; starting each new shell slightly behind tail of previous shell.
For Elongated Shells: Extend tail while relaxing pressure, until desired length is achieved.
For Upright Shells: Hold bag at 90° angle to cake sides. Follow same procedure as elongated shells.

Note: Once you've mastered the motion of shell making, you can create unique borders with other tip groups such as leaf and ruffle.

Reverse Shells
Hold bag at 45° angle with tip slightly above surface. Squeeze to let icing fan out as if you were making a typical shell, then swing tip around to the left in a semi-circular motion as you relax pressure to form tail of a shell. Stop pressure, pull tip away. Repeat procedure, only this time, swing tip around to the right as you form tail of shell. Continue procedure alternating directions for a series of reverse shells.

Fleur-De-Lis
Make a shell. Keep bag at 45° angle and starting at the left of this shell, squeeze bag to fan icing into shell base. Then as you relax pressure to form tail, move tip up slightly around to the right, relaxing pressure, forming tail similar to reverse shells. Join to tail of the first shell. Repeat procedure to right side of first shell.

Scrolls
Hold bag at 45° angle to surface so that end of bag points to the right. Use tip 3 to draw an inverted "C" center and use circular motion to cover inverted "C." You may overpipe (go over lines) with tip 13 or any small star tip. Use a heavy pressure to feather the scroll, relaxing pressure as you taper end. Add side petals like reverse shells.

Reverse Scrolls
With tip 3 squeeze out an inverted "C" scroll. Then, starting at the top of this "C," squeeze and move tip down, up and around for a backward "C." Cover outlines with tip 13. Add reverse shell side petals.

Hint: Use our Scroll Pattern Presses to imprint an easy-to-follow guide on cake top or sides.

Rosettes
Hold bag at 90° angle with tip slightly above surface. Squeeze and move hand to the left, up and around in a circular motion to starting point. Stop pressure and pull tip away. For a fancy effect, trim center with a star.

Spirals
Follow rosettes technique. Starting at outer edge, move tip in a clockwise direction in a continuous circular motion decreasing size of circles until center is reached. Stop pressure and pull tip away.

Drop Flower Tips
These are the easiest flowers for a beginning decorator to do. The number of openings on the end of the tip determines the number of petals the flower will have. Each drop flower tip can produce two different flower varieties–plain or swirled. Swirled drop flowers cannot be made directly on cake. Some form center holes. Small tips include numbers 107, 108, 129, 217, 220, 224, 225; medium tips are 109, 131, 135, 140, 177, 190, 191, 193, 194, 195; for large flowers, tips 1B, 1C, 1E, 1G, 2C, 2D, 2E and 2F.

Drop Flowers
Icing consistency should be slightly stiffer. Hold bag at a 90° angle with tip touching surface and pipe as you would a star. For swirled flowers: Curve wrist around to the left and as you squeeze out icing, bring hand back to the right. Stop pressure, pull tip away. Add tip 2 or 3 dot centers.

LEAF TIPS
The v-shaped openings of these tips give leaves pointed ends. With any leaf tip you can make plain, ruffle or stand-up leaves. Make leaves with center veins from small 65s, 65-70, to large, 112-115 and 355. Other popular numbers are 71-76, 326, 349, 352.

Basic Leaf
Use thin icing consistency and hold bag at 45° angle to surface, back of bag facing you. Squeeze and hold tip in place to let icing fan out into base, then relax and stop pressure as you pull tip towards you and draw leaf to a point.

Stand Up Leaf
Hold bag at a 90° angle. Touch tip lightly to surface and squeeze, holding tip in place as icing fans out to form base. Relax and stop pressure as you pull tip straight up and away, creating stand-up leaf effect.

Holly Leaf: With tip 68, follow basic leaf method and use medium consistency royal icing to pipe desired size leaf. While icing is wet, pull out tiny points around edge with a dampened Decorator's Brush. Let dry on flower formers for a curved look. Do not make directly on cake.

Petal Tips

These tips have an opening that is wide at one end, narrow at the other. This teardrop-like shaped opening yields a variety of petals that form flowers like the rose, carnation, daisy, pansy and more (see pages 101-103). Petal tips can also make ribbons, drapes and swags; bows and streamers. Plain rose tips include numbers 101s, 101, 102, 103, 104, 124, 125, 126, 127 and giant roses, tip 127D. Swirled rose tips that make instant-curled petals are 97, 116, 118 and 119. Others include 59s, 59, 60, 61, 121, 122, 123, 62, 63, 64 and 150.

Ruffle
Use medium icing consistency. Hold bag at a 45° angle to surface, finger tips on bag facing you. Touch wide end of tip to surface, angle narrow end out about ¼-in. away from surface. As you squeeze, move hand up and down slightly to ruffle the icing. **For Stand-Up Ruffle** just turn tip so wide end is at the top.

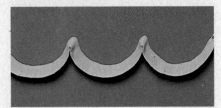

Swag/Drape
Use same procedure as for ruffle. As you squeeze, swing tip down and up to the right forming ribbon drape.

Bows
Creating bows with a petal tip is different from a round or star tip because of the shape of tip but otherwise the technique is the same. With tip 104 and medium icing consistency, hold bag at a 45° angle to surface. The wide end of the tip should touch the surface and the narrow end should point straight up. While squeezing, move the tip up and around to the starting point and continue around, making a second loop on the left. The two loops should form a figure 8. Still holding bag in the same position return to the center and squeeze out two streamers.

Stripe/Basketweave Tips

These are decorating tips with a smooth side for making smooth, wide icing stripes and/or one serrated side for making ribbed, wide icing stripes. When short ribbed horizontal stripes are interwoven in vertical rows the effect is that of a basketweave. Tips are 46 and 47. For smooth stripes, 44 and 45. For ribbed stripes, 48 and 327. Large ribbon tips include 1D, 2B and 789 (Cake Icer).

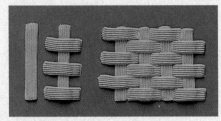

Basketweave
Use star or basketweave tips and medium consistency icing. For an interesting effect, use a round tip to make vertical lines.

• Hold bag at 45° angle to cake with serrated side of tip facing up (or use round tip). Touch tip lightly to surface and squeeze out a vertical line of icing.

• Next, hold bag at 45° angle to surface, finger tips gripping bag facing you. Touch tip, serrated side facing up, to top left side of vertical line and squeeze out a horizontal bar. Add two more horizontal bars, each about a tip width apart, to cover vertical line.

• With bag and tip at 45° angle, make another vertical line of icing to right of first one, overlapping ends of horizontal bars. Use same procedure as step two to cover this line with horizontal bars, working them in spaces of bars in first row.

• Repeat entire procedure, alternating vertical lines and horizontal bars, to create a basketweave effect. Other tips may be used for basketweave, but serrated tips 46-48 give icing a ribbed basket effect.

Stripes
• This versatile technique can be made with star and ribbon tips. They can be piped straight, curved or side-by-side to fill in an area. Hold decorating bag at 45° angle to surface. As you squeeze out icing with steady, even pressure, move tip in vertical direction laying out a ribbed stripe of icing. Stop pressure and pull tip up and away. When covering an area, stripes can be slightly overlapped for added dimension.

Ribbon Stripe Bow
• To make a bow with a basketweave tip as shown, hold bag at a 45° angle with the ribbed side of tip up. Start in center and move bag up and to the right. As you bring bag down to form loop, turn tip so that the ribbed side is now down. Repeat procedure for left loop. Pipe streamers with smooth or ribbed side up.

Flutes
• A pretty effect to add between rows of shells. Hold tip 104 at 45° angle so that wide end of tip is between two shells. Squeeze and move tip up slightly as icing fills in between shell. Stop pressure, lower tip, pull away.

Making a Rose

The flower nail (p. 132) is a decorating tool used to make the most popular flower of all, the rose. It is also used to make pretty flowers, like the violet, apple blossom and daisy. Flower nails come in a variety of sizes. No. 7 and No. 9 are the popular choices for small and average size blooms. Large flowers would use a 2 or 3-in. flower nail.

The key to making any flower on the nail is to coordinate the turning of the nail with the formation of a petal. The stem of the nail is held between your left thumb and forefinger, so you can turn the flat nailhead surface at the same time you're piping a flower with your right hand. Using the flower nail takes practice, but the beautiful results are well worth the effort!

Note: Left-handed decorators should use the nail opposite of above instructions.

Make all flowers on the nail with royal or stiffened buttercream icing (see p. 93-94), and the tips specified for each flower. Air dry flowers made in royal icing, and freeze buttercream flowers (buttercream roses can also be placed directly on iced cake) until firm at least 2 hours. Then, when you're ready to decorate, remove the frozen flowers, a few at a time, and position them on the cake. (Snow White Buttercream Icing flowers can be air dried.)

For each flower you make, attach a 2-in. square of waxed paper to the nailhead with a dot of icing. Make a flower; remove waxed paper and flower together. For more about rose making, order the **Wilton Celebrates The Rose**, p. 116.

Make The Rose Base
- Use tip 10 or 12. Hold the bag perpendicular at a 90° angle to nail with tip slightly above center of nailhead.
- Squeeze with a heavy pressure, keeping bottom of tip in icing until you've made a full, round base.
- Ease pressure as you raise tip up and away from nailhead, narrowing base to a dome head. The base is very important for successful rose-making. Be sure that it is secure to nail and can support all the petals. Practice until you feel comfortable with the technique.

The Center Bud
- Use tip 104. Hold bag at a 45° angle to nail with wide end of tip just below top of dome, and narrow end pointed in slightly. Back of bag should be pointed over your shoulder.
- Now you must do three things simultaneously...squeeze, pull tip up and out away from top of dome stretching icing into a ribbon band, as you turn the nail counterclockwise.
- Relax pressure as you bring band of icing down around dome, overlapping the point at which you started.

  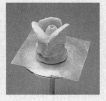  

1st Row of 3 Petals
- Hold bag at 45° angle with end of bag pointed over your shoulder. Touch wide end of tip 104 to midpoint of bud base. Turn nail counterclockwise and move tip up and back down to midpoint of bud base forming first petal of rose.
- Start slightly behind end of 1st petal and squeeze out 2nd petal same as first.
- Start slightly behind end of 2nd petal and add a 3rd petal, ending this petal overlapping starting point of 1st petal. Now you have a full rosebud made on a nail to use just as you would a rosebud made on a flat surface (see p. 102).

2nd Row of 5 Petals
- Touch wide end of tip 104 slightly below center of a petal in 1st row, angle narrow end of tip out slightly more than you did for 1st row of petals. Squeeze and turn nail counterclockwise, moving tip up, then down to form 1st petal in second row.
- Start slightly behind this last petal and make a 2nd petal. Repeat this procedure for a total of 5 petals, ending last petal overlapping the 1st petal's starting point.

ahead of time so you can continue rose making without stopping. HINT: An easy way to place a buttercream icing rose directly on your cake is to slide open scissors under base of rose and gently lift flower off waxed paper square and flower nail. Position flower on cake by slowly closing scissors and pushing base of flower with stem end of flower nail. Practice & watch your talent grow!

3rd Row of 7 Petals
- Touch wide end of tip 104 below center of petal in 2nd row, again angling narrow end of tip out a little more. Squeeze and turn nail counterclockwise and move tip up and down forming 1st petal. Repeat for a total of 7 petals.
- Slip waxed paper and completed rose off nail. Attach another square of waxed paper and start again. Have several squares of waxed paper cut

Two-Tone Roses
Create a dramatic effect by making the center petals of your rose contrast with the outer petals. You'll need to pipe the base, center bud and 1st row of petals with one color. Then in your contrasting shade, add remaining petals.

Flowers

Flat Surface Flowers:
Rosebuds, Half Roses & Sweet Peas

These are flowers you can make right on a cake, or any other flat surface. To make all these, use tip 104 and royal or stiffened buttercream icing. Attach a sheet of waxed paper to the back of a cookie sheet with dots of icing or use Wilton Practice Board.

Make your practice flowers in horizontal rows and when you've filled the entire sheet, loosen the waxed paper with a spatula to remove it and start again.

When you're decorating a cake with lots of flat-surface flowers, make all the ones you need ahead of time using the same cookie sheet method. Air dry flowers made with Royal or Snow-White Buttercream. Freeze flowers made with buttercream until hard (at least 2 hours). Remove buttercream flowers with your spatula, a few at a time as you decorate, so they stay firm. Note: When you make flowers directly on a cake, use buttercream, not royal icing.

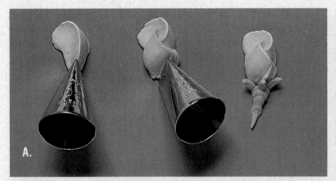

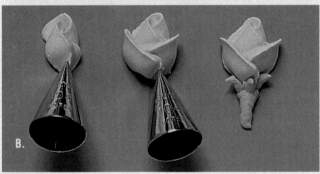

A. Rosebud
• Make base petal. Hold bag at a 45° angle so that the end of bag points over your right shoulder, finger tips gripping bag facing you. Touch wide end of tip 104 to surface, point narrow end to the right. Squeeze, move forward ¼-in.; hesitate so icing fans out, then move back as you stop pressure.

• Make overlapping center petal. Hold bag in same position as above with wide end of tip touching inside right edge of base petal, narrow end of tip pointing slightly up above base petal. Squeeze as icing catches inside edge of base petal and rolls into interlocking center bud, Stop pressure; touch large end back to surface and pull tip away.

• Make sepals and calyx directly on cake with tip 3 and thinned icing. Hold bag at a 45° angle to base of bud with end of bag pointing towards you. Touch tip to bud. Squeeze and pull tip up and away from flower, relaxing pressure as you draw calyx to a point. Add three tip 3 sepals.

B. Half Rose
• Make a rosebud without sepals and calyx. To make left petal: Hold bag at a 45° angle so the end of bag points to the right, finger tips gripping the bag should face you. Touch wide end of tip 104 to bottom left side of bud. Squeeze, move it up, around to the right and down, relaxing pressure.

• To make right petal: Hold bag in opposite position as for left petal. Touch wide end of tip to bottom right side of bud base. Squeeze, move up, around to the left and down to center of bud base. Stop pressure, pull tip away.

• Make sepals and calyxes with tip 3 and thinned icing. Follow same procedure as for step 3 of rosebud, starting at bottom center of half rose.

C. Sweet Pea
• Make center petal. Hold bag at a 45° angle to surface so that back end of bag points towards you. Touch wide end of the tip to surface with narrow end of tip straight up. Squeeze, raise tip slightly and let icing roll into center petal. Stop pressure, lower tip, pull away.

• Make side petals. Touch wide end of tip to bottom left edge of center rolled petal, point narrow end up and out to the left. Squeeze, lift tip slightly, stop pressure, lower tip, pull away. Repeat procedure for right petal, starting at bottom edge of center petal.

• Add calyx to flower base with tip 3 and thinned icing. Hold bag at 45° angle to surface so that end of bag points towards you. Insert tip into flower base and hold in place as you squeeze to build up pressure as you draw tip down, narrowing calyx to a point.

D. To Attach Flowers & Leaves To Wire Stems.
• **For flowers:** On waxed paper square, using royal icing, pipe a dot base with tip 4. Make 1/8-in. hook on one end of 4-in. florist wire and insert hook into base. With slightly moistened decorator's brush, smooth and taper icing on the wire. Push other end of wire into a piece of styrofoam to dry base. Remove waxed paper and attach flower with dots of icing. **For Leaves:** Pipe tip 3 royal icing dot on a waxed paper square and immediately push in hooked end of wire. Use tip 352 and royal icing to pipe a leaf directly on top of wire. Again, push into styrofoam to dry. Then remove waxed paper square. Entwine stems together. Note: Use only royal icing for attaching flowers to stems.

Flower Nail Flowers

For best results, use royal icing to pipe these impressive blooms. To curve petals, dry on convexed or concaved flowers formers. Instructions will indicate the number of flowers needed, so make extras to allow for breakage.

Daisy

Use royal icing and tip 103. Dot center of nail with icing as guide for flower center. Hold bag at a 45° angle with tip almost parallel to nail surface, wide end of tip pointing to nail center, narrow end pointing out. Now, starting at any point near outer edge of nail, squeeze and move tip towards center icing dot. Stop pressure, pull tip away. Repeat procedure for a total of twelve or more petals.

• Add tip 4 yellow flower center and press to flatten. For pollen-like effect, dampen your finger, press in edible glitter, then flatten center.

Chrysanthemum

• Hold bag at 90° angle to nail and pipe tip 6 mound of icing on nail center. Use tip 79 and very stiff royal icing for short petal effect. Hold bag at a 45° angle to outer base edge of mound, with half-moon opening of tip 79 pointing up. Squeeze row of ½-in. long cupped base petals using pull-out star technique.

• Add second row of shorter petals atop and in between those in first row. Repeat procedure making each additional row of petals shorter than the previous row. When entire mound is covered, add a few stand-up petals to top and tip 1 center dots.

Bachelor Button.

• Like the chrysanthemum, start with a tip 7 dot base. Pipe a cluster of short pull-out dots in the center with tip 1. With tip 14, cover the rest of the mound with pull-out stars.

Daffodil And Jonquil

• Use tip 104 for daffodil or tip 103 for jonquil. Hold bag at a 45° angle to nail, with large end of tip touching nail, narrow end pointed out and almost parallel to nail surface. Squeeze and as you turn nail, move tip out about ½-in. and back to center of nail to form petal. Repeat procedure for five more petals. Dip fingers in cornstarch and pinch ends of petals to form points. Pipe row-upon-row of tip 2 string circles and top with tip 1 zigzag for center.

Narcissus

• Use tip 102 and same procedure as for daffodil to make six ¾-in. long petals. Add tip 1 coil center and tip 1 zigzag.

Apple Blossom

• Use tip 101 or 101s and hold bag at a 45° angle to flower nail with wide end of tip touching nail center, narrow end pointed out 1/8-in. away from nail surface.

• Squeeze bag and turn nail as you move tip 1/8-in. out from nail center and back, relaxing pressure as you return to starting point.

• Repeat procedure to make four more petals. Add five tip 1 dots for center.

Forget-Me Nots

• Very similar to the apple blossom. Use tip 101 and move tip out just 3/8-in. from center, curve around and return, letting the turn of the nail form petals. Dot center with tip 1. Use large flower nail No. 7 and pipe several at once!

Violet

• Use tip 59s and same procedure as for apple blossom to make three ¾-in. long petals and two ¼-in. base petals. Add two tip 1 center dots.

Pansy

• Fit two decorating bags with tip 104. Fill one with yellow icing, the other with violet. Hold bag with yellow icing at a 45° angle to nail center, squeeze and move tip out to edge of nail. Turn nail as you squeeze, relax pressure as you return to nail center. Repeat to form second yellow petal. Use same procedure to add two shorter yellow petals atop the first two.

• Now with bag of violet icing, squeeze out a base petal that equals the width of the yellow petals, using a back and forth hand motion for a ruffled effect.

• Use a decorator's brush to add veins of violet icing color after flower has air dried. Add tip 1 string loop center.

Wild Rose

• Use tip 103 and hold bag at a 45° angle. Touch nail with wide end of tip with narrow end just slightly above nail surface. Begin at center of nail and press out first petal, turning nail as you move tip out toward edge of nail, and return to center of nail as you stop squeezing. Repeat 4 more times. Pull out tiny stamens with tip 1.

Poppy

• Hold wide end of tip 103 down, narrow end pointed out at 45° angle. Starting in center, pipe out a large, rounded, ruffled petal. Jiggle hand as you move up and out to edge of nail and down again into a point. Make four petals around nail.

• Pipe a second row of smaller, cupped petals inside first row, starting first petal between piped petals.

• Pipe tip 6 dot center and tip 14 pull-out star stamens.

• **For half poppy:** With wide end of tip 103 touching center of nail, small end pointed out at 45° angle, squeeze out a ruffle semicircle. Overpipe with another ruffle petal.

Lily Nail Flowers

The Wilton Lily Nail Set lets you make natural-looking flowers with bell-like shapes and cupped, turned-up petals. Different lily nail sizes relate to the size of flowers you can make. The larger the nail, the larger the flowers. Always use royal icing for flowers made on the lily nail since softer icing will not hold their deeply-cupped shapes. To make any flower on the lily nail, place an aluminum foil square in bottom half of nail. Press in top half to form a foil cup. Remove the top half. Lightly spray foil with vegetable oil spray. This makes it easier to remove from foil after icing has dried and reduces breakage. Pipe a flower on the foil cup and lift out flower and foil to dry.

Petunia

• Prepare 1 5/8-in. lily nail. Then with wide end of tip 102 held down, narrow end up, start piping icing deep inside nail.

• Move up to outer edge as you turn nail, jiggling hand slightly all the while to form ruffled petal edge, then go back to starting point.

• Pipe 5 separate petals in all. Add tip 14 green star center. Push in artificial stamens.

Bluebell

• Use 1¼ in. lily nail. With tip 66, pipe three ¾ in. long petals, pulling only to top of nail. Between these petals, add three more.

• Push in three short artificial stamens.

Borders and More...

Triple Shell: With tip 16, pipe row of curved shells. Directly below first row, pipe another row of curving shells in the opposite direction. With a contrasting color, pipe a row of straight shells in center of curved pairs.

Overlapping Double Drop Strings (p. 31)
With toothpick, dot mark specified intervals on sides of your cake. Touch tip 3 to a mark, allow your string to skip the next mark and attach to the following one. Repeat for 2nd drop string. Return to the mark that was skipped and drop a string to connect the next mark. Be sure to keep depth of strings even.

Jiggly-motion Seaweed (p. 16)
With tip 352, hold bag at a 45° angle and use medium pressure. As you squeeze out icing, jiggle hand with a very tight up and down motion. When desired length is reached, relax pressure and pull-out icing to form end.

Piping With Royal Icing

Lace Points (p. 34)
Trace Lacework Pattern on paper (several on each sheet). Tape paper to a cake board or circle. Tightly cover board with waxed paper or plastic wrap. Hint: If board is sprayed very lightly with vegetable oil, lace pieces are easier to remove.

Using thin consistency royal and tip 1, hold bag at a 90° angle and outline pattern design. To end, stop pressure and touch surface.

Let dry completely. For a curved effect, dry on flower formers.

Because these pieces are extremely fragile, we suggest you make almost double the amount needed.

Overpiped Stringwork (p. 70)
With tip 2, pipe a ½ in. deep drop string. Allow ¼ in. interval between next two strings. Use tip 3, then tip 5. Overpipe 2nd drop string with tip 2. Overpipe 3rd with tip 3, then tip 2.

Overpiped C-Scrolls (p. 70)
Cover scroll designs with tip 14 zigzags. Overpipe with tip 5 string, then tip 3 (on outer edge of previous one).

Musical Note Border (p. 9)
Use tip 7. Add a vertical string staff next to bead. Add 2 pull-out beads to staff. Repeat procedure, alternate color. Pipe a bead at base.

Bricks (p. 49)
Use tip 47 with the ribbed side up. Starting at base, pipe a horizontal ribbed stripe. Outline edges of stripe with tip 3 and add vertical lines. Repeat procedure for each row.

Pull-out Grass or Fur
Use tip 233 or 234 and medium icing consistency. Hold bag at a 90° angle. As you squeeze out icing, pull tip up and away from surface. When icing strand is long enough (about ½ in.), stop pressure and pull tip away.

Lattice
Lattice is piped from edge to edge and dropped on. Work from the center of design, outward. Use thinned icing and a tip 2 or 3, hold bag at a 45° angle at the top of design with tip slightly above cake. Squeeze out a diagonal line to the right, all the way to the edge of your design. On both sides of the first line, fill in more lines, evenly spaced and going in the same direction. Return to starting point in center and pipe diagonal lines to left.

Sotas (p. 59)
This cornelli-like lacework is a Philippine technique. Randomly pipe tip 2 curls, V's and C's so that they touch.

Lambeth-Method Borders
Use royal or snow-white buttercream icing in medium consistency. To avoid decorations from shifting or collapsing from the weight of the moist icing, pipe no more than one row at a time and allow work to dry completely.

Fancy Overpiped Zigzag Scrolls (p. 82)
Pipe tip 362 zigzag scrolls. Overpipe with tip 3 zigzags. Then add tip 3 string.

Special Effects

Drum Strings: Break thin uncooked spaghetti into 4 in. pieces (15 are needed, but make extras in case of breakage). Fill decorating bag, fitted with tip 3 with royal icing. Insert piece of spaghetti into open end of bag until only a small end protrudes. As you pull end of spaghetti out of bag, move bag in back and forth motion to create a rope-like effect. Push into a craft block to dry.

Drum Stick: Follow the same procedure, but pull spaghetti out straight for a smooth look.

Whiskers: Can be pushed into open end of tip, then pulled out . Or use a Decorator Brush and "paint" uncooked spaghetti with icing color.

Pearl Beading: In the idea section several cakes were dripping with pearls and the effects ... spectacular. To work with pearl beading, we suggest that the complete length (5 yds.) be used. Cut strand after wrapping around cake to insure that strand won't be too short. For safety, it is advisable to only decorate with long strands of pearl beading. Remove pearls before cutting.

Figure Piping

Medium icing consistency and pressure control are essential to successful figure piping. Let your decoration set slightly before shaping or flattening with finger tip dipped in cornstarch. Most of the figure piping shown here can be done with buttercream icing directly on cake. You'll get very good results using our Snow-white Buttercream or Boiled Icing recipes, but remember, these don't hold their shape or resist humidity like royal icing. More intricate figures such as the animals should be done on waxed paper with royal icing. When dry, position on cake.

Basic Icing Build-Up Technique

Lightly touching tip to the surface, exert pressure as you lift the tip to let the form build up. It's essential that the tip remains buried in the icing as it is squeezed out. When desired shape builds up, stop pressure as you bring the end of the tip to the surface and use end of tip to cut away points. Smooth away rippled or unwanted points with finger dipped in cornstarch.

Skull & Bones (p. 13):
Cover skull pattern with waxed paper. Using tip 8, hold bag at a 90° angle and cover ends of bones with a bead-motion. Pipe short side first, then long side. Fill skull area with a large dot, then flatten lower portion with finger dipped in cornstarch. With tip 4, outline patch and mouth; pipe in patch; add dot eye and nose.

Palm trees: Can be made with royal or buttercream icing. Use pretzel sticks for small trees, pretzel rods for large. Begin piping tip 70 leaves about a 4th of the way from top of pretzel. Pipe a row of pull-out leaves. Add bunch of bananas using tip 3 or a larger round tip. Squeeze out a dot of icing, then cover with tip 3 pull-out strings. Continue adding overlapping rows of leaves. Push directly into decorated cake or push into a craft block to dry.

Lace, Ribbons, Tulle, Flower Puffs & Fabric Leaves are lovely and easy to work with, but here are a few things to remember. Nylon lace will not absorb grease so it is the best choice. Be sure to use a waterproof, satiny ribbon for the same reason. Before attaching real trims, let icing crust a bit, then anchor in place with dots of icing.

Tinted coconut: Place shredded coconut in a plastic sandwich bag. Add a few drops of icing color, diluted slightly with water. Shake bag until color is evenly distributed.

Jungle Animals (p. 18):

Lion: Use tip 12 and hold bag at a 90° angle. With heavy pressure, build up rear of lion. Gradually ease pressure as you move bag forward to form a pear-shaped body. With tip 12 and medium pressure, squeeze out C-motion back legs. Tuck tip 12 into front of body and pull-out front legs. Pipe tip 12 ball head. Add tip 3 outline ears, snout and tail. Outline paws and facial features with tip 1. Pipe tip 13 pull-out star mane and tail.

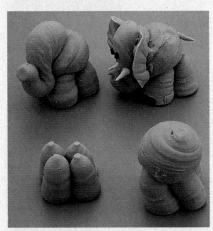

Elephant: Use tip 12 and hold bag at a 90° angle. With medium pressure, squeeze out four side-by-side legs, about 1 in. high. With tip 2A and heavy pressure, pipe a large ball body. Tuck tip 12 into "neck" and squeeze out icing with a shell-like motion gradually relaxing pressure as you lift tip upwards to form trunk.

Gorilla: Use tip 12 and hold bag at a 90° angle. Squeeze out icing with heavy pressure until body builds up to desired height. Tuck tip 12 into body and pull-out curved legs and arms. Pipe tip 12 dot head; tip 3 dot hands and feet. Add tip 1 facial features and banana. Cover with tip 233 pull-out fur.

Bunny (p. 25): With tip 1A and medium pressure, hold bag at a 90° angle. Pipe ears, relaxing pressure as you near head area. With tip 1A, pipe large dot head. Overpipe ears and paws (on dowel rod wand) with tip 12. Add tip 2 facial features and outline whiskers.

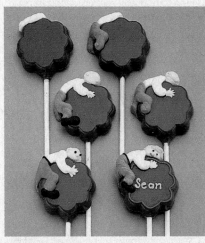

Kid Pops (p. 18):
Place lollipops on waxed paper. Hold bag at a 90° angle. For body: Use tip 4 to squeeze out shirt and pants. Tuck tip 3 into body and pull out arm. Add tip 3 dot head and shoe. Pipe hand, fingers, facial features and belt with tip 1; hair with tip 13. Use same tips and procedure for other kids.

Ghost (p. 65):
With tip 9, pipe a ball shape for head and pull out a body, tapering off the end as you gradually decrease pressure. Tuck tip into body and pull out arms. Add tip 3 dot eyes.

Pumpkins (p. 67):
With tip 7 and heavy pressure, pipe two quotation-motion marks that touch at top and bottom. Overpipe and fill space between with another pair. In center, pipe a straight oval shape line. Add tip 3 stem.

All About Tier Cakes

There are many methods of constructing tiered cakes. Here are some of the most popular:

Dowel Rod

Stacked

Mark Center Back

Pillar

Mark Where Legs Go

Push-In Leg

To Prepare Cake For Assembly

Place base tier on a sturdy base plate or 3 or more thicknesses of corrugated cardboard. For heavy cakes, use masonite or plywood. Base can be covered with Fanci-Foil Wrap and trimmed with Tuk-N-Ruffle. Each tier in your cake must be on a cake circle or board cut to fit. Smear a few strokes of icing on boards to secure cake. Fill and ice layers before assembly.

To Dowel Rod Cakes For Pillar & Stacked Construction

Center a cake circle or plate one size smaller than the next tier on base tier and press it gently into icing to imprint an outline. Remove circle. Measure one dowel rod at the cake's lowest point within this circle. Using this dowel rod for measure, cut dowel rods (to fit this tier) the same size using pruning shears. If the next tier is 10-in. or less, push seven ¼-in. dowel rods into cake down to base within circle guide. Generally the larger and more numerous the upper tiers, the more dowels needed. Very large cakes need ½-in. dowels in base tier.

Stacked Construction

This method is often combined with pillar construction. Dowel rod bottom tier. Center a corrugated cake circle, one size smaller than the tier to be added, on top of the base tier. Position the following tier. Repeat procedure for each additional tier. To keep stacked tiers stable, sharpen one end of a dowel rod and push through all tiers and cardboard circles to base of bottom tier. To decorate, start at top and work down.

Pillar Construction

Dowel rod tiers. Optional: Snap pegs into separator plates to prevent slipping (never substitute pegs for dowel rods). Position separator plates on supporting tiers, making sure that pillar projections on each tier will line up with pillars below. Mark center backs of cakes. Decorate cakes. At reception, align pillar projections and assemble cakes on pillars.

Fast & Easy Push-In Leg Construction

Dowel rods are not needed because legs attached to separator plates push right through the tiers down to the plate below.

Ice cakes on cake circles. To mark where legs will go, simply center separator plate for tier above (projections down) and gently press onto the tier. Lift plate off. Repeat this procedure for each tier (except top). Position upper tiers on separator plates. Decorate cakes.

To assemble: Insert legs into cake at marks. Push straight down until legs touch cake board. Add plate with cake to legs. Be sure plates are securely fastened to legs. Continue adding tiers in this way until cake is assembled.

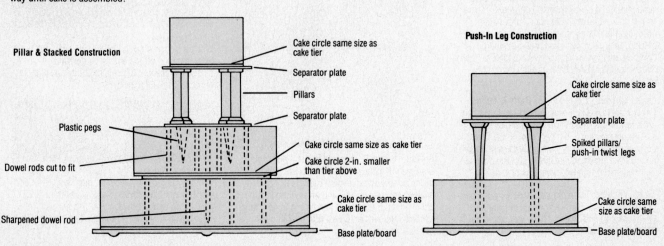

Pillar & Stacked Construction

- Cake circle same size as cake tier
- Separator plate
- Pillars
- Separator plate
- Cake circle same size as cake tier
- Cake circle 2-in. smaller than tier above
- Cake circle same size as cake tier
- Base plate/board

Plastic pegs

Dowel rods cut to fit

Sharpened dowel rod

Push-In Leg Construction

- Cake circle same size as cake tier
- Separator plate
- Spiked pillars/ push-in twist legs
- Cake circle same size as cake tier
- Base plate/board

Hints for Assembling & Transporting Tiered Cakes

• Before placing separator plate or cake circle atop another tier, sprinkle a little confectioners sugar or coconut flakes to prevent plate or circle from sticking. Letting icing crust a bit before positioning plate on cake will also prevent sticking.

• You will have less crumbs when icing, if cakes are baked a day in advance.

• When filling or torting large layers, use less than you usually would. Your dam of icing should also be far enough from edge so filling doesn't form a bubble.

• The cake icer tip (789) is an invaluable timesaver in icing wedding tiers.

• The 16-in. bevel pan takes 1½ cake mixes. So your beveled sides bake properly, pull batter out from center to add depth to the sides.

• When transporting tiers, place cakes on damp towels or carpet foam and drive carefully.

• Some of the plates of the Tall Tier Stand will not sit level when not on the stand. Pack atop crumpled foil, tissue or towels when transporting. To decorate, set plates on pan or bowl. The column cap nut of the Tall Tier Stand attaches under the top tier cake. Therefore, this cake must be positioned after assembling the Tall Tier Stand. Place top tier on a cake circle slightly larger than the cake to make positioning easier. Add base borders after assembling the top tier.

• To keep balance, cut cakes on the Tall Tier Stand from top tier down.

• To divide tiers, use the Cake Dividing Set. The Wheel Chart makes it easy to mark 2-in. intervals on 6 to 18-in. diam. cakes. The triangle marker gives precise spacing for stringwork and garlands. The raised lines on separator plates can also be followed for easy dividing.

• When using Spiked Pillars and stacked construction, double cake boards or use separator plates between layers to prevent the weight of tiers from causing the pillars to pierce through cake.

Wedding Cake Data

One cake mix yields 4 to 6 cups of batter. Pans are usually filled ½ to ⅔ full; 3-in. deep pans should be filled only ½ full. Batter amounts on this chart are for pans two-thirds full of batter. Icing amounts are very general and will vary with consistency, thickness applied and tips used. These amounts allow for top and base borders and a side ruffled border. For large cakes, always check for doneness after they have baked for one hour.

The charts to the right show how to cut popular shaped wedding tiers into pieces approximately 1-in. x 2-in. by two layers high (about 4-in.). Even if you prefer a larger serving size, the order of cutting is still the same.

Number of servings are intended as a guide only.

Pan Shape	Size	# Servings 2 Layer	Cups Batter/ 1 Layers 2"	Baking Temps	Baking Time	Approx. Cups Icing to Frost and Decorate
Oval	7¾ x 5¾"	13	2½	350°	25	3
	10¾ x 7⅞"	30	5½	350°	30	4
	13 x 9¾"	44	8	350°	30	5½
	16 x 12¾"	70	11	325°	30	7½
Round	6"	14	2	350°	25-30	3
	8"	25	3	350°	30-35	4
	10"	39	6	350°	35-40	5
	12"	56	7½	350°	35-40	6
	14"	77	10	325°	50-55	7¼
	16"	100	15	325°	55-60	8¾
Round 3" Deep (# Servings for 1 layer)	8"	15	5	325°	60-65	2¾
	10"	24	8	325°	75-80	4¾
	12"	33	11	325°	75-80	5¾
	14"	45	15	325°	75-80	7
Half Round 2" layer	18"	127†	9*	325°	60-65	10½
3" layer		92††	12*	325°	60-65	10½
Petal	6"	8	1½	350°	25-30	3½
	9"	20	3½	350°	35-40	6
	12"	38	7	350°	35-40	7¾
	15"	62	12	325°	50-55	11
Hexagon	6"	12	1¾	350°	30-35	2¾
	9"	22	3½	350°	35-40	4¾
	12"	50	6	350°	40-45	5¾
	15"	72	11	325°	40-45	8¾
Heart	6"	11	1½	350°	25	2½
	9"	24	3½	350°	30	4½
	12"	48	8	350°	30	5¾
	15"	76	11½	325°	40	8¾
Square	6"	18	2	350°	25-30	3½
	8"	32	4	350°	35-40	4½
	10"	50	6	350°	35-40	6
	12"	72	10	350°	40-45	7½
	14"	98	13½	350°	45-50	9½
	16"	128	15½	350°	45-50	11
	18"	162	18	350°	50-55	13

*Batter for each half round pan.   †Four half rounds.   ††Two half rounds.

Wedding Cake Cutting Guide

The first step in cutting is to remove the top tier, and then begin the cutting with the 2nd tier followed by 3rd, 4th and so on. The top tier is usually saved for the first anniversary so it is not figured into the serving amount.

Cutting guides for shapes not shown can be found in other Wilton publications. The diagrams below show how to cut popular shaped wedding tiers into pieces approximately 1-in. x 2-in. by two layers high (about 4-in.). Even if you prefer a larger serving size, the order of cutting is still the same.

To cut oval tiers, move in 2-in. from the outer edge and cut across. Then slice 1-in. pieces of cake. Now move in another 2-in. and slide again until the entire tier is cut.

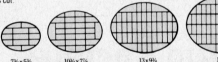

7¾ x 5¾   10¾ x 7⅞   13 x 9¾   16 x 12¾

To cut round tiers, move in two inches from the tier's outer edge; cut a circle and then slice 1-in. pieces within the circle. Now move in another 2-in., cut another circle, slice 1-in. pieces and so on until the tier is completely cut. The center core of each tier and the small top tier can be cut into halves, 4ths, 6ths and 8ths, depending on size.

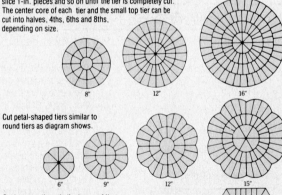

8"   12"   16"

Cut petal-shaped tiers similar to round tiers as diagram shows.

6"   9"   12"   15"

Cut hexagon tiers similar to round tiers.

6"   9"   12"   15"

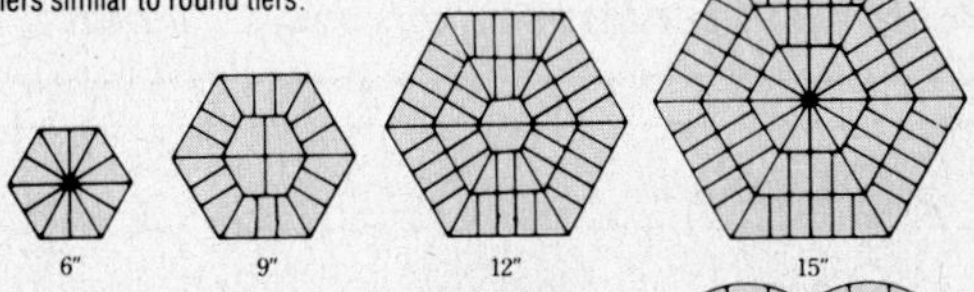

To cut heart-shaped tiers, divide the tiers vertically into halves, quarters, sixths or eighths. Within rows, slice one inch pieces of cake.

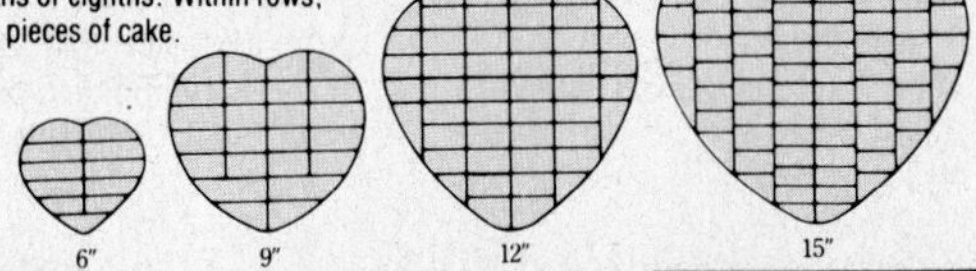

6"   9"   12"   15"

To cut square tiers, move in 2-in. from the outer edge and cut across. Then slice 1-in. pieces of cake. Now move in another 2-in. and slice again until the entire tier is cut.

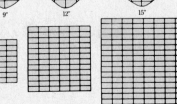

8"   12"   16"

Color Flow

Color Flow Technique

• Tape pattern and waxed paper overlay to your work surface. (The back of a cookie pan makes a great work surface.) For curved decorations, use flower formers. Use full-strength Color Flow icing and tip 2 or 3 to outline the pattern with desired colors. If you're going to use the same color icing to fill in the outlines, let the icing outlines dry a few minutes until they "crust." If you're going to fill in with icings that differ in colors from the outlines, then let outlines dry thoroughly (1-2 hours) before filling in.

• Soften icing for filling in pattern outlines as specified in recipe. Don't use a tip for filling in outlines; instead, cut a very small opening in end of parchment bag. Begin filling in along the edges of the outline first, squeezing gently and letting the icing flow up to the outline almost by itself. Work quickly; filling in design from the outside edges in and from top to bottom. If you have several outlined sections, fill in one at a time.

Color Flow Icing Recipe

(Full-Strength for Outlining)
¼ cup water + 1 teaspoon
1 lb. sifted confectioners sugar (4 cups)
2 Tablespoons Wilton Color Flow Icing Mix

In an electric mixer, using grease-free utensils, blend all ingredients on low speed for 5 minutes. If using hand mixer, use high speed. Color Flow icing "crusts" quickly, so keep it covered with a damp cloth while using. Stir in desired icing color. In order to fill in an outlined area, this recipe must be thinned with a ½ teaspoon of water per ¼ cup of icing (just a few drops at a time as you near proper consistency.) Color Flow icing is ready for filling in outlines when a small amount dropped into the mixture takes a full count of ten to disappear. Use grease-free spoon or spatula to stir slowly.
Note: Color Flow designs take a long time to dry, so plan to do your Color Flow piece at least 2-3 days in advance.

Cookie Recipes

Grandma's Gingerbread Recipe

5 to 5½ cups all-purpose flour
1 tsp. baking soda
1 tsp. salt
2 tsps. ginger
2 tsps. cinnamon
1 tsp. nutmeg
1 tsp. cloves
1 cup shortening
1 cup sugar
1¼ cups unsulphured molasses
2 eggs, beaten
Thoroughly mix flour, soda, salt and spices.
Melt shortening in large saucepan. Cool slightly. Add sugar, molasses and eggs; mix well. Add four cups dry ingredients and mix well.

Turn mixture onto lightly floured surface. Knead in remaining dry ingredients by hand. Add a little more flour, if necessary, to make a firm dough. Roll out on a lightly floured surface to ¼ in. thickness for cut-out cookies.

If you're not going to use your gingerbread dough right away, wrap dough in plastic and refrigerate. Refrigerated dough will keep for a week, but be sure to remove it 3 hours prior to rolling so it softens and is workable. 1 recipe of this gingerbread dough will yield 40 average-size cookies.

If you're filling in a large area, have two half-full parchment bags ready, otherwise icing could "crust" before you finish filling in the pattern.

Hint: The back of a cookie pan makes a great work surface. For curved decorations, use flower formers. Since buttercream icing will break down color flow, either position color flow decoration on cake shortly before serving or place a piece of plastic wrap cut to fit on area first on set atop sugar cubes.

Roll-Out Cookies

1 cup butter
1 cup sugar
1 large egg
2 tsps. baking powder
1 tsp. vanilla
2¾ cups flour

Preheat oven to 400°. In a large bowl, cream butter and sugar with an electric mixer. Beat in eggs and vanilla. Add baking powder and flour, one cup at a time, mixing after each addition. The dough will be very stiff; blend last flour in by hand. Do not chill dough. **Note:** Dough can be tinted with Icing Color. Add small amounts until desired color is reached. **For chocolate cookies:** Stir in 3 ounces melted, unsweetened chocolate (if dough becomes too stiff, add water, a teaspoon at a time).

Divide dough into 2 balls. On a floured surface, roll each ball into a circle approximately 12 inches in diameter and 1/8 in. thick. Dip cutters in flour before each use. Bake cookies on top rack of oven for 6-7 minutes, or until cookies are lightly browned.

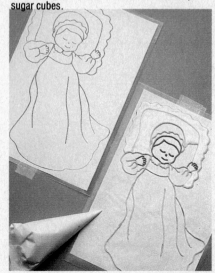

Candy Making

Wilton Candy Melts™ brand confectionery coating take the guesswork out of making candy at home. They melt easily, right to the ideal consistency for molding and dipping, and have a creamy, rich flavor. For a change of taste, they can be flavored with Wilton Candy Flavors. See our complete collection of candy making products (p. 118-121).

Candy Melts Are So Easy To Use

For melting, molding and dipping directions, simply refer to the back of the Candy Melts package. Remember that constant stirring is very important to insure even heating, when using the double boiler method. Here's a no-mess way of melting in microwave: Fill an uncut disposable decorating bag half-full of Candy Melts. Microwave 1 minute at half power; knead candy. Repeat at 30-second intervals until candy is completely melted. Then cut the tip and squeeze melted coating out into candy molds.

To Flavor: The creamy, rich taste can be enhanced by adding approximately ¼ teaspoon Wilton oil-based Candy Flavor (p. 118) to 1 lb. of melted Candy Melts. Never use alcohol based flavorings; they will cause coatings to harden.

To Color: Add Wilton Candy Colors (p. 119) to melted Candy Melts a little at a time. Mix thoroughly before adding more color. Colors tend to deepen as they're mixed. Pastel colored candies are most appetizing, so keep this in mind when tinting.

To Mold Multi-Color Candy

"Painting" Method: Use a decorator's brush dipped in melted Candy Melts. Paint features or details desired. Let set. Fill mold. Refrigerate until set. Unmold. **"Layering" Method:** Pour melted coating into dry molds to desired height. Refrigerate until partially set. Pour contrasting color melted coating to desired height. Refrigerate until partially set. Repeat until desired numbers of layers are formed. Let candy harden in refrigerator. Unmold. Wilton Classic Candy Molds are available in a wonderful variety of unique and traditional shapes. Their generous depth makes painting and layering fun and easy. See page 121 for our outstanding Classic Candy Molds selection.

To Mold Candy Plaques

Molding a section or the entire pan out of Candy Melts is easy and impressive.

• Pour melted coating into center of pan. Tap pan gently on counter to break up bubbles and spread coating evenly over bottom (approximately ¼ in. thick). For control, use a decorating bag fitted with tip 2 or snip off a very small end off disposable bag.

• Place pan in refrigerator for approximately 5 to 10 minutes (check occasionally, if coating becomes too hard it will crack). Unmold onto hand or soft towel (tap pan gently, if necessary).

• Cookie cutters work great, too. Place cutter on waxed paper; pour in candy. Unmold when set per instructions above.

• For multi-color effect: Paint desired area with a decorator's brush, Let set. Pour in melted coating to fill remaining area.

For Open-Heart Plaque

• Trace pattern and place on a heavy board or piece of glass, cover with waxed paper and tape securely.

• Fill a parchment or disposable bag with melted Candy Melts. Cut a very small opening in end (approximately the size of a tip 3). Outline edges of heart collar and let set 5 to 10 minutes. Flow in candy (to smooth surface, skim area with end of bag immediately) and let set. Edge with scallops, then add bead borders. Allow to set completely 10 to 15 minutes. To add strength (optional), turn collar over and repeat procedure.

TO MAKE CANDY LEAVES

On the back of clean, thoroughly dried, grape or rose leaves, paint on melted Candy Melts with a soft pastry or decorator's brush. Pull out pointed or curved edges to resemble certain kinds of leaves such as the "oak" leaves.
Let coating set and when completely dry, carefully peel off candy.

Ganache Glaze

So easy to make with our delicious Candy Melts™* brand confectionery coating. Elegantly covers cakes with a luscious, satiny-smooth finish. Can be used for decorating and as a filling. Just allow mixture to cool so it sets, then whip. It can now be used to fill cakes, pipe borders, scrolls and even roses.

Ganache Glaze Recipe

14 oz. package of Candy Melts
½ cup whipping cream

Finely chop wafers (use food processor). Heat whipping cream just to boiling point (do not boil) in a sauce pan. Add chopped wafers and stir until smooth and glossy. If mixture is too thin to pour, wait a few minutes until cool. To cover, place cake on a wire rack over a drip pan. Pour glaze into center and work towards edges.

Modeling Candy "Clay"
- 14 oz. bag of Candy Melts
- ⅓ cup light corn syrup
- Candy or Icing Color (optional)

Melt candy as directed on package. Stir in corn syrup and mix only until blended.

Shape mixture onto a 6 in. square of waxed paper and let set at room temperature until dry.

Wrap well and store at room temperature until needed. Modeling candy handles best if hardened overnight.

To use: If you wish to tint candy, add candy or icing color. Knead a small portion at a time. If it gets too soft, set aside at room temperature or refrigerate briefly. Lasts for several weeks in a well-sealed container.

When rolling out candy, sprinkle surface with cornstarch to prevent sticking. Thickness of rolled-out candy should be approximately ⅛ in. Hint: Secure pieces together with dots of buttercream icing, if necessary.

MODELING A ROSE
Start with the base and mold a cone that's approximately 1½-in. high from a 3/4-in. diameter ball of modeling candy. Next, make petals. Flatten 3/8-in. ball of modeling candy into a circle that's about ¼-in. thick on one side and about the diameter of a dime. Make several petals this size.
- Wrap first petal around the point of the cone to form a bud. Now press three more petals around the base of the bud.
- Gently pinch edges of petals. Make five more petals using slightly larger balls of modeling candy. Flatten, then thin edge with finger and cup petals. Press petals under first rows of petals. Continue adding petals, placing them in between and slightly lower than previous row. For a fuller flower, continue adding petals in this manner.

To Make Flowers (p. 34)
Use tools and instructions included in our Gum Paste Flowers Kit for making daffodil, violet and leaves.

Make 1 recipe of Modeling Candy with white Candy Melts. Tint ½ of recipe yellow. Divide remainder into 3rds. One remains white, tint rest green and violet with icing colors.

For Daffodil: Do steps 1 through 3 (in gum paste kit instruction book), except use cornstarch instead of grease. Let petals dry on flower formers. For trumpet or cup, roll out white modeling candy. Cut out trumpet with small carnation cutter. With a knife, cut away a triangular 4th. Dip modeling stick (included in kit) in cornstarch and form trumpet around it. Let dry. Attach trumpet to petals with royal icing. Edge top with tip 2 royal icing zigzags. Make 15.

For leaves: Roll out green modeling candy. Cut out leaves with large leaf cutter. Dip leaf mold into cornstarch, then press candy into mold. Remove leaf from mold and allow it to dry on flower former. Make 23 leaves.

For violets: Follow steps 1 thru 3 in gum paste kit instruction book. Let flowers dry on flower formers. For centers, make tiny balls from yellow modeling candy. Attach with dots of royal icing.

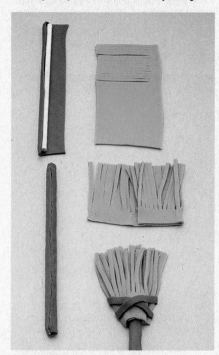

To Make Snowman's Attire (p. 46)
Make 1 recipe of Modeling Candy using White Candy Melts.

For nose: Remove a small piece (about a quarter-size). Knead in orange color, then shape into a cone.

For hat band & berries: Remove a golf ball size

piece of candy. Add red color. Shape 3 pea-size berries. Roll out and cut Hatband Pattern.

For Broom Bristles: Shape candy into a 3 in. long, 1 in. thick cylinder. Tint light brown with brown color. Roll out and cut Broom Bristles Pattern.

Divide remaining candy in half.

- For scarf & holly leaves: Tint candy green. Cut out candy using Holly Leaf (cut 2) and Scarf Patterns.
- Tint remaining candy brown. Shape 6 pea-size balls for mouth; 2 dime-size rounds for eyes; 2 nickle-size pieces for buttons. Roll out remaining candy and cut out Hat, Broomstick & Broom Band (need 2) Patterns.
- To decorate cake: Ice cake with buttercream icing (lightly ice hat area). Lift up hat piece and place on cake. Mold it around cake with finger. Position hatband and holly leaves. Lay scarf on cake. With tip 3 and buttercream icing, outline leaves and edges of scarf. Trim scarf with relaxed zigzags. Add candy facial features and buttons. Wrap broom handle piece around dowel rod. Fold broom bristle into 3rds and wrap top portion around broom handle. Position broom on cake and add crisscrossed broom bands. Place broom bands

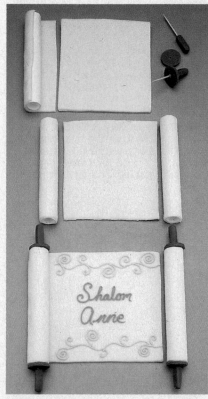

To Make Torah (p. 70)
Before making 1 recipe of Modeling Candy with White Candy Melts, paint rose leaves with melted candy. Make candy roses. Remove about an ⅛th from remaining candy and knead in brown color.

- Roll out white modeling candy, then cut a 5½ in. square and two 5½ x 3 in. rectangles. Cut 2 plastic dowel rods to 5½ in. lengths. Roll a rectangle piece around each dowel rod once. Trim away excess. Place some candy inside dowel rods to fill ends. With brown modeling candy, cut 4 round pieces to fit ends of scrolls. Divide remainder into 4 pieces and mold each around a toothpick. Allow about ⅓ of toothpick to remain uncovered. Push toothpick into ends of scrolls. Position scroll center and side pieces on cake, then decorate as per instructions.

The Wilton School
Of Cake Decorating and Confectionary Art

Learn how to decorate from the experts! Since 1929, when Dewey McKinley Wilton first opened the Wilton School, thousands of students have learned the fundamentals of decorating the Wilton Way. The Wilton Method of Cake Decorating stresses classic decorating—beginning with a thorough understanding of the fundamentals. Students are then encouraged to express themselves creatively.

The Wilton School is approved by the Illinois State Board of Education under the provisions of the Illinois Private Business and Vocational Schools Act. Students receive instruction, supervision and guidance by expert instructors/decorators.

World renown, the Wilton School has greatly expanded its curriculum since the Wilton Method was first introduced 60 years ago. Today the basic Master Course is supplemented by courses in foreign methods, Lambeth, chocolate artistry, gum paste, pulled sugar, catering cakes and more. The following is a summary of courses we offer:

MASTER COURSE—2 weeks, 70 hours. Focuses on the fundamentals of cake decorating. Designed for the cake decorating shop owner, baker, caterer, chef or enthusiast.
TUITION: $550

INTRODUCTION TO GUM PASTE COURSE—12 hours—four afternoons during the Master Course. This mini-course teaches the art of making lovely gum paste flowers, bouquets and more.
TUITION: $125

ADVANCED GUM PASTE/FOREIGN METHODS COURSE—2 weeks, 80 hours. Designed for the more serious decorator. Covers: Nirvana, the English method of cake decorating that uses color flow panels; South African and Australian Methods, which use delicate royal icing wings and are done on rolled fondant-covered cakes; gum paste flowers and arrangements. A gum paste doll is constructed. Previous decorating experience is required.
TUITION: $550

LAMBETH CONTINENTAL COURSE—1 week, 40 hours. Teaches intricate overpiping of borders on royal icing and rolled fondant- covered cakes. All students decorate cakes using a combination of over-piped borders. Previous decorating experience is required.
TUITION: $300

PULLED SUGAR COURSE—9 hours, 3 afternoons during Master Course. Learn how to use pulled sugar to cover a cake, make flowers, candy dishes, ribbons, bows and more
TUITION: $150

CHOCOLATE ARTISTRY WITH ELAINE GONZALEZ—5 days, 30 hours. Well-known chocolatier and author of *Chocolate Artistry* presents an in-depth course devoted exclusively to making and decorating candy. Professional techniques for creating fabulous candies from molded treats to delicious truffles.
TUITION: $300

CAKES FOR CATERING—A 5 day, 40-hour course where students learn to ice and decorate cakes to serve large or small groups. The class covers wedding and other tiered cakes, sheet cakes, large rounds and squares and petit fours, including small cakes and cookies. Learn to design theme party cakes and get special tips for quick and easy, but spectacular designs.
TUITION: $300

The Wilton School is located in Woodridge, Illinois (a suburb of Chicago). Course enrollment is limited. For more information, or to enroll, write to: School Secretary, Wilton School of Cake Decorating and Confectionary Art, 2240 W. 75th St., Woodridge, IL 60517. Or call 708-963-7100 for free brochure and schedule. You may charge your courses on VISA or MasterCard.

Home Study
Wilton
Course in
Candy Making

In just five easy lessons, you'll learn how to make and mold luscious candies that rival expensive store-bought delights.

You'll soon be impressing family and friends with your delicious homemade sweets and discovering that making candy is a real treat!

Step-by-step instructions, illustrations and photographs will take you from basic melting and molding techniques to adanced cooked candies. Special tools, supplies and ingredients are included.

LESSON 1
Melt and mold an assortment of candy treats in various shapes, flavors and colors. Make candy clusters and candies with nut centers. Combine creamy caramel, pecans and chocolaty coating to create chewy Caramel Turtles!

Lesson 1 includes:
- Notebook Easel and Lesson Pages
- 4 pkgs. Candy Melts™ brand confectionery coating
- 2 Plastic Sheet Molds
- Disposable Decorating Bags
- Lollipop Sticks
- Pink Candy Color
- Peppermint Candy Flavor
- Caramel Filling (16 oz. container)
- *Let's Make Candy Book*

LESSON 2
Shape and dip creme center candies! Learn to use Wilton Creme Center Mix to make vanilla, peppermint and peanut butter creme centers. It's easy to mold and dip these candies! Covered cherries are another tasty treat you'll learn to make.

Lesson 2 includes:
- Lesson Pages
- 5 pkgs. Candy Melts™ brand confectionery coating
- 2 Plastic Sheet Molds
- Panda 3-D Stand-Up Mold
- 3 Pkgs. Creme Center Mix
- Disposable Decorating Bag
- Plastic Dipping Spoon
- Decorator's Brush
- Candy Box, Liner, Label and Paper Candy Cups.

LESSON 3
Learn to turn plain candies into extraordinary treats by decorating with melted coating. Learn to make molded, layered and piped truffle candies—so very creamy and rich! Try your hand at making ice cream candies to thrill a sweet tooth!

Lesson 3 includes:
- Lesson Pages
- 6 pkgs. Candy Melts™ brand confectionery coating
- Heart Box 3-D Mold
- Plastic Coupler and Decorating Tips
- Disposable Decorating Bags
- Green and Yellow Candy Colors
- Lollipop Sticks
- Lemon Candy Flavor
- Foil Candy Cups.

Try it!

Once you experience the joy and rewards of making your own candy, you'll never reach for store-bought candy again.

Our home study course makes candy creating so effortless. Simple, how-to instructions take you through five informative lessons. Soon you'll be amazed at how easy it is to master these techniques. Try it today!

LESSON 4
Mix and fix the most delicious candies! Mold candy cups to fill with liqueur or brandy. Learn how to make two cooked candies—light-as-air divinities and chewy nougats. Learn to shape an edible rose from special modeling candy recipe.

Lesson 4 includes:
- Lesson Pages
- 4 pkgs. Candy Melts™ brand confectionery coating
- Cordial Cup Plastic Sheet Mold
- Candy Box and Liner
- Professional Quality Candy Thermometer.

LESSON 5
Make some super, sensational sweets! Learn how to make chewy jellied candies and shimmering hard candies in hard candy molds. Make delicate mints and petit fours with their smooth and creamy fondant-like icing.

Lesson 5 includes:
- Lesson Pages
- 1 pkg. Candy Melts™ brand confectionery coating
- 2 Hard Candy Molds
- Nylon Candy Funnel
- Candy Water & Fondant Mix
- Disposable Decorating Bags
- Lollipop Sticks

Even if you've never tried cake decorating before, the Wilton Home Study Course will show you how to decorate beautiful cakes for every occasion. Easy-to-follow 5-lesson course includes the specialty tools you need plus the step-by-step instructions, illustrations and photographs that make it easy!

LESSON 1

Discover the easy way to pipe buttercream icing stars, zigzag borders and more! Learn how to prepare and color icing for your decorating bag, the correct angle to use, and how to control the pressure for expert results. Make a "Happy Birthday" cake.

Lesson 1 includes:
• Notebook Easel and Lesson Pages
• Decorating Tips 4, 16 and 18
• Quick-Change Plastic Coupler
• Two Jars of Paste Icing Color
• Shaped "Happy Birthday" Cake Pan
• 12" Featherweight Decorating Bag
• Pattern Sheets and Practice Board
• Cardboard Cake Circle
• *Cake Decorating Easy As 1-2-3 Book*

LESSON 2

Make royal icing drop flowers, star flowers and leaves. Mold a sugar basket. Create a blooming basket cake. Learn how to achieve special effects with color and floral sprays plus how to print or write personalized messages!

Lesson 2 includes:
• Lesson Pages
• Flower Basket Sugar Mold
• Large Stainless Steel Angled Spatula
• Decorating Tips 3, 20, 67 and 131
• 2 Jars of Paste Icing Color
• Meringue Powder (4 oz. canister)
• Pack of 50 Parchment Paper Triangles
• Cardboard Cake Circle
• 6 Pattern Sheets

LESSON 3

Learn the proper techniques for making shells, rosebuds, sweet peas ruffles, bows and more! Learn to make bouquets on a heart-shaped cake ideal for anniversaries, birthdays, Valentine's Day, weddings, showers.

Lesson 3 includes:
• Lesson Pages
• Two 9" Heart-Shaped Aluminum Pans
• Decorating Tips 22, 103 and 104
• 12" Featherweight Decorating Bag
• Quick-Change Plastic Coupler
• Cardboard Cake Circle
• Jar of Paste Icing Color
• 4 Pattern Sheets

LESSON 4

Pipe daisies and chrysanthemums using a flower nail. Weave basketweave stripes. Create symmetrical cake designs, pipe rope borders and more. Use your new cake turntable to decorate a round cake.

Lesson 4 includes:
• Lesson Pages
• Trim 'N Turn Cake Stand
• Decorating Tips 48 and 81
• Cardboard Cake Circle
• Flower Nails 7 and 9
• Jar of Paste Icing Color
• Wilton Cake Marker
• 6 Pattern Sheets

LESSON 5

Shape a magnificent icing rose! Pipe stringwork and create a mini-tiered cake using the pans and separator set we'll send. After this lesson you'll qualify for your Wilton Certificate of Completion!

Lesson 5 includes:
• Lesson Pages
• Round Mini-Tier Kit (includes 3 cake pans, separator plates and columns)
• Decorating Tips 2, 12, 87 and 102
• Cardboard Cake Circle
• 4 Pattern Sheets

You can do it!

We'll show you how. Even if you don't know a decorating bag from a coupler, by the end of this course, you'll be a pro.

Learn creative techniques on which you will constantly rely. Piping, drop flowers, shells, daisies, chrysanthemums and magnificent roses. The ideas and options are endless. You will quickly realize, with confidence, that "you can do it."

How To...
Videos

Video Home Study

IT'S FUN AND EASY...in just three lessons, you'll learn the basic skills of cake decorating. You'll receive the video tapes and all the pans and tools you'll create six wonderful, decorated cakes for birthdays, holiday and any occasion you want to make special.

Lesson 1
Have fun learning the fundamentals of baking and frosting shaped cakes, about icings, how to use decorating tools and more! Learn how to decorate 2 fun, shaped cakes.
Includes
Lesson I 30 minute VHS video, Lesson Plan/Guide, Huggable Bear shaped pan, 10 in. Soft Touch decorating bag, 3 disposable decorating bags, 4 metal decorating tips, 2 quick-change couplers, practice board with practice sheets, 2 jars of icing color, heavy duty cake board, Trim 'N Turn cake stand, 1991 Wilton Yearbook of Cake Decorating.

Lesson 2
Learn how to torte, how to ice a cake smooth, how to make shells, drop flowers, leaves, figure pipe. Learn how to decorate 2 cakes and a clown cupcake, using figure piping and drop flowers.
Includes
Lesson II 30 minute VHS video, Lesson Plan/Guide, 9" Round Pan Set, 3 metal decorating tips, large angled spatula, 2 jars of icing color, 3 disposable decorating bags, 30 parchment sheets, 2 cake circles, Clown Heads cake tops.

Lesson 3
Learn how to make the rose and other icing flowers, how to make bows, and how to position flower sprays on cakes. Learn how to decorate 2 heart-shaped cakes with basketweave and flowers.
Includes
Lesson III 30 minute VHS video, Lesson Plan/Guide, 9" Happiness Heart Pan Set, 3 metal decorating tips, #7 flower nail, 2 jars icing color, a container of meringue powder, 2 cake circles, a decorating comb and a Certificate of Completion.

HOW TO MAKE WEDDING CAKES.
Receive invaluable lessons on how to design and assemble dramatic tier cakes for weddings, showers, anniversaries and other special occasions. Hints for transporting and serving are also included.
VHS. 901-W-128 $19.99 each

HOW TO MAKE ICING FLOWERS.
Add blooming beauty to all cakes. Learn how to make roses, Easter lilies, violets, pansies, daises, poinsettias and more! Five lovely cake designs incorporate all the beautiful flowers included in this video.
VHS. 901-W-119 $19.99 each

CAKE DECORATING – EASY AS 1-2-3!
Zella Junkin, Director of the Wilton School, takes you through the basics. See how to level and frost a cake perfectly, make simple borders, flowers, leaves and more.
VHS. 901-W-115 $19.99 each

CANDY MAKING – EASY AS 1,2,3!
Have fun learning how to make truffles, candy novelties, dipped fruit, molded and filled candy. Melting candy in the microwave included.
VHS. 901-W-125 $19.99 each

IT'S CONVENIENT...see actual decorating techniques demonstrated right in your own home. Learn, step-by-step, how to create these wonderful icing techniques yourself...then practice them on your practice board right in front of your TV. Start with the basics and build up to a beautiful rose. You'll love all the decorating fun and ease of learning it with this great new video.

IT'S A TREAT...learn from our experts. Now you can gather all the secrets of experienced cake decorators. See and hear all the hints and tips that make decorating easy. You'll be surprised at how much you can learn and accomplish with this new Wilton Video Home Study Cake Decorating Course.

ENROLL IN THE WILTON VIDEO HOME STUDY COURSE NOW. The cost is only **$29.99*** per lesson...and the videos and all the pans and tools are yours to keep. Don't delay. Return the card on page 128 with your first payment of $29.99* to Wilton and we'll send you Lesson I. If you are not completely satisfied, you can return both the video and the materials within 30 days for a full refund or credit.

*plus $3.50 shipping and handling.

Publications

CAKE DECORATING – EASY AS 1-2-3
Shows and explains the basics of cake decorating in simple terms. Perfect for beginners! Soft cover; 36 pages; full color; 5½ X 8½ in.
902-W-1792 $1.99 each

USES OF DECORATING TIPS
Extremely valuable quick reference/idea book. Shows the versatility and range of many tips by depicting design variations. Full color; soft cover; 48 pages; 8½ X 11 in.
902-W-1375 $6.99 each

DISCOVER THE FUN OF CAKE DECORATING
Find over 100 irresistible cake ideas, from fast and easy sheet cakes to wedding cakes with complete easy-to-follow, step-by-step instructions. Includes patterns and cake serving ideas. 184 color pages; 8⅞ X 11 in.
904-W-206 $12.99 each

THE WILTON WAY OF CAKE DECORATING –
As easy as one, two, three. Explore this must-have trilogy of techniques, tools, ideas, instructions and hints. All found in three invaluable volumes you'll be constantly consulting.

VOLUME ONE – BEGIN WITH THE BASICS!
More than 600 full-color photos portray the Wilton method of decorating. Specialty techniques, such as Color Flow, Figure Piping, Sugar Molding and Marzipan Modeling are easy to master. Includes recipes. Hard cover; 328 color pages; 8½ X 11 in. Printed in Italy.
904-W-100 $29.99 each

VOLUME TWO – ADVANCED TECHNIQUES
Our 328-page encyclopedia is brimming with Wilton-American and foreign techniques: English (Nirvana and over-piped), Australian, Continental, Mexican, Philippine and South African. Includes gum paste flowers and figures and the art of pulled sugar taught and demonstrated by Norman Wilton. Soft cover; 328 color pages; 8½ X 11 in. Printed in U.S.A.
904-W-119 $26.99

VOLUME THREE – USING DECORATING TIPS
More than 400 color photos highlight over 40 beautiful borders, plus dozens of flowers and other decorative motifs. Exciting figure piped and gum paste creations are demonstrated and explained. Hard cover; 328 color pages; 8½ X ll in. Printed in U.S.A.
ENGLISH VERSION
904-W-348 $29.99 each
VOLUME THREE – SPANISH VERSION (not shown)
Like the English version, this book is totally devoted to tips. Also features a full chapter of quinceanos cakes and easy-to-follow "pictorial dictionary."
904-W-1348 $34.99 each

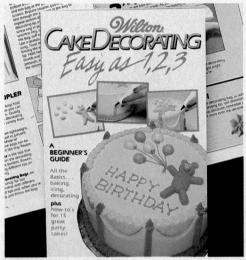

Publications

WEDDING CAKES – A WILTON ALBUM

Mark those cherished occasions with a culinary masterpiece. Create wedding, shower and anniversary cakes – from classic to contemporary. Complete, easy-to-follow instructions, patterns, recipes and wedding cake data and cutting guide are also included. Soft cover; 82 color pages; 8¼ x 10¾ in.

908-W-100 $6.99 each

CELEBRATE! WEDDING CAKES BY WILTON

From intricate cakes that serve hundreds to dainty creations for the most intimate gathering, this book has everything for that special bride. Scores of designs using innovative techniques including foreign methods, stairways and fountains. Instructions and patterns included. Hard cover; 192 color pages; 8¾ x 11 in.

916-W-847 $12.99 each

DRAMATIC TIER CAKES

With this complete Wilton guide learn the fundamentals of constructing and decorating lavish tier cakes, from the basics of building a cake to the safest way to transport wedding tiers to the reception. Includes uses of stairways and fountains, plus tested recipes, decorating descriptions and a complete selection of products needed to make the cakes shown. A must-have for any decorator. Soft cover; 80 color pages; 8½ x 11 in.

902-W-1725 $6.99 each

WILTON CELEBRATES THE ROSE

The rose. Learn all about this most popular icing flower. Includes easy-to-follow classic rose-making directions plus a quick, impressive method. Also learn how to create petal-perfect candy flowers, how to model marzipan and gum paste roses, and how to stencil cakes. Recipes and patterns included. Full-color; soft cover; 66 pages; 8½ x 11 in.

916-W-1218 $6.99 each

CELEBRATE WITH PARTY SPECTACULARS FROM A TO Z

Entertain all year 'round without making the same cake twice. Make your selections from over 150 of the most unique confections. Fun-loving cakes for children, foreign decorating methods to explore, holiday treats and much more! Even how to model Candy Melts* into flowers and figures. Soft cover; 160 color pages; 8½ x 11 in.

916-W-936 $11.99 each
*brand confectionery coating

CELEBRATE! VI

A cherished annual for cake decorators and those who love decorated cakes! A multitude of impressive designs for weddings, showers, holidays and birthdays. Methods include Australian, Philippine and English overpiped styles. Soft cover; 160 color pages; 8⅞ x 11¼ in.

916-W-618 $11.99 each

Publications

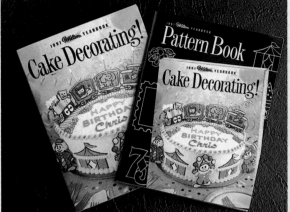

NEW! 1991 YEARBOOK OF CAKE DECORATING
Order a few! What an exciting way to introduce a friend or relative to the wonderful world of cake decorating. Soft cover; 192 pages. 8⅞ x 11 in.
1701-W-901 $5.99 each

NEW! 1991 PATTERN BOOK
All the patterns needed to duplicate certain cakes in the 1991 Yearbook. A real timesaver for busy decorators. Soft cover. 8⅞ x 11 in.
408-W-910 $3.99 each

NEW! ADVENTURES IN COOKIE LAND
This fun cookie cutter activity book contains a variety of games, puzzles, coloring activities and craft ideas for children. Soft cover; 32 pages. 8½ x 11 in.
900-W-1990 $1.49 each

LET'S MAKE CANDY
A step-by-step guide to candy making. Kids of all ages will appreciate the expertise and caring that go into these treasures. Learn techniques for beginning and experienced candy makers. Basic candy making techniques such as molding, and dipping, plus specialty ideas, such as candy clay and candi-pan are clearly explained. Soft cover; 44 pages, 5½ x 8½ in.
902-W-2100 $1.99 each

THE COMPLETE WILTON BOOK OF CANDY
What better way to let them know you fussed. Treat family and friends to these luscious molded and dipped chocolates, dessert shells, fudge, truffles, confectionery coating candies, marzipan, hard candies. Find out just how easy it is with our delicious recipes and helpful hints. Soft cover; full color; 176 pages; 7½ x 10½ in.
902-W-1243 $10.99 each

HOLIDAY
Need we say more? A complete collection of cakes, cookies, centerpieces and candy for holiday baking and making. Find dozens of unusual festive ideas you'll love to make from gingerbread, cookie dough, cakes, candy and other confections, plus unique cookie baskets. Rediscover holiday characters, trimmed ornaments – even create your own heirloom. Make baking and decorating a family affair with these festive designs you'll use again and again. Soft cover; 80 full color pages; 8½ x 11 in.
902-W-1225 $6.99 each

12 Days of Christmas Centerpiece Tree

Essential Candy Making Tools

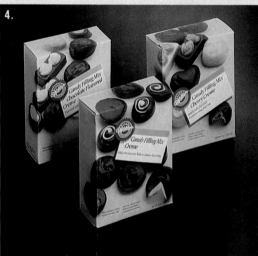

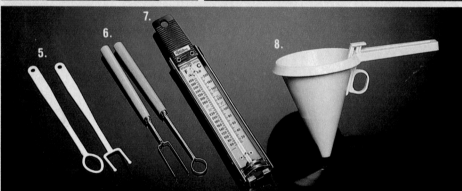

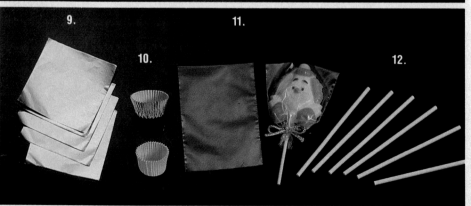

1. CANDY FILLINGS
Delicious and ready to use.
CARAMEL 16 oz.
1911-W-1400 $4.49 each
COCONUT 16 oz.
1911-W-1028 $4.49 each
NOUGAT 10 oz.
1911-W-1488 $4.49 each

2. 4-PC. CANDY FLAVOR SET
Cinnamon, Cherry, Creme De Menthe and Peppermint. ¼ oz. bottles.
1913-W-1029 $3.99 set

3. CANDY WAFER & FONDANT MIX
Makes satiny smooth candies or icing for cakes. 16 oz.
1911-W-1427 $3.99 each

4. CANDY CENTER MIXES
Creates creamy centers that can be dipped or molded for classic favorites. 9 oz.
$2.49 each
CREME CENTER MIX   1911-W-1901
CHOCOLATE FLAVORED   1911-W-1903
CHERRY   1911-W-1905

5. 2-PC. CANDY DIPPING SET
White plastic spoon and fork, each 7¾ in. long.
1904-W-800 $2.99 set

6. 2-PC. DIPPING SET
Sturdy metal with wooden handles. 9 in. long.
1904-W-925 $8.49 set

7. CANDY THERMOMETER
Scale necessary for hard candy, nougat, more.
1904-W-1168 $14.99 each

8. EASY-POUR FUNNEL
Push button controls the flow. 5 x 4 in. wide; nylon.
1904-W-552 $3.99 each

9. FANCY CANDY WRAPPERS
Gold foil to protect and fancy up your candy. 125 sheets, each 3 x 3 in.
1912-W-2290 $3.29 pack

10. CANDY CUPS
Crisply pleated cups, just like professionals use. Choose gold foil or white glassine-coated paper in 1 in. diameter. White also available in 1¼ in. size. Packs of 100.
GOLD FOIL 1912-W-1227 $3.99 pack
WHITE   1912-W-1243 $1.19 pack
NEW! WHITE 1¼ in. diameter
1912-W-1245 $1.29 pack

11. LOLLIPOP BAGS
Plastic bags for lollipops and other candies. 3 x 4 in. 50 bags in a pack.
1912-W-2347 $2.49 pack

12. LOLLIPOP STICKS
Sturdy paper sticks are easy to add to candy molds. 4½ in. long. 50 sticks per pack.
1912-W-1006 $1.49 pack

PLEASE NOTE: All prices, certain products and services reflect the U.S.A. domestic market and do not apply in Australia and Canada.

Plastic dipping fork and spoon made in Hong Kong. Thermometer made in Japan. Metal dipping set made in Japan.

Candy Making

1. CANDY MELTS™ *

brand confectionery coating. Creamy, easy-to-melt wafers are ideal for all your candy making needs – molding, dipping and coating. Delicious taste that can be varied with our Candy Flavors. 14 oz. bag.

Certified Kosher   **$2.50 each**
WHITE 1911-W-498
LIGHT COCOA (All natural, cocoa flavor.) 1911-W-544
DARK COCOA (All natural, cocoa flavor.) 1911-W-358
PINK 1911-W-447
YELLOW 1911-W-463
GREEN 1911-W-404
CHRISTMAS MIX (RED, GREEN) (Available 9/4 - 12/15) 1911-W-1624
SPRING MIX (Pink, Lavender, Blue.) (Available 12/1/ - 5/31) 1911-W-1637
ORANGE (Available 7/16 - 10/31) 1911-W-1631

Discover the fun and ease of making candy the Wilton Way!

2. CANDY COLORS KIT

Rich, concentrated oil-based color that blends beautifully into Wilton Candy Melts. Contains red, green, yellow and orange; ¼ oz. jars. Convenient and economical.
1913-W-1299 $3.99 kit

3. THE COMPLETE WILTON BOOK OF CANDY

Create candy that rivals the fanciest store-bought kinds. Filled with delicious recipes, step-by-step instructions and more. Full-color photographs are a treat to see. Hard cover.
902-W-1243 $10.99 each

4. LET'S MAKE CANDY

A step-by-step 4-color guide to candy making. A little treasure of candy making ideas and techniques for beginning and experienced candy makers. Basic candy making techniques such as molding and dipping, plus specialty ideas, such as candy clay and candi-pan are clearly explained. Soft cover; 44 pages, 5½ x 8½ in.
902-W-2100 $1.99 each

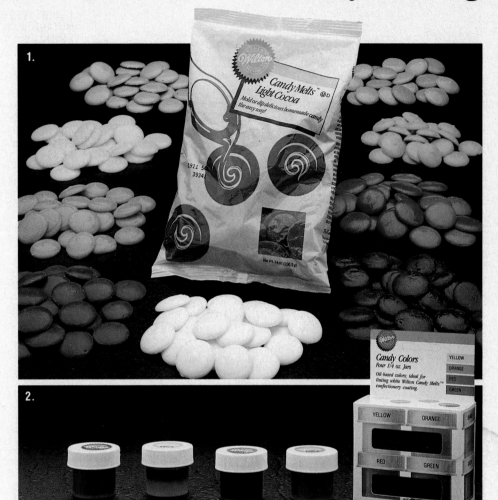

Candy Molds

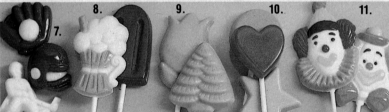

NEW! 1.

2.

3.

NEW! **NEW!**

1. NEW! TEENAGE MUTANT NINJA TURTLES®
7 molds; 7 designs
2114-W-90110
$1.99 each
© & ® 1990 Mirage Studios, U.S.A.
Exclusively licensed by Surge Licensing, Inc.

2. NEW! BATMAN™
7 molds; 6 designs
2114-W-90105
$1.99 each
TM & © 1989 D C Comics Inc.

3. NEW! GARFIELD
7 molds; 6 designs
2114-W-90100
$1.99 each
GARFIELD Characters:
© 1978 United Feature Syndicate, Inc.

4. TEDDY BEARS & GUMBALL MACHINES
8 molds; 2 designs.
2114-W-94232
$1.99 each

5. BEARS
4 cute designs. Perfect for lollipops.
2114-W-94055 $1.99 each

6. ALUMINUM PANDA MOLD
Ideal for baking or molding a great treat. Sides clip together, base opens for easy filling. 5 x 5 in. Instructions, base and clips included.
518-W-489 $4.99 each

7. SPORTS
Baseball, hockey, football, basketball designs-8 molds on sheet.
2114-W-1102 $1.49 each

8. TREATS
5 lollipops per sheet.
2114-W-3006 $1.49 each

9. LOLLIPOPS I
5 molds; 5 designs.
2114-W-90882
$1.99 each

10. LOLLIPOPS II
5 molds; 5 designs on sheet.
2114-W-90861
$1.99 each

11. CLOWNS
4 funny lollipop designs.
2114-W-4110 $1.49 each

12. ROSES 'N BUDS
10 molds on sheet; 2 designs; 2 lollipops.
2114-W-1101 $1.49 each

13. ROSES
10 molds; 3 designs on sheet.
2114-W-91511
$1.99 each

14. LEAVES
10 molds; 2 designs on sheet.
2114-W-90629
$1.99 each

15. FANCY CHOCOLATES I
12 molds; 2 designs.
2114-W-91269
$1.99 each

16. ANIMALS
5 lollipops per sheet.
2114-W-3008 $1.49 each

17. DINOSAURS
9 molds; 4 designs per sheet.
2114-W-98888 $1.99 each

18. MINT DISCS
12 molds; 1 design on sheet; ¼ in. deep.
2114-W-91226
$1.99 each

19. ACCORDIAN RUFFLES
10 molds; 1 design on sheet.
2114-W-91013
$1.99 each

20. ROUNDS
8 molds; 2 designs on sheet
2114-W-90466
$1.99 each

21. BON BONS
12 molds; 1 design on sheet.
2114-W-91072
$1.99 each

For Hard Candy

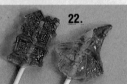

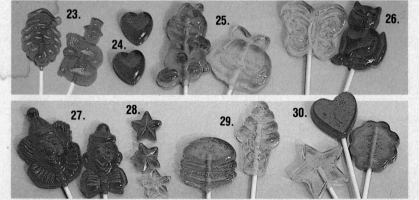

22.

23. 24. 25. 26. 27. 28. 29. 30. 19.

22. HALLOWEEN
5 different designs.
2115-W-324 $1.99 each

23. HOLIDAY LOLLIPOPS
5 designs on sheet.
2115-W-358 $1.99 each

24. HEARTS
15 molds on sheet.
2115-W-322 $1.99 each

25. GARFIELD
Zany! 4 lollipops; 4 designs on sheet.
2115-W-360 $1.99 each

26. ANIMALS
5 animals on sheet. 5 molds.
2115-W-350 $1.99 each

27. CLOWNS
5 lollipops on sheet.
2115-W-344 $1.99 each

28. STARS
16 molds on sheet.
2115-W-336 $1.99 each

29. TREATS
What fun! 5 lollipops on sheet.
2115-W-352 $1.99 each

30. VARIETY OF LOLLIPOPS II
5 molds on sheet.
2115-W-338 $1.99 each

Candy Molds

1. NUMBERS
18 molds per sheet.
2114-W-2912 $1.49 set

2. ALPHABET SET
Capital letters; two of each vowel; plus two t's and s's.
2114-W-2910 $2.99 set

3. SCRIPT WORDS I
Best, Wishes, Congratulations.
2114-W-2914 $1.49 set

4. SCRIPT WORDS II
Happy, Birthday, Anniversary.
2114-W-2915 $1.49 set

5. 3-D PUMPKIN
About 3 in. high.
2114-W-1447 $1.99 each

6. JACK-O-LANTERNS
2½ in. wide. 3 jolly-faced molds on sheet.
2114-W-91056
$1.99 each

7. PUMPKIN
12 identical smiling molds.
2114-W-90740
$1.99 each

8. HALLOWEEN VARIETY SET
2 sheets of molds. 11 designs. 18 molds.
2114-W-1031 $2.99 set

9. THANKSGIVING
3 traditional designs, including turkey lollipops. 9 molds. 2 lollipops.
2114-W-91128 $1.99 each

10. 3-D SANTA
About 4 in. tall.
2114-W-1374 $1.99 each

11. CHRISTMAS TREES
14 molds on sheet.
2114-W-91099
$1.99 each

12. SNOWFLAKES
8 molds. 2 designs on sheet.
2114-W-90661
$1.99 each

13. CHRISTMAS II
10 molds, 9 joyful designs per sheet.
2114-W-94152
$1.99 each

14. CHRISTMAS CLASSICS II
Trees, trims & holiday friends. 6 designs. 18 molds.
2114-W-1225 $2.99 set

15. CHRISTMAS I
8 festive molds; 7 designs.
2114-W-94136
$1.99 each

16. CHRISTMAS CLASSICS
Santas, Sleigh, Reindeer and Toys. 6 designs, 18 molds.
2114-W-1224 $2.99 set

17. HEARTS I
11 molds, 3 designs on sheet.
2114-W-91030
$1.99 each

18. HEARTS II
8 molds; 2 designs on sheet.
2114-W-90645 $1.99 each

19. HEARTS
15 classic molds on sheet.
2114-W-90214
$1.99 each

20. BIT O' IRISH
10 St. Pat's day molds on sheet; 4 designs.
2114-W-91105 $1.99 each

21. EGG MOLD SET
2-pc. plastic molds. Includes one each: 5 x 4 in.; 4½ x 3 in.; 3 x 2 in.
1404-W-1040 $3.99 set

22. 3-D LAMB
3¼ in. high.
2114-W-3229 $1.99 each

23. 3-D BUNNY
4½ in. high.
2114-W-1390 $1.99 each

24. NEW! PLAYFUL BUNNIES
8 designs. 8 molds.
2114-W-90999
$1.99 each

25. EASTER BUNNIES
12 cottontails per sheet.
2114-W-91200
$1.99 each

26. EGGS
Each 1 x 1½ in. long; 12 molds per sheet.
2114-W-90998
$1.99 each

27. NEW! EASTER TREATS
8 designs. 8 molds.
2114-W-91000
$1.99 each

28. EASTER VARIETY SET
2 sheets per set. 13 designs. 26 molds.
2114-W-3131 $2.99 set

29. BABY
4 designs, 10 molds per sheet.
2114-W-2816 $1.49 each

30. GRADUATION
4 designs, 11 molds per sheet.
2114-W-2818 $1.49 each

31. WEDDING
3 designs for bridal showers and weddings; 12 molds, including 2 lollipops, on sheet.
2114-W-1104 $1.49 each

32. 4TH OF JULY
Flags, bells, fireworks! 8 molds on sheet.
2114-W-1103 $1.49 each

Cookie Kit and Cutters

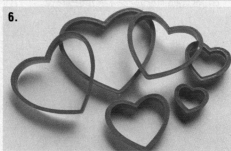

1. HAUNTED HOUSE KIT
Construct a gingerbread mansion to conjure up some Halloween fun. Kit includes patterns, sturdy plastic cookie cutters, 4 disposable bags, 1 round tip, liquid colors, easy-to-follow instructions, and cookie recipe.
2104-W-1031 $7.49 each

2. 4-PC. HALLOWEEN COOKIE CUTTERS SET
Four haunting shapes for little goblins. Ghost and tombstone, cat, pumpkin and witch. 5¼ to 5½ in. Recipe on label.
2304-W-994 $2.99 set

3. HALLOWEEN CANISTER SET
Ten not-so-spooky characters in a handy reusable container. 3 to 4¼ in. Recipe on label.
2304-W-1031 $3.99 set

4. NEW! 4-PC. JACK-O-LANTERN CUTTER SET
This silly jack-o-lantern goes through four funny moods. 3 to 3¾ in. Recipe on label.
2304-W-90 $2.99 set

5. 4-PC. HAPPY EASTER
The season's most popular quartet. Bunny, lamb, chick and egg. 3¼ to 3¾ in. Recipe on label.
2304-W-110 $2.99 set

6. NESTING HEARTS SET
An invaluable collection of 6 different-sized nesting hearts. 1¼ to 4⅛ in. Recipe on label.
2304-W-115 $2.99 set

7. CHRISTMAS CANISTER SET
10 festive holiday shapes. 2½ to 3½ in. Reusable sturdy plastic container. Recipe on label.
509-W-1225 $3.99 set

8. 4-PC. SWEETHEART BEARS COOKIE CUTTER SET
Four romantic shapes and messages; recipe on label. 4 to 4½ in.
2304-W-1214 $2.99 set

9. NEW! 4-PC. CHRISTMAS TREATS SET
Fun-loving yuletide favorites. Cottage, holly, reindeer, snowman. 4¾ to 5½ in. Recipe on label.
2304-W-1290 $2.99 set

10. 4-PC. GINGERBREAD FAMILY
Set includes two 5½ x 4 in. adults and two 2½ x 1½ in. children. Recipe on label.
2304-W-121 $2.99 set

11. 4-PC. CHRISTMAS SET
Favorite holiday shapes. Angel, Santa, Wreath, Tree. Recipe on label. 4¼ to 5 in.
2304-W-995 $2.99 set

12. HOLIDAY SHAPES SET
Santa, angel, tree, boy and girl – 3⅝ to 6 in. high. Recipe on label.
2304-W-105 $2.99 set

1. GINGERBREAD HOUSE KIT
An enchanted cottage where holiday memories begin. Creative kit includes patterns, 3 plastic gingerbread people cutters, disposable bags, tips and instruction booklet.
2104-W-2946 $7.49 each

2. NEW! NO-BAKE GINGERBREAD HOUSE KIT
Looks like real gingerbread! Just assemble and decorate house pieces provided in kit. Or cover with real graham crackers. Can also be used as a pattern for an edible gingerbread house. Candy and all necessary tools are included.
2104-W-2990 $9.99 each

3. CHRISTMAS COOKIE TREE KIT
What a fun holiday idea for the whole family. Ice, stack and trim cookie stars. Kit includes 10 plastic star cutters in graduated sizes, plus instruction book.
2105-W-3424 $5.99 each

4. NEW! SANTA SLEIGH AND REINDEER COOKIE KIT
It's the jolly old man himself. Create quite a unique centerpiece or holiday ornament. Two-sided cookie cutters make flat or stand-up santas and reindeer. Kit is complete with 4 plastic cutters, disposable bags, tips and easy-to-follow instruction book.
2104-W-1500 $7.99 each

5. 12 DAYS OF CHRISTMAS KIT
Create holiday magic. The words and music of a favorite Christmas ballad come to life in an elaborate gingerbread centerpiece decorated with sweets. Kit includes patterns, 4 sheets of candy molds, liquid colors, decorating brush, tips, disposable bags and easy-to-follow instructions.
2104-W-2950 $8.99 each

6. SANTA'S STABLE KIT
A magical Christmas fantasy for the entire family. Recreate the reindeer's North Pole headquarters on a holiday tabletop. Kit includes patterns, sturdy plastic cookie cutters liquid colors, disposable bags, tips, and easy-to-follow instructions.
2104-W-2949 $7.99 each

7. COOKIE SHEETS
An important staple in any baker's kitchen. High quality pans will not rust, bake evenly and have a smooth finish.
10 x 15 in.
2105-W-1265 $5.99 each
12½ x 16½ in.
2105-W-2975 $7.99 each

8. COOKIE/JELLY ROLL PAN
One-inch deep sides are ideal for jelly rolls or cookies. Non-rust, smooth finish makes baking easy.
12 x 18 x 1 in.
2105-W-4854 $9.99 each
10½ x 15½ x 1 in.
2105-W-1269 $8.99 each

Cookie Cutters Galore!

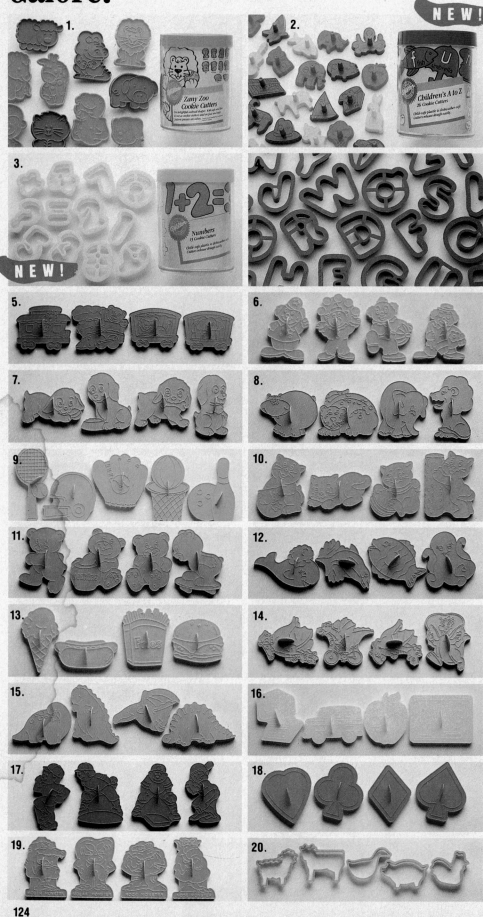

NEW!

NEW!

1. ZANY ZOO COOKIE CANISTER SET
10 plastic animal-shaped cutters in plastic storage container, cookie recipe included.
509-W-9550 $3.99 set

2. NEW! CHILDREN'S A TO Z CANISTER SET
Spell out F-U-N so many ways with this educational 26-piece set. Sturdy, reusable plastic storage container. Recipe on label.
2304-W-91 $5.99 set

A TO Z COOKIE CUTTERS ONLY
2304-W-104 $4.99 set

3. NEW! NUMBERS CANISTER SET
Addition, subtraction, multiplication and equal signs included in this 13-piece set. Sturdy, reusable plastic storage container.
2304-W-92 $5.99 set

NUMBERS COOKIE CUTTERS ONLY
2304-W-103 $4.99 set

4. ALPHABET SET
26-piece set. 2 x 1⅛ in. each.
2304-W-102 $7.99 set

Exciting New and Favorite Cookie Cutter Shapes!
4-pc. and 5-pc. cookie cutter sets are made of sturdy plastic and include a cookie recipe on label.

5. NEW! 4-PC. CIRCUS TRAIN SET
2304-W-1513 $2.99 set

6. NEW! 4-PC. COMICAL CLOWNS SET
2304-W-1516 $2.99 set

7. NEW! 4-PC. PUPPY PALS SET
2304-W-1505 $2.99 set

8. NEW! 4-PC. JUNGLE CRITTERS SET
2304-W-1510 $2.99 set

9. 5-PC. SPORTS SET
2304-W-2101 $2.99 set

10. NEW! 4-PC. CUTE KITTENS SET
2304-W-1509 $2.99 set

11. NEW! 4-PC. CUDDLY TEDDY BEARS SET
2304-W-1504 $2.99 set

12. NEW! 4-PC. SEA FRIENDS SET
2304-W-1508 $2.99 set

13. NEW! 4-PC. FUN FOODS SET
2304-W-1515 $2.99 set

14. NEW! 4-PC. PLAYFUL DRAGONS SET
2304-W-1507 $2.99 set

15. 4-PC. DINOSAURS SET
2304-W-1990 $2.99 set

16. NEW! 4-PC. SCHOOL DAYS SET
2304-W-1514 $2.99 set

17. NEW! 4-PC. BASEBALL STAR SET
2304-W-1511 $2.99 set

18. NEW! 4-PC. PLAYING CARDS SET
2304-W-1512 $2.99 set

19. NEW! 4-PC. MONSTERS! SET
2304-W-1503 $2.99 set

20. 5-PC. FARMYARD FRIENDS SET
2304-W-432 $2.99 set

Cookie Cutters and More!

1. NEW! TEENAGE MUTANT NINJA TURTLES® SET*
Raphael, Michaelangelo, Leonardo and Donatello.
2304-W-1500 $2.99 set

© & ® 1990 Mirage Studios, U.S.A., Exclusively licensed by Surge Licensing, Inc.

2. NEW! SUPER MARIO BROTHERS® SET*
2304-W-1502 $2.99 set

© 1989 Nintendo of America Inc.

3. NEW! 4-PC. GARFIELD™ SET*
Trouble-making duo: Garfield and Odie.
2304-W-1501 $2.99 set

GARFIELD Characters: © 1978 United Feature Syndicate, Inc.

4. NEW! 4-PC. BATMAN™ SET*
Caped-crusader and his arch rival, Joker.
2304-W-1506 $2.99 set

TM & © 1989 DC Comics Inc.

5. 4-PC. LOONEY TUNES™ SET*
Bugs Bunny, Porky Pig, Sylvester and Tweety.
2304-W-404 $2.99 set

© 1988 Warner Bros. Inc. Wilton Enterprises Authorized User.

6. 4-PC. SESAME STREET SET*
Big Bird, Cookie Monster, Ernie and Bert.
2304-W-129 $2.99 set

Sesame Street Characters
© Jim Henson Productions, Inc.
All rights reserved.

7. 6-PC. NESTING OVAL SET*
3¼ to 7 in. long. 2⅛ to 4¾ in. wide.
2304-W-388 $2.99 set

8. 6-PC. NESTING STAR SET*
From 1⅝ to 4⅝ in.
2304-W-111 $2.99 set

9. 6-PC. NESTING HEART SET*
1¼ to 4⅛ in.
2304-W-115 $2.99 set

10. 6-PC. NESTING ROUND SET*
1½ to 4 in.
2304-W-113 $2.99 set

11. SPRITZ COOKIE PRESS SET*
Easy-squeeze trigger-action. Includes 10 plastic disks in classic holiday shapes.
2104-W-313 $12.99 set

12. NEW! STARS, HEART & ROUNDS CANISTER SET*
14 cookie cutters in all. Sturdy, reusable plastic canister.
2304-W-93 $6.99 set

13. COOLING GRID
Even the smallest shapes won't fall through. Chrome-plated steel. 10 x 16 in.
2305-W-128 $4.99 each

14. ROLL ALONG COOKIE CUTTERS SET*
18 interchangeable holiday designs. Cuts 6 different designs at once.
2104-W-2404 $6.99 set

*Cookie recipe included.

Be sure to order our NEW! Children's activity book, *Adventures in Cookieland!* See p. 117.

1.

2.

3.

4.

5.

6.

7.

8.

9.

10.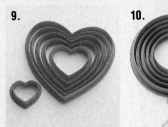

11.

12.

13.

14.

125

Color is vital to your decorating. With color you can add realism and vitality to all your character cakes, personalize special events cakes, highlight holiday cakes and add beauty and vibrance to all your cakes.

Wilton Icing Colors are concentrated in a rich, creamy base, are fast-mixing and easy to use, and will not change your icing consistency. Our extensive range of icing colors makes it convenient for you to achieve the colors you need and want.

DAFFODIL YELLOW*	LEMON YELLOW	GOLDEN YELLOW	ORANGE	PINK	CHRISTMAS RED	RED-RED	RED (no taste)
IVORY	TEAL	TERRA COTTA	ROSE	COPPER	BROWN	ROSE PETAL PINK	CREAMY PEACH
VIOLET	BURGUNDY	ROYAL BLUE	CORNFLOWER BLUE	SKY BLUE	WILLOW GREEN	KELLY GREEN	LEAF GREEN

MOSS GREEN

BLACK

WILTON CONCENTRATED PASTE ICING COLORS are available in 1 oz. and 4 oz. jars. Specified colors are available in 20 oz. jars.

WILTON CONCENTRATED LIQUID ICING COLORS are available in 13 oz. jars.

ICING COLORS	CONCENTRATED PASTE						CONCENTRATED LIQUID
	1 OZ.		4 OZ.		20 OZ.		13 OZ.
Black	610-W-981	1.69	611-W-17	5.79	612-W-17	18.99	603-W-100	7.99
*Cornflower Blue	610-W-710	1.49	611-W-19	4.99	Not Available		603-W-119	7.69
Royal Blue	610-W-655	1.49	611-W-10	4.99	612-W-10	16.99	603-W-106	7.69
Sky Blue	610-W-700	1.49	611-W-12	4.99	Not Available		603-W-111	7.69
Brown	610-W-507	1.69	611-W-8	5.79	612-W-8	18.99	603-W-103	6.99
Burgundy	610-W-698	1.99	611-W-11	5.79	Not Available		603-W-114	7.99
Copper	610-W-450	1.49	611-W-7	4.99	Not Available		Not Available	
Kelly Green	610-W-752	1.49	611-W-13	4.99	Not Available		603-W-113	6.99
Leaf Green	610-W-809	1.49	611-W-14	4.99	612-W-14	16.99	603-W-104	6.99
Moss Green	610-W-851	1.49	611-W-15	4.99	Not Available		Not Available	
*Willow Green	610-W-855	1.49	611-W-22	4.99	Not Available		603-W-120	7.69
*Ivory	610-W-208	1.49	611-W-23	4.99	Not Available		603-W-121	7.69
*Creamy Peach	610-W-210	1.49	611-W-21	4.99	Not Available		603-W-117	7.69
Pink	610-W-256	1.49	611-W-4	4.99	Not Available		603-W-105	7.69
*Rose Petal Pink	610-W-410	1.49	611-W-20	4.99	Not Available		603-W-118	7.69
Christmas Red	610-W-302	1.49	611-W-5	4.99	Not Available		603-W-107	7.99
Red-Red	610-W-906	1.99	611-W-16	5.79	612-W-16	20.99	603-W-102	7.99
Red (no taste)	610-W-998	1.99	611-W-18	4.99	Not Available		603-W-101	7.99
Rose	610-W-401	1.49	611-W-6	4.99	Not Available		Not Available	
Orange	610-W-205	1.49	611-W-3	4.99	Not Available		603-W-109	6.99
*Teal	610-W-207	1.49	611-W-25	4.99	Not Available		603-W-115	6.99
*Terra Cotta	610-W-206	1.49	611-W-24	4.99	Not Available		603-W-116	7.69
Golden Yellow	610-W-159	1.49	611-W-2	4.99	Not Available		603-W-110	6.99
Lemon Yellow	610-W-108	1.40	611-W-1	4.99	Not Available		603-W-108	7.69
Violet	610-W-604	1.49	611-W-9	4.99	Not Available		603-W-112	7.99
Daffodil Yellow	610-W-175	1.99	Not Available		Not Available		Not Available	

*Special Blend Color

All Icing Colors are Certified Kosher.

*Daffodil Yellow is an all-natural color. It does not contain Yellow #5. The color remains very pale.

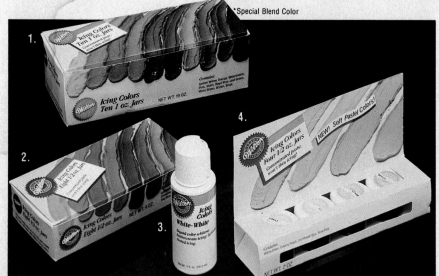

1. 10-ICING COLOR KIT
1 oz. jars of icing colors. Violet, Leaf Green, Royal Blue, Brown, Black, Pink, Watermelon, Moss Green, Orange and Lemon Yellow.
601-W-5569 $12.99 kit

2. 8-ICING COLOR KIT
½ oz. jars of colors. Christmas Red, Lemon Yellow, Leaf Green, Sky Blue, Brown, Orange, Pink, and Violet.
601-W-5577 $8.99 kit

3. WHITE-WHITE ICING COLOR
Just stir into icing to make icing made with butter or margarine white. Perfect for wedding cakes. 2 oz. plastic bottle.
603-W-1236 $2.99 each

4. 4-COLOR ICING KIT
(SOFT PASTEL COLORS) ½ oz. jars of paste colors. Petal Pink, Creamy Peach, Willow Green, Cornflower Blue.
601-W-5588 $3.29 kit

Icings and Flavorings

1. NEW! CAKE AND PASTRY FILLING
Luscious and delicious, chunky real fruit filling ready to use from the 10 oz. resealable glass jar. Perfect to fill and torte up to 10" round cake, a real treat in tarts, pies and fancy pastries!

Filling	Stock No.	Price
Cherry – 10 oz.	709-W-3	$1.99
Strawberry – 10 oz.	709-W-1	$1.99
Raspberry – 10 oz.	709-W-2	$1.99

2. READY-TO-USE DECORATOR ICING
Perfect for decorating and frosting. Use for borders, flowers, writing, etc. Just stir and use! Delicious homemade taste! 16 oz.
710-W-117 $1.99 each

3. CREAMY WHITE ICING MIX
Convenient mix that provides rich, home-made taste. Just add butter and milk. Ideal for frosting as well as decorating. Yields 2 cups.
710-W-112 $1.99 each

4. PIPING GEL
Clear gel. Can be tinted with paste color. Use for glazing, writing, more. 10 oz.
704-W-105 $3.29 each

5. GLYCERIN
A few drops stirred into dried-out icing color restores consistency. 2 oz.*
708-W-14 $1.99 each

6. BUTTER FLAVOR
Gives a rich, buttery taste to icing, cakes, cookies. Adds no color! 2 oz.*
604-W-2040 $1.69 each

7. CLEAR VANILLA EXTRACT
Perfect for decorating because it won't change the color of your icing. 2 oz. Great for baking, too!*
604-W-2237 $1.69 each

8. ALMOND EXTRACT
Delicious almond flavor for icing, cookies, cakes. 2 oz.*
604-W-2126 $1.69 each

9. COLOR FLOW MIX
Add water and confectioners sugar for smooth icing for color flow designs. 4 oz. can yields about ten 1½ cup batches.
701-W-47 $6.99 each

10. MERINGUE POWDER MIX
For royal icing, meringue, boiled icing.
4 OZ. CAN 702-W-6007 $4.49 each
8 OZ. CAN 702-W-6015 $6.99 each

*Certified Kosher

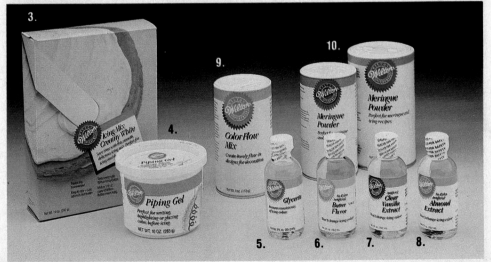

Gum Paste

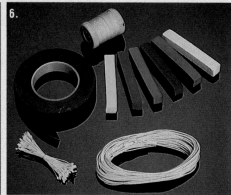

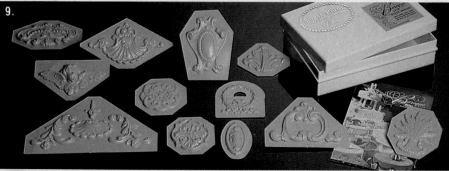

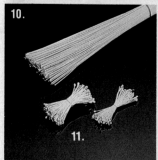

1. GUM PASTE FLOWERS KIT
Make lifelike, beautiful gum paste flowers. Create bouquets or single blooms for cakes, centerpieces, favors and more. Full-color how-to book contains lots of ideas and step-by-step instructions. Kit includes 24 plastic cutters, 1 leaf mold, 3 wooden modeling tools and 2 squares of foam for modeling. 30-pc. kit.
1907-W-117 $14.99 kit

2. WILTON PEOPLE MOLDS
Create an entire gum paste family. Use as table or cake decorations, or as center-pieces. Includes 4 (man, woman, two chil-dren) 3-part molds and instruction book.
1906-W-5154 $16.99 set

3. GUM PASTE MIX
Easy to use! Just add water and knead. Results in a workable, pliable dough-like mixture to mold into beautiful flowers and figures. 1 lb. can.
707-W-124 $4.99 each

4. GLUCOSE
Essential ingredient for making gum paste. 24 oz. plastic jar.
707-W-109 $4.29 each

5. GUM-TEX™ KARAYA
Makes gum paste pliable, elastic, easy to shape. 6 oz. can.
707-W-117 $6.49 each

6. GUM PASTE ACCESSORY KIT
Includes 90' green florist tape, 30' fine florist wire, 20 pieces medium florist wire (18 in. long), 12-pc. chalk set and 144 yellow stamens.
1907-W-227 $10.99 kit

7. FLOWER FORMERS
Plastic stands used to dry icing leaves and flowers in a convex or concave shape. Set of nine (11 in. long) in three widths: 1½, 2, 2½ in.
417-W-9500 $5.99 set

8. TREE FORMERS
Use to make icing pine trees and to dry royal icing or gum paste decorations. Set of four, 6½ in. high.
417-W-1150 $1.99 set

9. BAROQUE GUM PASTE MOLDS
Create lovely gum paste trims. Includes 12 classic super-flex molds, full-color idea/instruction booklet, plastic storage box.
1906-W-1299 $10.99 set

10. FLORIST WIRE
Medium weight for a multitude of projects. 175 white wires (18 in. long) per pack.
409-W-622 $8.99 pack

11. STAMENS
Make flowers more realistic. 144 per pack.
PEARL WHITE
1005-W-102 $1.49 pack
YELLOW
1005-W-7875 $1.49 pack

12. EDIBLE GLITTER
Sprinkles sparkle on scores of things. ¼ oz. plastic jar.
WHITE
703-W-1204 $2.29 each

Enclose in envelope provided on Order Form or call (708) 963-7100

Enclose in envelope provided on Order Form or call (708) 963-7100

Enclose in envelope provided on Order Form or call (708) 963-7100

Enclose in envelope provided on Order Form or call (708) 963-7100

1. FEATHERWEIGHT DECORATING BAGS

Lightweight, strong, flexible polyester bags are easy to handle, soft, workable and never get stiff. Specially coated so grease won't go through. May be boiled. Dishwasher safe. Instructions included.

Size	Stock No.	Each
18 IN.	404-W-5184	$7.29
16 IN.	404-W-5168	$6.69
14 IN.	404-W-5140	$5.79
12 IN.	404-W-5125	$4.49
10 IN.	404-W-5109	$3.49
8 IN.	404-W-5087	$2.29

2. DISPOSABLE DECORATING BAGS

Use and toss – no fuss, no muss. Perfect for melting Candy Melts™* in the microwave, too. Strong, flexible, and easy-to-handle plastic. 12 in. size fits standard tips and couplers.

*brand confectionery coating
2104-W-358 $3.99 pack of 12
24-COUNT VALUE PACK
2104-W-1358 $6.29 pack of 24

3. PARCHMENT TRIANGLES

Make your own disposable decorating bags with our quality, grease-resistant vegetable parchment paper.
12 IN. 2104-W-1206
$3.99 pack of 100
15 IN. 2104-W-1508
$4.99 pack of 100

4. TIP SAVER

Reshape bent tips. Molded plastic.
414-W-909 $2.79 each

5. TIP SAVER BOXES

Keep decorating tips clean and organized.
A. 26-TIP CAPACITY
405-W-8773 $4.99 each
B. 52-TIP CAPACITY
405-W-7777 $6.99 each

PLASTIC COUPLERS

Use to change tips without changing bags when using the same color icing.

6. LARGE COUPLER

Fits 14 in. to 18 in. Featherweight Bags. Use with large decorating tips.
411-W-1006 $1.19 each

7. ANGLED COUPLER

Reaches around sharp angles. Fits all bags and standard decorating tips.
411-W-7365   79¢ each

8. STANDARD COUPLER

Fits all decorating bags, standard tips.
411-W-1987   59¢ each

9. TIP COVER

Slip over tip and save to take filled bags of icing along for touch-ups. Plastic.
414-W-915   Package of 4   99¢ each

10. MAXI TIP BRUSH

Gets out every bit of icing fast and easy.
414-W-1010 $1.69 each

11. TIP BRUSH

Plastic bristles clean tips thoroughly.
418-W-1123 $1.19 each

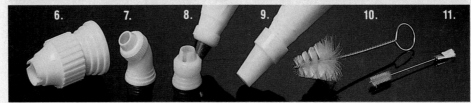

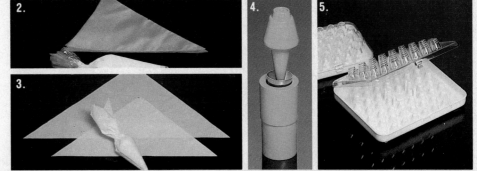

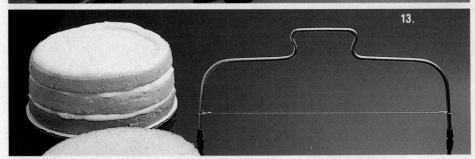

12. DESSERT DECORATOR

Easy-to-control lever lets you decorate cakes, pastries, cookies with one hand. Includes 5 easy-to-change decorating nozzles.
415-W-825 $10.99 each

13. CAKE LEVELER

Levels and tortes cakes up to 10 in. wide and 2 in. high.
415-W-815 $2.99 each

Decorating Tools

Sturdy plastic tools leave easy-to-follow designs on cake tops and sides. Valuable timesavers for busy decorators.

1. NEW! ALL-OCCASION SCRIPT PATTERN PRESS SET
Press and pipe messages easily with sized seasonal words and phrases: Merry Christmas, Happy New Year, Easter, Thanksgiving, God Bless You, I Love You and Good Luck.
2104-W-2090 $3.99 set

2. 15-PC. DECORATOR PATTERN PRESS SET
Traditional designs ready to solo or use in combination. Many can also be reversed for symmetrical designs.
2104-W-2172 $4.99 set

3. 9-PC. PATTERN PRESS SET
Discover fancy florals, classic curves make any occasion so special.
2104-W-3101 $4.29 set

4. SCRIPT PATTERN PRESS MESSAGE SET
Lets you put it into words so beautifully. Combine the words Happy, Birthday, Best, Wishes, Anniversary, Congratulations and make a lasting impression.
2104-W-2061 $2.99 set

5. MESSAGE BLOCK LETTER PATTERN PRESS SET
Have just the right words at your fingertips. Includes the same six words as the Script Set. 2 X 6¾ X ¾ in. high.
2104-W-2077 $3.49 set

6. CAKE DIVIDING SET
Handy when chart marks 2-in. intervals on 6 to 18-in. diameter cakes. Triangle marker for precise spacing for stringwork, garlands, more. Includes instructions.
409-W-800 $8.99 set

7. DECORATING COMB
An easy technique that makes it look like you fussed. Makes ridges in icing. 12-in. long, plastic.
409-W-8259 $1.29 each

8. DECORATING TRIANGLE
Each side adds a different contoured effect to icing. 5 X 5-in. plastic.
409-W-990   99¢ each

9. DECORATOR'S BRUSHES
Perfect for smoothing icing, painting candy molds and colorful touches. Set of 3.
2104-W-846 $1.49 set

STAINLESS STEEL & ROSEWOOD SPATULAS

10. 8 IN. TAPERED
409-W-517 $2.59 each

11. 8 IN. SPATULA
409-W-6043 $2.59 each

12. 11 IN. SPATULA
409-W-7694 $4.49 each

13. 8 IN. ANGLED SPATULA
409-W-738 $2.59 each

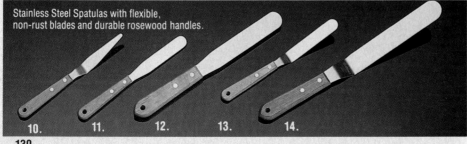

Stainless Steel Spatulas with flexible, non-rust blades and durable rosewood handles.

Decorating Sets

Beginners and expert decorators will like the convenience of buying a complete line of tools they'll need – all in one handy kit. Excellent gift ideas for any busy decorator.

1. STARTER CAKE DECORATING SET
- 4 metal decorating tips
- Instruction booklet
- Six 12-in. disposable decorating bags
- Two tip couplers
- Five liquid color packets

2104-W-2530 $6.99 set

2. BASIC CAKE DECORATING SET
- 5 professional quality metal tips
- Twelve 12-in. disposable bags
- Two tip couplers
- Flower nail no. 7
- Four ½ oz. icing colors
- Instruction booklet.

2104-W-2536 $9.99 set

3. DELUXE CAKE DECORATING SET
Contains 36 essentials!
- 10 nickel-plated metal tips
- Four ½ oz. icing colors
- Plastic storage tray
- Eighteen 12-in. disposable bags
- Two tip couplers
- No. 7 flower nail
- Cake Decorating, Easy As 1,2,3 book.

2104-W-2540 $18.99 set

4. SUPREME CAKE DECORATING SET
52 tools in all!
- 18 metal tips
- Two tip couplers
- Five ½ oz. icing colors
- 8-in. angled spatula
- No. 9 flower nail
- Twenty-four disposable 12 in. bags
- Cake Decorating Easy as 1,2,3 book
- Storage Tray

2104-W-2546 $26.99 set

5. TOOL CADDY
You can take it with you and keep it all beautifully organized. (Tools not included.) Holds 38 tips, 10 icing color jars, couplers, spatulas, books and more. Lightweight, stain-resistant molded polyethylene. 16⅝ x 11½ x 3 in.

2104-W-2237 $17.99 each

6. DELUXE TIP SET
- 26 decorating tips
- 2 flower nails
- Tip coupler
- Tipsaver plastic box

2104-W-6666 $18.99 set

7. MASTER TIP SET
- 52 metal tips
- Tipsaver box
- Two flower nails
- Two couplers

2104-W-7778 $34.99 set

8. PRACTICE BOARD WITH PATTERNS
Practice is a must for decorating that gets an A +. Slip practice pattern onto board under wipe-clean vinyl overlay and trace in icing. Includes stand and patterns for flowers, leaves, borders and lettering – 31 designs included.

406-W-9464 $6.99 each

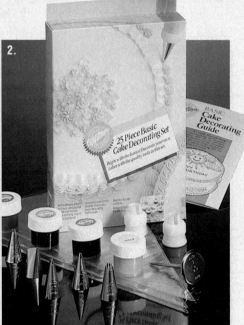

Instant Beauty

Flower Nails

1. READY-TO-USE ICING ROSES

Save decorating time! Stock up on all colors and sizes for your next cake.

Color	Size		Stock No.	Price
WHITE	LARGE	1½ in.	710-W-411	$3.99 for 9
WHITE	MEDIUM	1¼ in.	710-W-311	$3.99 doz.
WHITE	SMALL	1 in.	710-W-211	$2.99 doz.
RED	LARGE	1½ in.	710-W-412	$3.99 for 9
RED	MEDIUM	1¼ in.	710-W-312	$3.99 doz.
RED	SMALL	1 in.	710-W-212	$2.99 doz.
PINK	LARGE	1½ in.	710-W-413	$3.99 for 9
PINK	MEDIUM	1¼ in.	710-W-313	$3.99 doz.
PINK	SMALL	1 in.	710-W-213	$2.99 doz.
YELLOW	LARGE	1½ in.	710-W-414	$3.99 for 9
YELLOW	MEDIUM	1¼ in.	710-W-314	$3.99 doz.
YELLOW	SMALL	1 in.	710-W-214	$2.99 doz.
PEACH	LARGE	1½ in.	710-W-415	$3.99 for 9
PEACH	MEDIUM	1¼ in.	710-W-315	$3.99 doz.
PEACH	SMALL	1 in.	710-W-215	$2.99 doz.

2. FANCI-FOIL WRAP

Serving side has a non-toxic grease-resistant surface. FDA approved for use with food. Continuous roll: 20 in. x 15 ft.

ROSE	**804-W-124**
GOLD	**804-W-183**
SILVER	**804-W-167**
BLUE	**804-W-140**
WHITE	**804-W-191**

$6.99 each

3. TUK-N-RUFFLE

Attach to serving tray or board with royal icing or tape. Order 60 ft. bolt or by the foot.

Color	Per Foot	
PINK	801-W-708	35¢
BLUE	801-W-200	35¢
WHITE	801-W-1003	35¢

Color	60-Ft. Bolt	
PINK	802-W-702	$13.99
BLUE	802-W-206	$13.99
WHITE	802-W-1008	$13.99

NOTE: ORDER PRE-CUT LENGTHS BASED ON YOUR CAKE SIZE:
8″ and 10″ round, order 3 ft.
12″ and 14″ round, order 4 ft.
16″ round, 12″ and 14″ square, order 5 ft.
16″ square and 18″ round, order 6 ft.

Essential turnables for creating impressive icing flowers such as the rose.

4. FLOWER NAIL NO. 9 1¼ in. diameter.
402-W-3009   69¢ each

5. FLOWER NAIL NO. 7 1½ in. diameter.
402-W-3007   89¢ each

6. 2 IN. FLOWER NAIL
Use with curved and swirled petal tips, 116-123, to make large blooms.
402-W-3002 $1.09 each

7. 3 IN. FLOWER NAIL
Has extra large surface, ideal with large petal tips.
402-W-3003 $1.19 each

8. 1-PC. LILY NAIL
1⅝ in. diameter.
402-W-3012   89¢ each

9. LILY NAIL SET
Essential for making cup flowers, such as poinsettias and lilies. To use 2-pc. nails: Place aluminum foil in bottom half of nail and press top half in to form cup. Pipe flower petals. Set includes ½, 1¼, 1⅝ and 2½ in. diam. cups. Sturdy white plastic.
403-W-9444 $1.99 8-pc. set

1. NEW! SERVING TRAYS

Elegant, reusable trays in sturdy laminated plastic. Perfect for decorated cakes and desserts. Inner recessed area designed to securely fit round or rectangular cake circles and boards.

Stock No.	Description	
415-W-0908	10⅛ in. holds 8-in. cake circle	$1.99
415-W-0910	12⅛ in. holds 10-in. cake circle	$2.49
415-W-0912	14⅜ in. holds 12-in. cake circle	$2.99
415-W-0914	16¾ in. holds 14-in. cake circle	$3.49
415-W-0916	12⅛ in. x 16¾ in. holds 10 x 14 in. cake board	$3.49

2. SHOW 'N SERVE CAKE BOARDS

Scalloped edge. Protected with food-safe, grease-resistant coating.

8 IN.   2104-W-1125
$3.99 pack of 10
10 IN.   2104-W-1168
$4.49 pack of 10
12 IN.   2104-W-1176
$4.99 pack of 8
14 IN.   2104-W-1184
$5.49 pack of 6
14 x 20 IN. RECTANGLE
2104-W-1230 $5.99 pack of 6

3. CAKE CIRCLES & BOARDS

Sturdy corrugated cardboard.

6 IN.	2104-W-64	$2.19 pack of 10
8 IN.	2104-W-80	$3.29 pack of 12
10 IN.	2104-W-102	$3.99 pack of 12
12 IN.	2104-W-129	$3.99 pack of 8
14 IN.	2104-W-145	$3.99 pack of 6
16 IN.	2104-W-160	$4.99 pack of 6
18 IN.	2104-W-180	$4.99 pack of 6
10 x 14 IN.	2104-W-554	$3.99 pack of 6
13 x 19 IN.	2104-W-552	$4.49 pack of 6

4. DOILIES

Grease-resistant, glassine-coated paper doilies are ideal for iced cakes. Round and rectangle shapes have lace borders sized to fit around your decorated cakes. Ideal for serving cookies and canapes, too!

8 IN. ROUND   2104-W-90004
$1.99 pack of 16
10 IN. ROUND   2104-W-90000
$1.99 pack of 16
12 IN. ROUND   2104-W-90001
$1.99 pack of 12
14 IN. ROUND   2104-W-90002
$1.99 pack of 8
10 x 14 IN. RECTANGLE
2104-W-90003 $1.99 pack of 12

5. PROFESSIONAL CAKE STAND

Heavy-duty aluminum stand is 4⅝ in. high with 12 in. rotating plate. Super strong; essential for decorating tiered wedding cakes.

307-W-2501 $36.99 each

6. LAZY DAISY SERVER

Stationary stand. Sturdy white plastic with scalloped edges. 5 in. high with 12 in. plate.

307-W-700 $8.99 each

7. TRIM 'N TURN CAKE STAND

Flute-edged. Plate turns smoothly on hidden ball bearings. Just turn as you decorate. White molded plastic; holds up to 100 lbs. 12 in.

2103-W-2518 $7.99 each

8. REVOLVING CAKE STAND

Now with easy, rotating ball bearings! Plate turns smoothly in either direction for easy decorating and serving; 3 in. high with 11 in. diameter plate in molded white plastic.

415-W-900 $9.99 each

Bases, Boards & Cake Stands

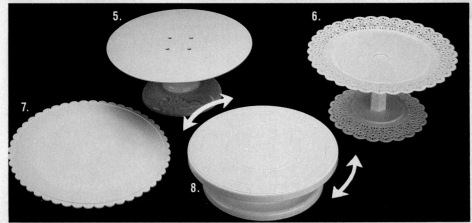

Decorating Tips Guide

Tip Openings and Techniques shown are actual size.

ROUND—outline, lettering, dots, balls, beads, stringwork, lattice, lacework.

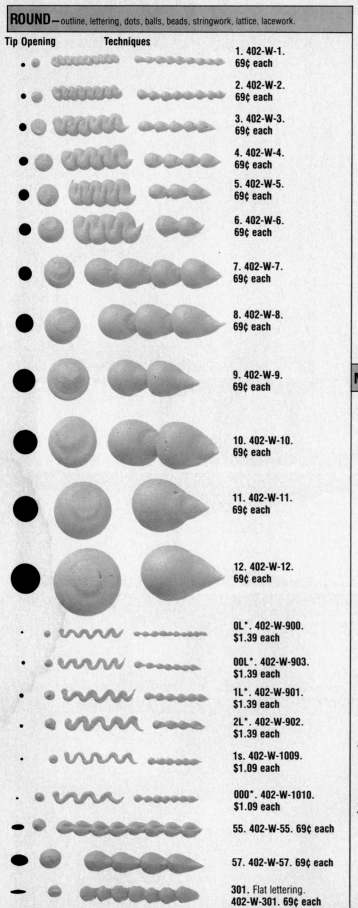

Tip Opening Techniques

1. 402-W-1. 69¢ each
2. 402-W-2. 69¢ each
3. 402-W-3. 69¢ each
4. 402-W-4. 69¢ each
5. 402-W-5. 69¢ each
6. 402-W-6. 69¢ each
7. 402-W-7. 69¢ each
8. 402-W-8. 69¢ each
9. 402-W-9. 69¢ each
10. 402-W-10. 69¢ each
11. 402-W-11. 69¢ each
12. 402-W-12. 69¢ each
0L*. 402-W-900. $1.39 each
00L*. 402-W-903. $1.39 each
1L*. 402-W-901. $1.39 each
2L*. 402-W-902. $1.39 each
1s. 402-W-1009. $1.09 each
000*. 402-W-1010. $1.09 each
55. 402-W-55. 69¢ each
57. 402-W-57. 69¢ each
301. Flat lettering. 402-W-301. 69¢ each

134

*Use with parchment bags only.

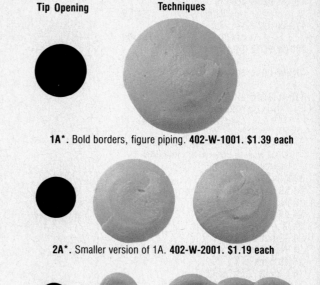

Tip Opening   Techniques

1A*. Bold borders, figure piping. 402-W-1001. $1.39 each

2A*. Smaller version of 1A. 402-W-2001. $1.19 each

230. For filling bismarcks & eclairs. 402-W-230. $1.99 each

MULTI-OPENING—rows and clusters of strings, beads, stars, scallops.

Tip Opening   Techniques

41. 402-W-41. 69¢ each

42. 402-W-42. 69¢ each

43. 402-W-43. 69¢ each

89. 402-W-89. 69¢ each

134*. 402-W-134. $1.39 each

233. 402-W-233. $1.19 each

234. 402-W-234. $1.39 each

235*. 402-W-235. $1.19 each

TRIPLE STAR*. 402-W-2010. $2.19 each

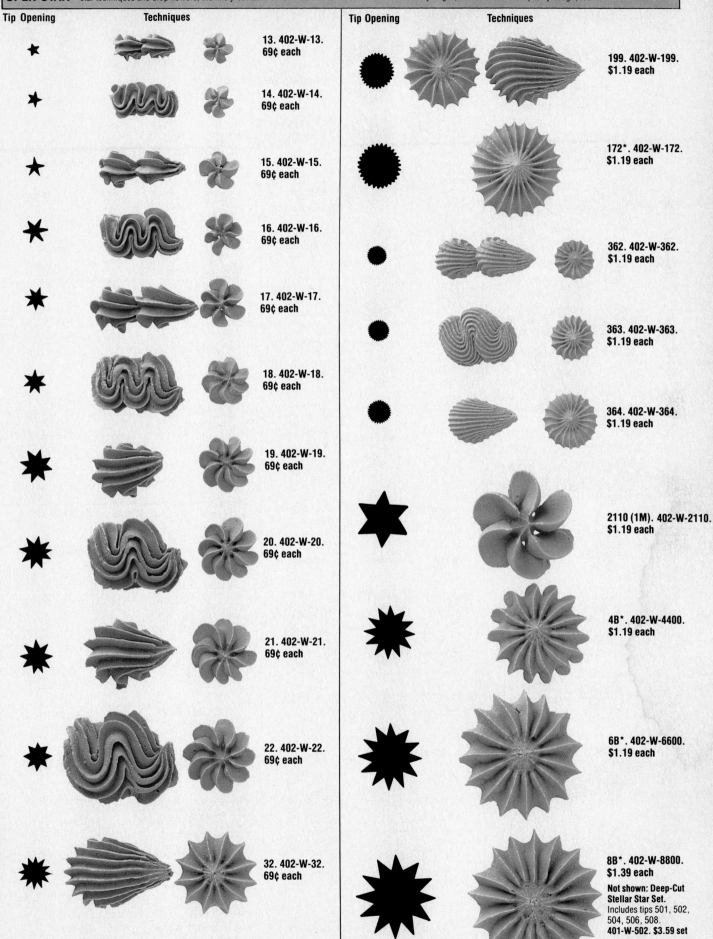

Tip Opening	Techniques		
★			13. 402-W-13. 69¢ each
★			14. 402-W-14. 69¢ each
★			15. 402-W-15. 69¢ each
✳			16. 402-W-16. 69¢ each
✳			17. 402-W-17. 69¢ each
✳			18. 402-W-18. 69¢ each
✳			19. 402-W-19. 69¢ each
✳			20. 402-W-20. 69¢ each
✳			21. 402-W-21. 69¢ each
✳			22. 402-W-22. 69¢ each
✳			32. 402-W-32. 69¢ each

Tip Opening	Techniques		
●			199. 402-W-199. $1.19 each
●			172*. 402-W-172. $1.19 each
●			362. 402-W-362. $1.19 each
●			363. 402-W-363. $1.19 each
●			364. 402-W-364. $1.19 each
★			2110 (1M). 402-W-2110. $1.19 each
✳			4B*. 402-W-4400. $1.19 each
✳			6B*. 402-W-6600. $1.19 each
✴			8B*. 402-W-8800. $1.39 each

Not shown: Deep-Cut Stellar Star Set. Includes tips 501, 502, 504, 506, 508.
401-W-502. $3.59 set
*Fits large coupler only.

CLOSED STAR — Create deeply grooved shells, stars and fleurs-de-lis.

LEAF

Tip Opening	Techniques	
✱		23. 402-W-23. 69¢ each
✱		24. 402-W-24. 69¢ each
✳		25. 402-W-25. 69¢ each
✱		26. 402-W-26. 69¢ each
✱		27. 402-W-27. 69¢ each
✱		28. 402-W-28. 69¢ each
✳		29. 402-W-29. 69¢ each
✳		30. 402-W-30. 69¢ each
✳		31. 402-W-31. 69¢ each
✳		33. 402-W-33. 69¢ each
✳		34. 402-W-34. 69¢ each
✳		35. 402-W-35. 69¢ each
✳		132. 402-W-132. 69¢ each
✳		133. 402-W-133. 69¢ each

Tip Opening	Techniques	
+		49. 402-W-49. 69¢ each
+		50. 402-W-50. 69¢ each
+		51. 402-W-51. 69¢ each
+		52. 402-W-52. 69¢ each
+		53. 402-W-53. 69¢ each
+		54. 402-W-54. 69¢ each

LEAF — so realistic! Ideal for shell-motion borders, too.

65S. 402-W-659. $1.09 each
65. 402-W-65. 69¢ each
66. 402-W-66. 69¢ each

67. 402-W-67. 69¢ each
68. 402-W-68. 69¢ each
69. 402-W-69. 69¢ each

70. 402-W-70. 69¢ each
71. 402-W-71. 69¢ each

72. 402-W-72. 69¢ each
73. 402-W-73. 69¢ each
74. 402-W-74. 69¢ each

75. 402-W-75. 69¢ each
76. 402-W-76. 69¢ each
349/352s. 402-W-349. $1.09 each

352. 402-W-352. $1.09 each
326. 402-W-326. $1.09 each
355. 402-W-355. $1.09 each

112*. 402-W-112. $1.19 each
113*. 402-W-113. $1.19 each

114*. 402-W-114. $1.19 each
115*. 402-W-115. $1.19 each

Tip Opening **Techniques**

106. 402-W-106. $1.19 each

107. 402-W-107. $1.19 each

108**. 402-W-108. $1.19 each

109**. 402-W-109. $1.39 each

129. 402-W-129. $1.19 each

217. 402-W-217. $1.19 each

220. 402-W-220. $1.19 each

224. 402-W-224. $1.19 each

225. 402-W-225. $1.19 each

131. 402-W-131. $1.19 each

177. 402-W-177. $1.19 each

Tip Opening

190**. 402-W-190. $1.39 each

191. 402-W-191. $1.19 each

193. 402-W-193. $1.19 each

194**. 402-W-194. $1.39 each

135**. 402-W-135. $1.39 each

140. 402-W-140. $1.39 each

195**. 402-W-195. $1.19 each

2C*. 402-W-2003. $1.19 each

2D*. 402-W-2004. $1.19 each

Tip Opening

2E*. 402-W-2005. $1.19 each

2F*. 402-W-2006. $1.19 each

1B*. 402-W-1002. $1.39 each

1C. 402-W-1003. $1.39 each

1E*. 402-W-1005. $1.39 each

1F*. 402-W-1006. $1.39 each

1G*. 402-W-1007. $1.39 each

*Fits large coupler only.
**use parchment bag only.

PETAL—realistic flower petals, dramatic ruffles, drapes, swags and bows.

RUFFLE—plain, fluted, shell-border, special effects.

Tip Opening   Techniques

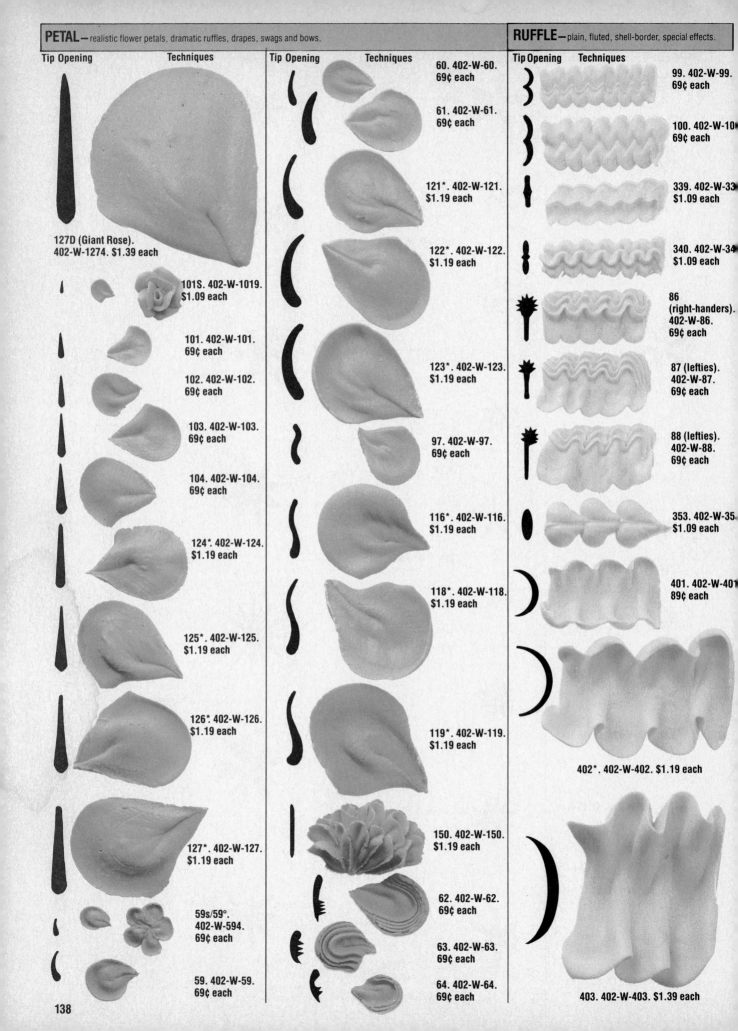

127D (Giant Rose).
402-W-1274. $1.39 each

101S. 402-W-1019.
$1.09 each

101. 402-W-101.
69¢ each

102. 402-W-102.
69¢ each

103. 402-W-103.
69¢ each

104. 402-W-104.
69¢ each

124*. 402-W-124.
$1.19 each

125*. 402-W-125.
$1.19 each

126*. 402-W-126.
$1.19 each

127*. 402-W-127.
$1.19 each

59s/59°.
402-W-594.
69¢ each

59. 402-W-59.
69¢ each

Tip Opening   Techniques

60. 402-W-60.
69¢ each

61. 402-W-61.
69¢ each

121*. 402-W-121.
$1.19 each

122*. 402-W-122.
$1.19 each

123*. 402-W-123.
$1.19 each

97. 402-W-97.
69¢ each

116*. 402-W-116.
$1.19 each

118*. 402-W-118.
$1.19 each

119*. 402-W-119.
$1.19 each

150. 402-W-150.
$1.19 each

62. 402-W-62.
69¢ each

63. 402-W-63.
69¢ each

64. 402-W-64.
69¢ each

Tip Opening   Techniques

99. 402-W-99.
69¢ each

100. 402-W-100.
69¢ each

339. 402-W-339.
$1.09 each

340. 402-W-340.
$1.09 each

86
(right-handers).
402-W-86.
69¢ each

87 (lefties).
402-W-87.
69¢ each

88 (lefties).
402-W-88.
69¢ each

353. 402-W-353.
$1.09 each

401. 402-W-401.
89¢ each

402*. 402-W-402. $1.19 each

403. 402-W-403. $1.39 each

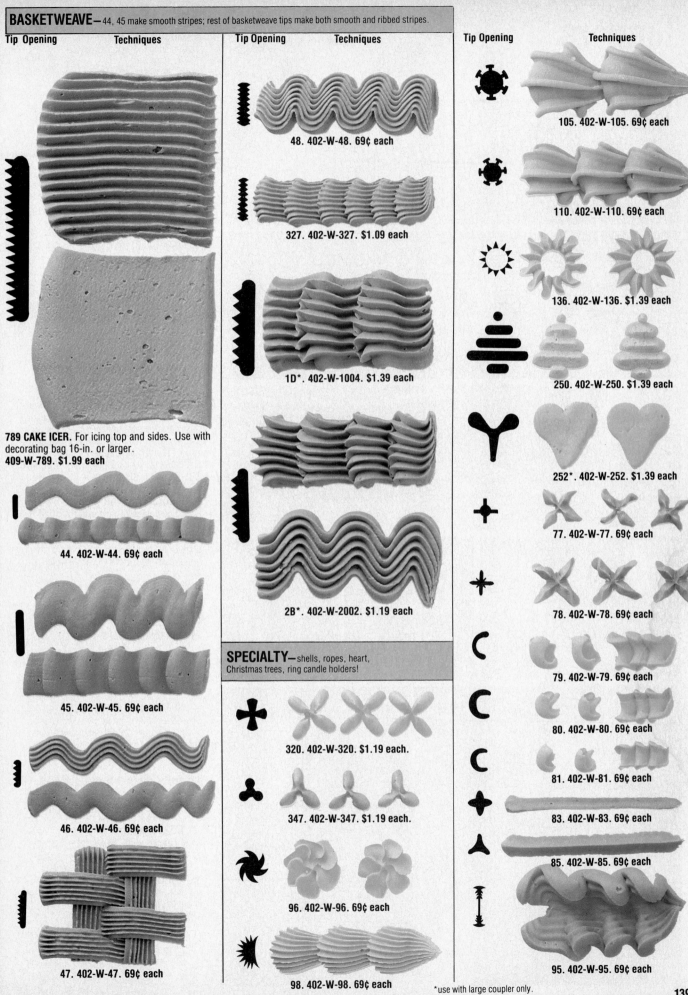

BASKETWEAVE — 44, 45 make smooth stripes; rest of basketweave tips make both smooth and ribbed stripes.

Tip Opening	Techniques

789 CAKE ICER. For icing top and sides. Use with decorating bag 16-in. or larger.
409-W-789. $1.99 each

44. 402-W-44. 69¢ each

45. 402-W-45. 69¢ each

46. 402-W-46. 69¢ each

47. 402-W-47. 69¢ each

48. 402-W-48. 69¢ each

327. 402-W-327. $1.09 each

1D*. 402-W-1004. $1.39 each

2B*. 402-W-2002. $1.19 each

SPECIALTY — shells, ropes, heart, Christmas trees, ring candle holders!

320. 402-W-320. $1.19 each.

347. 402-W-347. $1.19 each.

96. 402-W-96. 69¢ each

98. 402-W-98. 69¢ each

105. 402-W-105. 69¢ each

110. 402-W-110. 69¢ each

136. 402-W-136. $1.39 each

250. 402-W-250. $1.39 each

252*. 402-W-252. $1.39 each

77. 402-W-77. 69¢ each

78. 402-W-78. 69¢ each

79. 402-W-79. 69¢ each

80. 402-W-80. 69¢ each

81. 402-W-81. 69¢ each

83. 402-W-83. 69¢ each

85. 402-W-85. 69¢ each

95. 402-W-95. 69¢ each

*use with large coupler only.

139

Toppers

1. CIRCUS BALLOONS
12 in a bunch. 3 bunches per set.
6½ in. high.
2113-W-2366   **$2.49 set**

2. PETITE CLOWN CANDLES
6 mini mites clowning around. 1¼ to 2⅞ in.
2811-W-511   **$1.99 set**

3. JUGGLER CLOWN
Jolly fellow in action. 4½-in. high.
2113-W-2252   **$2.09 each**

4. COUNTDOWN CLOWN
Can adjust from age 1 to 6. 4¾ x 4 in. high.
2113-W-2341   **$1.39 each**

5. COMICAL CLOWNS
Varied expressions. 2-in. to 2½-in.
2113-W-2635   **$2.99 set of 4**

6. DERBY CLOWNS
A quartet of gigglers. On picks. 2-in. high.
2113-W-2333   **$2.49 pack of 4**

7. SMALL DERBY CLOWNS
Miniatures! Perfect for cupcakes. 1¾ in. high.
2113-W-2759   **$1.99 pack of 6**

8. CLOWN SEPARATOR SET
Two big-footed clowns balance a 6 in. round
cake on top plate. Perfect to set atop a large
base cake (be sure to dowel rod). They can
stand on their hands or feet. Set includes
two 7 in. scalloped-edged separator plates
and two snap-on clown supports. 4-in. high.
301-W-909   **$6.99 set**

9. CAROUSEL SEPARATOR SET
Galloping ponies will add excitement for that
special little one. Contains: 2 brown and 2
white snap-on pony pillars, two 10 in. round
plates—one clear acrylic, one plastic. Two
10 in. cardboard circles to protect plates.
9 in. high.
2103-W-1139   **$9.99 set**

10. LI'L COWPOKE
Wee buckaroo; 5 ⅛ in. high.
2113-W-2406   **$2.69 each**

11. DOLLY DRESS-UP
High style; 4½ in. high.
2113-W-1485   **$2.69 each**

12. SPACESHIP TOPPER SET
Spacecraft is 3¾ in. high; 4 ⅛ in. wide on
1¼ in. platform. 2¼ in. robot and 2 ⅛ in.
spaceman hold standard candles.
2111-W-2008   **$3.69 set**

13. APPALOOSA ROCKING HORSES
Four painted ponies; 2½ in. high.
2113-W-2015   **$3.49 set of 4**

14. HONEY BEAR
Hand-painted. 4 in. high.
2113-W-2031   **$2.69 each**

15. CAROUSEL CAKE TOP SET
A fast, easy, circus in seconds for 10 in. or
larger cakes. 9 in. high.
1305-W-9302   **$4.99 set**

Toppers

1. BIRTHDAY NUMBERS SET
Numbers 2 in. high. With picks, about 3¼ in. high, 11 numbers in set.
1106-W-7406 $1.39 set

2. TRAIN SET WITH CANDLES
Train 1¼-1⅝ in. high. Candles 2½ in. high. 6 train and 6 candle pieces.
2113-W-9004 $2.49 set

3. TEEN DOLL PICK
4½ in. tall
2815-W-101 $2.99 each

4. FRECKLE-FACED LITTLE GIRL
6½ in. tall.
2113-W-2317 $2.99 each

5. SMALL DOLL PICKS   3 in. on pick.
1511-W-1019 $4.99 pack of 4

6. TELEPHONE TEENS
Get in on the conversation track with these teens. 3 girls, 1½ in. high x 2¼ in. long. 3 boys, 1¾ in. high x 2¾ in. long.
1301-W-706 $3.69 6-pc. set

7. COMMUNION ALTAR
Tulle veil on girl. Each, 3 in. high.
BOY 1105-W-7886 $2.09 each
GIRL 1105-W-7878 $2.09 each

8. SHINING CROSS
Detachable pick. 3¾ in. high.
1105-W-7320 $1.09 each

9. SLEEPING ANGELS
1½ in. high x 3 in. long.
2113-W-2325 $1.99 pack of 2

10. 3 A.M. FEEDING 5 in. high.
2113-W-3333 $3.99 each

11. CRYSTAL-CLEAR BOOTIES
Add ribbon laces. 2 in. high x 4¼ in. long.
1103-W-9332 $1.69 pack of 2

12. BABY SHOES CAKE PICKS
1¼ in. on 1¾ in. picks.
2113-W-3811 $1.39 pack of 6

13. STORK CAKE PICKS
1 in. on 1¾ in. picks.
2113-W-3805 $1.39 pack of 6

14. DAINTY BASSINETTE
Fill with surprises. 3½ in. high.
2111-W-9381 $1.09 each

15. MAMA STORK 3¾ in. high.
1305-W-6303 $1.69 each

16. MR. STORK
115-W-1502 $6.00 each

17. PETITE LULLABY
115-W-1987 $8.00 each

18. BABY BRACELETS 1⅛ in. high.
2111-W-72 $1.69 pack of 4

19. TINY TODDLER 4½ in. high.
BLUE 1103-W-7429 $1.99 each
PINK 1103-W-7437 $1.99 each

20. BABY RATTLES
Great as gift trimmers, too! 3½ in. long.
2113-W-3283 $1.09 pack of 2

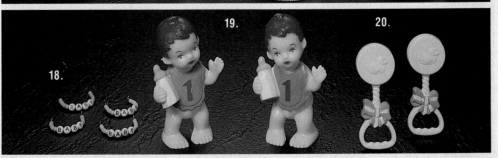

Toppers

1. SOFTBALL PLAYER
4¼ in. high
2113-W-3705 $2.99 each

2. BASEBALL SET
Batter, catcher, pitcher and 3 basemen. Hand-painted. Each 2-2¾ in. high.
2113-W-2155 $2.99 6-pc. set

3. BASEBALL TOPPER SET
Umpire 3 in. high, catcher 2 in. high, slider 1½ in. high x 4½ in. long.
2113-W-2473 $2.99 3-pc. set

4. GOOD SPORT COACH 4½ in. high.
2113-W-4140 $2.69 each

5. CAMPUS CHEERLEADER 5½ in. high.
2113-W-2708 $1.69 each

6. BASKETBALL PLAYER 3¾ in. high.
2113-W-9354 $1.99 each

7. SUPER BOWL FOOTBALL SET
Eight 1½-2 in. high players and two 4½ in. high goal posts.
2113-W-2236 $2.99 10-pc. set

8. BUMBLING BOWLER 4½ in. high.
2113-W-2783 $2.69 each

9. GOLF SET*
Includes 4½ in. high golfer plus 3 each: 2½ in. wide greens, 3¾ in. high flags, 5 in. clubs and golf balls.
1306-W-7274 $2.09 13-pc. set

10. COMICAL GOLFER
2 in. high, 4¼ in. wide, 5 ⅛ in. long.
2113-W-2554 $2.09 each

11. FISHY SITUATION 5¼ in. high.
2113-W-2074 $2.69 each

12. END OF DOCK FISHERMAN
Just swirl icing with spatula to resemble water, set on top. 5 in. high.
2113-W-4832 $2.69 each

13. FRUSTRATED FISHERMAN 4½ in. high.
2113-W-2384 $2.99 each

14. GONE FISHIN' SIGN BOARD
Pipe on icing message. 4 ½ in. high.
1008-W-726 $1.39 pack of 2

15. SHARP SHOOTER 6 in. high.
2113-W-2422 $2.99 each

16. JAUNTY JOGGER 4 in. high.
2113-W-2066 $2.69 each

17. ARMCHAIR QUARTERBACK
Man 3½-in. high; TV 2¼-in. high.
2113-W-1302 $2.69 2-pc. set

18. LAZY BONES
2½ in. high x 5½ in. long.
2113-W-2414 $2.69 each

19. PARTY GUY 3 in. high.
2113-W-3739 $2.69 each

20. BACKYARD GARDENER 4⅜ in. high.
2113-W-1973 $2.09 each

21. ALL THUMBS 4¾ in. high.
2113-W-2686 $2.09 each

22. OL' SMOKY
Man 5 ⅛ in. tall; grill 2⅜ in. high.
2113-W-2694 $2.09 2-pc. set

23. BIG BOSS
2¾ in. high x 2½ in. long.
2113-W-3798 $2.69 each

*CAUTION: Contains small parts. Not intended for use by children 3 years and under.

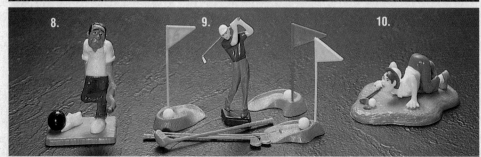

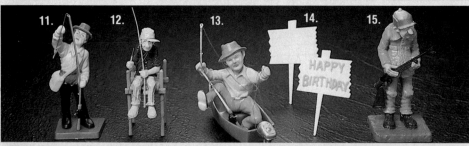

1. SESAME STREET SET. *
Big Bird 3 in., Oscar The Grouch 2 in.,
Cookie Monster 2¼ in., Bert 2¼ in. and
Ernie 2 in. high.
2113-W-1728 $2.99 5-pc. set

2. COOKIE MONSTER PICK*
1½ in. on 1¾ in. pick.
2113-W-3813 $1.99 pkg. of 6

3. BIG BIRD PICK*
1¾ in. on 1¾ in. pick.
2113-W-3815 $1.99 pkg. of 6

4. BIG BIRD WITH AGE*
Age indicator 1-6. 3 9/16 in. high x 3½ in.
long x 3 in. wide.
2113-W-1430 $2.09 each

*Sesame Street Puppet Characters. © 1990 Jim Henson
Productions, Inc. © 1990 Children's Television Workshop.

5. WACKY WITCH   5¼ in. high.
2113-W-6118 $2.09 each

6. HAPPY GHOST
4⅜ in. high x 4¼ in. long X 2¾ in. wide.
2113-W-3356 $1.09 each

7. JACK-O-LANTERNS   2-in.
2113-W-3135 $1.69 set of 4

8. BLACK CAT PICK
1¼ in. on 1¾ in. pick.
2113-W-4301 $1.39 pack of 6

9. JACK-O-LANTERN PICK
1⅝ in. on 1¾ in. pick.
2113-W-4328 $1.39 pack of 6

10. SANTA 'N TREE
Santa 2⅝ in. tall; tree 3⅜ in. high.
2113-W-1647 $1.69 2-pc. set

11. CHRISTMAS TREE PICK
Festive fir. 1⅝ in. on 1¾ in. pick.
2113-W-4344 $1.39 pack of 6

12. SNOWMAN PICK
Favorite roly poly. 1⅝ in. on 1¾ in. pick.
2113-W-4360 $1.39 pack of 6

13. VALENTINE PICK
1½ in. heart on 1 in. pick.
1502-W-1011 $1.39 pack of 12

14. SHAMROCK PICK
1¼ in. shamrock on 1⅞ in. pick.
2113-W-4387 $1.39 pack of 6

15. EASTER BUNNY PICK
2¼ in. on 1¾ in. pick.
2113-W-4476 $1.39 pack of 6

16. GOOD LUCK KEY PICK
2113-W-3801 $1.39 pack of 6

17. MORTARBOARD & DIPLOMA PICK
1½ in. on 1¾ in. pick.
2113-W-3803 $1.39 pack of 6

18. SUCCESSFUL GRAD   4½ in. tall.
2113-W-4549 $1.69 each

19. GLOWING GRAD   4½ in. tall.
2113-W-1833 $1.69 each

20. GLAD GRADUATE   5 in. tall.
2113-W-1817 $2.09 each

21. HAPPY GRADUATE   5 in. tall
2113-W-1818 $2.09 each

Candles

1. NEW! LITTLE DINOSAUR CANDLE SET
1¼ in. to 1½ in. high Collection of 4 fun dinosaurs.
2811-W-216 $2.99 set

2. PETITE CLOWN CANDLE SET
6 mini mites clowning around. 1¼ to 2⅞ in. high.
2811-W-511 $1.99 set

3. NEW! PARTY TEDDY BEAR CANDLE SET
1¾ in. high. 4 cuddly party favorites. 1¾ in. high.
2811-W-214 $2.99 set

4. PETITE ANIMALS CANDLES
6 animal menagerie! 1¼-in. to 2⅞-in. high.
2811-W-513 $1.99 set

5. NEW! BIRTHDAY TRAIN CANDLES SET
4-piece set is 1 in. to 1½ in. high.
2811-W-218 $2.99 set

6. NEW! TRAIN AND CANDLE SET
All aboard this 12-piece set. Train 1¼ in. to 1⅝ in. high, candles 2½ in. high.
2113-W-9004 $2.49 set

7. NEW! 24-COUNT CELEBRATION CANDLES
24 candles in assorted colors. 2½ in. high.
2811-W-1248   49¢ each

8. NEW! 12-COUNT CELEBRATION CANDLES
12 large candles 3¼ in. high.
2811-W-212   49¢ each box

9. SLENDERS
24 long, slender candles for all occasions. 6½ in. high.
2811-W-1188   79¢ each box

10. NEW! NUMERAL CANDLES
Number 0 through 9 and ? Multi-color confetti designs. All 3 in. high. **49¢ each**

NUMBER 0	2811-W-190
NUMBER 1	2811-W-191
NUMBER 2	2811-W-192
NUMBER 3	2811-W-193
NUMBER 4	2811-W-194
NUMBER 5	2811-W-195
NUMBER 6	2811-W-196
NUMBER 7	2811-W-197
NUMBER 8	2811-W-198
NUMBER 9	2811-W-199
QUESTION MARK	**2811-W-200**

Note: For safety reasons, these candles are fit with a short wick and will self-extinguish before burning completely.

Coordinated Cake Ornaments and Accessories

Wilton, the leader in wedding cake design and decoration for over a quarter of a century, proudly introduces the Ellen Williams' Designer Series. Exquisite wedding ornaments in fine porcelain, laces and trims now have their own coordinating collection of tier tops.

Each beautiful ornament has the option of mixing and matching with all the Designer Series' Cake Top Ornaments. Although the wedding cake ornaments listed at the side are the ones we feel coordinate best with each Tier Top, you may prefer other combinations.

PEARL LEAVES TIER TOP

• Opulence

• Beautiful

• True Love

BLOSSOM TIER TOP

• Masterpiece

• Dreams Come True

• Glorious

PEARL TIER TOP

• Crowning Glory

• Timeless

• Classique

SHIMMERING RIBBON TIER TOP

• Rejoice

• Rose Garden

145

1.

This superb Wilton ornament collection was designed with painstaking detail by renowned giftware designer, Ellen Williams. From expert detailing of the fine porcelain bisque figurines to the floral and lace arrangements, the artistry is quite evident.

The lovely wedding couples, designed by Ellen, were uniquely crafted for Wilton by **Roman, Inc.**, a leading giftware manufacturer.

1. CLASSIQUE
Timeless romantic beauty expertly created by Ellen Williams. The fine porcelain bisque figurine is beautifully placed between Gothic pillars, diaphanous blooms, shimmery pearls and crisp pleats of lace. 11″ high.
GREY COAT 118-W-410
BLACK COAT 118-W-415
$50.00 each

2. GLORIOUS
Dramatic porcelain bisque figurines afloat on lace-veiled base. A crystal-clear swirl and dancing-in-air floral and "pearl" cascade add romance to the occasion. 12½″ high.
GREY COAT 118-W-425
BLACK COAT 118-W-420
$60.00 each

3. DREAMS COME TRUE
Dainty, Ellen Williams' couple underneath a graceful arch of lavish ribbons, lace and posies, dotted with "pearls." Lovely wedding cake addition. 10½″ high.
GREY COAT 18-W-400
BLACK COAT 18-W-405
$60.00 each

4.

5.

2.

3.

4. MASTERPIECE
Ornately-trimmed bells toll out the happiest of wedding messages. Tied with ribbon and set in a lace-trimmed heart. 9½" high.
IVORY 103-W-425 **$40.00 each**
WHITE 103-W-430 **$40.00 each**

5. REJOICE
Our beautiful bells toll the joyous message of love and wedding good wishes. A glistening duo decked with bows, blooms and pearl sprays. 7½" high.
103-W-415 **$35.00 each**

6. TIMELESS
A radiant couple in blissful reverie under a lattice arch of pearls. Adorned with lovely floral and pearl bursts. 10" high.
GREY COAT 118-W-450
BLACK COAT 118-W-455
$75.00 each

7. ROSE GARDEN
Promises bloom beneath a stunning arch of roses, ribbons and pearl sprays. 11" high.
WHITE/GREY COAT 118-W-470
WHITE/BLACK COAT 118-W-475
IVORY/GREY COAT 118-W-460
IVORY/BLACK COAT 118-W-465
$75.00 each

8. BEAUTIFUL
The name says it all. The joyful couple is free standing in a mist of tulle, pearl leaves, flowers and lace. 7½" high.
GREY COAT 118-W-440
BLACK COAT 118-W-445
$70.00 each

1.

2.

3.

4.

5.

6.

7.

1. CROWNING GLORY
Two fluttering doves afloat on a lace traced heart and satiny bell. 9½" high.
103-W-405 $40.00 each

2. TRUE LOVE
Pearl-adorned swooning doves land on a pair of pearly wedding bands. Decorated with tufts of tulle and soft roses. In white, 8¼" high.
103-W-410 $40.00 each

3. EXUBERANCE
Two graceful swans floating on a lace-trimmed base. Under a shower of flowing tulle and flower buds with pearl sprays. 7" high.
103-W-440 $25.00 each

4. LOVE FOREVER
A pair of elegant swans carrying bouquets of blossoms on a base of lace ruffles. Open-heart backdrop is treated with lace and pearl stamens. 6¼" high.
103-W-435 $25.00 each

5. OPULENCE
Pearl-adorned wedding bands shimmer on a base of pearl leaves and accordian-pleated lace. 6½" high.
103-W-420 $40.00 each

6. BLESSED EVENT
Two satin and pearl adorned bells toll this most sacred union. "Gold" cross crowns the bloom-filled ornament. Beautifully finished with a shimmery bow. 9" high.
103-W-845 $40.00 each

7. INSPIRATION
The gilded cross is highlighted on a petal base flowing with tulle bursts. A soft bouquet of posies drapes cross and base. 6½" high.
106-W-355 $16.00 each

8. SWEET BEGINNINGS
Romantic porcelain couple steal a quiet moment beneath a lace and pearl trimmed heart. Delicate base and heart dotted with roses. 9" high.

118-W-490 BLACK COAT
118-W-495 GREY COAT
$60.00 each

9. EVERLASTING
In a gazebo showered with tulle bursts and lily of the valley, our porcelain couple solemnly stand. Lattice work trimmed with lace and edged with pearls. 11½" high.

118-W-500 GREY COAT
118-W-505 BLACK COAT
$60.00

10. DELICATE JOY
Dramatic solitary porcelain couple exchange vows on a lacy ruffled base adorned with pearly bursts of lily of the valley and other floral blooms. 6" high.

108-W-640 GREY COAT
108-W-645 BLACK COAT
$40.00 each

11. SMALL TOGETHER FOREVER FIGURINE
Petite Ellen Williams porcelain figure in a traditional romantic pose. Can be used with many other ornaments. 4½" high.

214-W-437 GREY COAT
214-W-439 BLACK COAT
$30.00

NEW!

1. NEW! FIRST WALTZ

A priceless moment to cherish forever. The tender, timeless couple of glazed porcelain was created by *Roman, Inc.* Gothic arched windows reflect their love. Delicate lace and tulle encircle the lovely pair. 7¼" high

118-W-435 $55.00 each

2. NEW! MOONLIGHT SERENADE

Our lovely couple share an embrace under a flowery archway on a lace-veiled base. Glazed porcelain figurine crafted by *Roman, Inc.* 8¾" high.

118-W-430 $55.00 each

3. NEW! FIRST KISS FIGURINE

Romantic couple of glazed porcelain by *Roman, Inc.* stand in solitary beauty. Can be used in combination with other settings. 4¾ in. high.

214-W-440 $35.00 each

© 1988 Roman, Inc.

4. PETITE HAPPY HEARTS

Ruffles of lace now highlight the base of this lighthearted couple. The ideal porcelain couple stands before sleek lucite-look heart. 6 in. high.

Coat	Color	Stock No.
BLACK	PINK	108-W-217
WHITE	PINK	108-W-219
BLACK	WHITE	108-W-525
WHITE	WHITE	108-W-526

$22.00 each

5. BRIDAL WALTZ

Making that all-important commitment in perfect unison. Charming arched windows share a view of our porcelain couple gliding in graceful harmony. Ruffles of lace and tulle decorate the bead-embossed base and outline windows. 7½ in. high.

Coat	Color	Stock No.
WHITE	WHITE	117-W-321
BLACK	WHITE	117-W-322
WHITE	PINK	117-W-323
BLACK	PINK	117-W-324
WHITE	PEACH	117-W-325
BLACK	PEACH	117-W-326
WHITE	TEAL	117-W-327
BLACK	TEAL	117-W-328
WHITE	IVORY	117-W-329
BLACK	IVORY	117-W-330

$40.00 each.

6. LOVE'S FANFARE

Lavish flourish and flair. Dramatic fan and ruffly froth of lace lavish our exquisitely detailed porcelain couple. A wreath of light-as-air flowers and pearl strands floats on lacy waves. 8 in. high. Scalloped base not included.

WHITE COAT	117-W-401
BLACK COAT	117-W-402

$50.00 each

7. SOPHISTICATION

Beautiful porcelain bride and groom under a burst of lily of the valley and soft tulle. Dotted with dramatic shimmery pearls. 8½ in. high.

WHITE COAT	117-W-202
BLACK COAT	117-W-201

$45.00 each

Wedding Ornaments

1. REFLECTIONS
Sophisticated and trendsetting.
Dramatic lucite-look backdrop reflects
porcelain couple, tulle burst, pearl
sprays and florals. 8 in. high.
BLUE 117-W-130
WHITE 117-W-268
PINK 117-W-297
$25.00 each

2. PROMISE
Sleek lucite-look heart frames white
porcelain couple. Crystal-look base is
covered with tulle, ribbons and fabric
flowers. 9 5/8 in. high.
BLUE 117-W-309
WHITE 117-W-315
PINK 117-W-311
$25.00 each

3. RHAPSODY
Contemporary belled arch is dotted
with flowers and tulle. Stylized porcelain couple stands on crystal-look
base, adorned with tulle puff and floral
spray. 9½ in. high.
PINK 117-W-305
WHITE 117-W-301
$25.00 each

4. ECSTASY
Sprays of flowers and leaves surround
the romantic porcelain pair. Delicate
tulle forms a lovely base.
9½ in. high.
WHITE 117-W-831
$40.00 each

5. SPLENDID
Dramatic curve of lucite surrounds
adoring porcelain pair. Cylindrical vase
holds a matching spray of flowers that
accents base. Add real flowers if you
prefer. 10½ in. high.
WHITE 117-W-506
PINK 117-W-507
BLUE 117-W-508
PEACH 117-W-450
$28.00 each

6. GARDEN ROMANCE
Lovely porcelain couple stands in a
gazebo decked with flowery vines.
Clusters of tulle and ribbons complete
this romantic hideaway.
10½ in. high.
IRIDESCENT 117-W-711
RAINBOW 117-W-713
$30.00 each

7. LUSTROUS LOVE
A burst of tulle peaks from behind lace
leaves; dotted white forget-me-nots
and rimmed with gleaming pearls.
Satiny roses bloom while pearls
are suspended on transparent
strings around the happy couple.
8 in. high.
WHITE 117-W-621
PINK 117-W-623
BLUE 117-W-625
$35.00 each

8. DEVOTION
Lucite arch is framed with gathered
tulle and lace. Glazed porcelain couple
stands on pedestal base in burst of
tulle, blooms and pearl strands.
9½ in. high.
WHITE 117-W-425
$25.00 each

1. SWEET CEREMONY
Seed pearl hearts frame glistening bell. Bride and heart frame are accented with tulle. 10 in. high.

WHITE COAT 101-W-22028
BLACK COAT 101-W-22011
GREY COAT 101-W-22045
$14.00 each

2. MORNING ROSEBUD
Doves in flight above open gate. Soft fabric flowers dot landscape. 8 in. high.

WHITE COAT 101-W-44020
BLACK COAT 101-W-44013   **$10.00 each**

3. MOONLIT SNOW
New! Now available with grey coats. An archway of flowers and pearls frames our couple. Base trimmed with a ruffle of lace. 9 in. high.   **$25.00 each**

COAT	COUPLE	COLOR	STOCK NO.
WHITE	WHITE	WHITE	114-W-201
BLACK	WHITE	WHITE	114-W-202
WHITE	BLACK	WHITE	114-W-207
BLACK	BLACK	WHITE	114-W-208
BLACK	WHITE	PEACH	114-W-205
WHITE	WHITE	PEACH	114-W-206
BLACK	WHITE	PINK	114-W-204
WHITE	WHITE	PINK	114-W-203
GREY	BLACK	WHITE	114-W-210
GREY	WHITE	WHITE	114-W-209

4. HEART-TO-HEART
Heart duo creates an eye-catching shadow-box effect around Kissing Couple. 9 in. high.

110-W-376   **$17.00 each**

5. PETITE DOUBLE RING COUPLE
The perfect pairs of people, birds and bands. 5½ in. high.

BLACK COAT 104-W-42413
WHITE COAT 104-W-42420   **$7.00 each**

6. NEW VERSIONS! LOVERS IN LACE
Now our handsome couple has the option of grey coat. All under lace-covered arches and a burst of tulle. 7 in. high.

COAT	COUPLE	
GREY	BLACK	104-W-842
GREY	WHITE	104-W-834
BLACK	BLACK	104-W-302
WHITE	BLACK	104-W-301
BLACK	WHITE	104-W-818
WHITE	WHITE	104-W-826

$10.00 each

7. EVERLASTING LOVE
Graceful arches of lace and filigree heart, dotted with tulle and wedding bands, surround floral filled bell. 10 in. high.

103-W-236   **$16.00 each**

8. SPRING SONG
Perching lovebirds sing their romantic love songs in a garden of posies and tulle. 9½ in. high.

111-W-2802   **$16.00 each**

9. VICTORIAN CHARM
Graceful ribbon loops and fantasy florals layer over romantic satin five-bell cluster. 7½ in. high.

IVORY   103-W-1586
WHITE   103-W-1587   **$20.00 each**

10. CIRCLES OF LOVE
Symbolic double rings and doves in a flowery hideaway of flowers and pearl sprays. 10 in. high.

WHITE   103-W-9004
PINK   103-W-300
PEACH   103-W-301
TEAL   103-W-302   **$25.00 each**

11. HEARTS TAKE WING
Romantic beak-to-beak birds perched on a setting of heart-shaped branches and tulle. 10½ in. high.

103-W-6218   **$12.00 each**

NEW!

Wedding Ornaments

12. WEDDING BELLS
Filigree bell cluster in a profusion of tulle and lace.
10½ in. high.
103-W-1356 $16.00 each

13. SATIN ELEGANCE
Lace-edged satin heart bursting with pearls, flowers
and tulle, bears a pair of wedding rings. 7 in. high.
Pearly stamens and dancing strands of pearls add
luster to the enchanting satin and chiffon petal flowers. An exuberance of tulle veils pretty floral
embossed base. 7 in. high.

TEAL	**109-W-1005**	
IVORY*	**109-W-1002**	
PINK	**109-W-1003**	
PEACH*	**109-W-1006**	
WHITE	**109-W-1001**	
BLUE	**109-W-1004**	**$20.00 each**

*on ivory bases

14. NATURAL BEAUTY
Filigree heart, floral spray and satin bow add charm
to perched pair. 6 in. high.

PEACH	**106-W-1104**	
PINK	**106-W-1120**	
WHITE	**106-W-1163**	**$10.00 each**

15. PETITE BELLS OF JOY
Eye-catching cluster of white filigree bells enhanced
with fabric roses, lace-covered arches and tulle.
7 in. high.

WHITE	**106-W-2658**	
PINK	**106-W-350**	**$12.00 each**

16. PETITE DOUBLE RING
Graceful doves land on band of love. Adorned with
tulle puff. 5½ in. high.
106-W-4316 $6.00 each

17. LA BELLE PETITE
Tolling bell surrounded by tulle glimmers with
iridescence. 5½ in. high.

WHITE	**106-W-248**	
PINK	**106-W-249**	
PEACH	**106-W-250**	**$9.00 each**

18. PETITE SPRING SONG
A song bird duet arched in flowers, pearls and
delicate tulle. 7 in. high.

WHITE	**106-W-159**	
PINK	**106-W-160**	
PEACH	**106-W-161**	**$11.00 each**

Anniversary Ornaments

1. 25 OR 50 YEARS OF HAPPINESS
In gold or silver, the number tells the happy story. Accented with blooms and shimmery leaves. 10 in. high.
25TH   102-W-207
50TH   102-W-223
$16.00 each

2. GOLDEN/SILVER JUBILEE
An event that calls for serious celebration. Say it in gold or silver tulle. Couple is on numeral wreath with orchids and ferns. 8½ in. high.
GOLD   102-W-1250
SILVER   102-W-1225
$16.00 each

3. DOUBLE RING DEVOTION
Our celebrating couple surrounded by rings and the shimmer of pearls and ferns. 5 in. high.
25TH SILVER   105-W-4613
50TH GOLD   105-W-4605
$9.00 each

4. PETITE ANNIVERSARY YEARS
The addition of beautiful blooms adds appeal to this versatile favorite. Embossed wreath holds snap-on numbers. 5 3/4 in. high.
105-W-4257
$7.00 each

5. PETITE ANNIVERSARY
Shining numeral wreath is highlighted by two fluttering doves resting on base. 5½ in. high.
25TH   105-W-4265
50TH   105-W-4273
$6.00 each

Loving TRADITIONS™

Create a modern day heirloom for that special couple. All these romantic mementos are beautifully gift packaged. Perfect for remembering weddings, showers, engagements and anniversaries.

1. WEDDING AND ANNIVERSARY LEADED CRYSTAL CHAMPAGNE GLASSES
Underscore this all-important occasion with a memorable toast. Sold in sets of 2 glasses. Leaded crystal, saucer style set. Embossed with our exclusive Loving Traditions design. Trimmed with lace, satin, ribbon and pearly trim.
BRIDE AND GROOM
120-W-210 $24.00 set
ANNIVERSARY WISHES
120-W-211 $24.00 set

2. WEDDING AND ANNIVERSARY SHERBERT GLASSES
Enhanced with satin ribbons.
BRIDE AND GROOM
120-W-203 $14.00 set
ANNIVERSARY WISHES
120-W-205 $14.00 set

3. BRIDAL AND ANNIVERSARY LEADED CRYSTAL TOASTING GLASSES
Leaded crystal glasses etched with beautiful roses. Pretty tiny flowers and satin ribbon accents. 8⅜ in. high.
BRIDAL SET   120-W-200
$24.00 set
ANNIVERSARY SET   120-W-202
$24.00 set

4. BRIDE'S GARTER

Traditional feminine accessory. Delicate and lacy, our garter is trimmed with a satin band, ribbons, faux pearls and shimmery stones.

WHITE   120-W-401
IVORY   120-W-403
PINK   120-W-400
BLUE   120-W-402
BLACK   120-W-404
$5.00 each

5. BRIDE'S PURSE

The perfect little carry-all that every bride will love. Dainty satin drawstring bag punctuated with fabric flowers and pearl trims. (11 X 13 in.).
120-W-601 $15.00 each

6. BRIDE'S HANDKERCHIEF

Just the right finishing touch for that Wedding Day. Lacy cotton handkerchief to carry or tuck into handbag. In white, ivory or "something blue."

WHITE   120-W-500
BLUE   120-W-502
IVORY   120-W-501
$5.00 each

7. RING BEARER'S PILLOWS

What better setting for wedding bands on that all-important day? Elegant satin tailored with classic or embellished treatments. Fine lace, dainty tulle, pearls, fabric flowers and satiny ribbons. To be cherished long after the wedding day.

PEARL HEART
WHITE 120-W-100 $16.00 each
FLORAL SQUARE
WHITE 120-W-104 $16.00 each
LACY SQUARE (not shown)
IVORY 120-W-107 $20.00 each
LACY SQUARE
WHITE 120-W-106 $20.00 each

8. CAKE AND KNIFE SERVERS

Shining stainless with beautifully detailed handles. Softly tied with sprays of flowers, ribbons and pearls.
CAKE KNIFE   120-W-701
$13.50 each
CAKE SERVER   120-W-702
$13.50 each
KNIFE & SERVER SET
120-W-700 $24.00 set

9. WEDDING BELL

Beautiful remembrance of that special day. Leaded crystal etched with traditional bridal couple design. Trimmed with satin ribbon bow and crystal-look clapper. 6-in. high.
120-W-900 $17.50 each

10. WEDDING ALBUM

An album to be cherished as much as the wedding day itself. Beautiful lace-covered album is handmade and painstakingly appointed with a satin ribbon bow, fabric flowers and pearl accents. Contains 21 pages to keep a detailed account of everything from engagement, showers, wedding guests, gifts, family trees and much more.
120-W-301 $30.00 each

4.

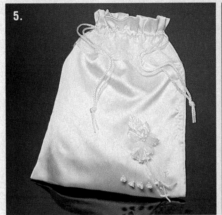

5.

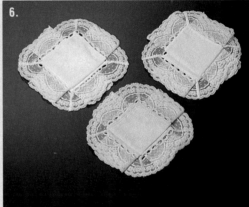

6.

7.

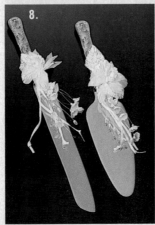

8.

9.

10.

Toppers and Accessories

TIER TOPS

The Fine Wilton Wedding Ornament tradition continues. Now an exquisite collection of Tier Tops from Ellen Williams. Each has been created to complement and enhance your wedding cake. Can be an elegant statement alone or with their matching Ellen Williams' ornaments.

1. PEARL TIER TOP*
Beautiful blossoms stream down from all sides. Pearl wisps decorate blooms and flower bursts. Base diameter 4 in.
211-W-1992 $12.50 each

2. PEARL LEAVES TIER TOP*
Delicate pearl leaves peek through tufts of tulle and graceful pearl-trimmed blossoms. Base diameter 4⅞ in.
211-W-1994 $15.00 each

3. SHIMMERING RIBBON TIER TOP*
Satin-striped ribbon bows underscore blooming flowers touched with pearl sprays. Base diameter 4⅞ in.
211-W-1993 $12.50 each

4. BLOSSOM TIER TOP*
Contemporary asymmetrical spray with bursts of tulle and pearl-decked flowers. Base diameter 4⅞ in.
211-W-1991 $7.50 each

* © 1990 EHW Enterprises

5. ARTIFICIAL LEAVES
144 leaves per package. Green or white cloth; gold or silver foil. Order 1005-W-number

Color		1⅛ in.		1¼ in.
Gold	6518	$2.59 pkg.	6712	$2.29 pkg.
Silver	6526	$2.59 pkg.	6720	$2.29 pkg.
Green	4655	$2.59 pkg.	4670	$2.29 pkg.
White	6501	$2.59 pkg.		

6. PEARL LEAVES
Dainty pearls edge appliqued tulle leaves. 2 per package. 2¼ in. long.
WHITE   211-W-1201 $2.99 pkg

7. PEARL LEAF PUFF – 5½ in.
WHITE   211-W-1125 $4.69 each

8. BEAUTY IN A BASKET
Dainty basket just ready to decorate a cake, gift or even a party favor. Satin roses in tulle puffs set in basket. Plastic basket. 3 X 2 X 2¾ in.
WHITE   2110-W-2309
PINK   2110-W-2305
$1.29 each

9. FLORAL PUFF ACCENT – 5½ in.
PINK   211-W-1013
WHITE   211-W-1011
$2.99 each

10. LIBERATED BRIDE
Swept away! 4½ in. high.
2113-W-4188 $3.99 each

11. RELUCTANT GROOM COUPLE
4½ in. high
1316-W-9520 $4.99 each

12. BRIDAL SHOWER DELIGHT
Lacy umbrellas with interlocking rings. 6 in. high.
115-W-201 $8.00 each

13. PARTY PARASOLS
4 in. parasols; 5 in. snap-on handles.
2110-W-9296 $1.69 pack of 4

1. NEW! FIRST KISS created by
Roman, Inc.
Couple's magic moment, 4½ in. high
214-W-440 $35.00 each

2. NEW! TOGETHER FOREVER
4½ in. high
Designed by Ellen Williams and crafted by
Roman, Inc.
GREY COAT COUPLE   214-W-437
BLACK COAT COUPLE   214-W-439
$30.00 each

© 1990 EHW ENTERPRISES, INC.
© 1988 Roman, Inc.

3. MOONLIT SNOW COUPLE 4¾" high
$4.49 each

Couple	Coat	Stock
White	White	214-W-563
White	Black	214-W-555
White	Grey	214-W-704
Black	White	214-W-302
Black	Black	214-W-301
Black	Grey	214-W-703

4-5. BISQUE PORCELAIN COUPLES
Exquisitely detailed partners.
Each 4½ in. high.   **$12.99 each**

4. SIDE-BY-SIDE COUPLE
BLACK COAT   214-W-201
WHITE COAT   214-W-202

5. DANCING COUPLE
WHITE COAT   214-W-320
BLACK COAT   214-W-321

6. CLASSIC COUPLE
Plastic, two sizes available.

Couple	Coat	Height	Stock No.	
White	Black	4½ in.	202-W-8110	4.69
White	White	4½ in.	202-W-8121	4.69
White	Black	3½ in.	2102-W-820	3.99
White	White	3½ in.	203-W-8221	3.99
White	Grey	4½ in.	202-W-300	4.99
White	Grey	3½ in.	203-W-304	3.99
Black	Black	4½ in.	214-W-301	4.49
Black	White	4½ in.	214-W-302	4.49
Black	Black	3½ in.	203-W-302	3.99
Black	White	3½ in.	203-W-301	3.99
Black	Grey	3½ in.	203-W-303	3.99

7. ANNIVERSARY COUPLE
Gold or silver gown. Plastic, 4½ in. tall.
25TH SILVER   203-W-2828 $3.99
50TH GOLD   203-W-1821 $3.99

8. KISSING COUPLE
Contemporary pair, 4 in. tall. Plastic.
202-W-172 $4.69 each

9. GLAZED PORCELAIN COUPLE
4⅝ IN. COUPLE
202-W-218 $15.99 each

10. BRIDESMAIDS
Plastic, 3½ in. tall.
WHITE   203-W-8324
PINK   203-W-8341
BLUE   203-W-8304
YELLOW   203-W-8325
$1.09 each

11. GROOMSMAN
Plastic, 3½ in. tall.
BLACK COAT   203-W-8402
WHITE COAT   203-W-8424
ALL WHITE   203-W-8829
$1.09 each

Wedding Couples
NEW!

INCOMPARABLE BEAUTY OF PORCELAIN
The ultimate touch of beauty to top the most important cake of your life. Timeless porcelain.

Beautiful Trims

1. CIRCLES OF LACE 10 in. high.
210-W-1986   **$8.99 each**

2. FLORAL ARCH 10-in. high.
210-W-1987   **$8.99 each**

3. FLORAL BASE
White, 1½ in. high, 4¾ in. diameter.
201-W-1815   **$1.99 each**

4. CRYSTAL-LOOK BASE
1¾ in. high, 4½ in. diameter.
201-W-1450   **$2.99 each**

5. PETITE PEDESTAL BASE
3½ in. top and 4 in. base. White.
201-W-1133   **$1.99 each**

6. HEART BASE
White openwork. 2 pcs. 1½ in. high.
4½ IN. 201-W-7332   **$2.99 each**
3¼ IN. 201-W-7847   **$2.69 each**

7. FLORAL SCROLL BASE
Victorian charm. 4½ X 2½ in. 2 pcs.
WHITE 201-W-1303   **$2.99 each**
IVORY 201-W-305   **$2.99 each**

8. FILIGREE BELLS

Height	Stock No.	Price/Pack
1 IN.	1001-W-9447	$1.79/12
2 IN.	1001-W-9422	$1.79/6
2¾ IN.	1001-W-9439	$2.29/6
3 IN.	1001-W-9404	$1.59/3
4½ IN.	1001-W-9411	$1.89/3

9. GLITTERED BELLS

Height	Stock No.	Price/Pack
1¼ IN.	1007-W-9061	$2.99/12
1¾ IN.	2110-W-9075	$1.09/6
2 IN.	1007-W-9088	$2.49/6
3 IN.	2110-W-9090	$2.49/6
5 IN.	1007-W-9110	$2.99/3

10. SMALL WEDDING RINGS
⅝ in. diam.
SILVER 1002-W-1016
GOLD 1002-W-1008
$1.59 pack of 24

11. FLOWER SPIKES
Fill with water, push into cake and add flowers.
3 in. high.
1008-W-408   **$2.49 pack 12**

12. LARGE FLUTTER DOVES
4 X 2¾ in.
1002-W-1806   **$2.99 pack of 2**

13. WHITE BIRD ON STAND
4¾ in. high.
1316-W-1202   **$3.99 each**

14. PETITE WHITE BIRDS 2⅛ IN.
1316-W-1210   **$2.99 each**

15. KISSING LOVE BIRDS
Beak-to-beak romantics. 5½ in. high.
1002-W-206   **$4.99 each**

16. SMALL DOVES 2 X 1½ in.
1002-W-1710   **$1.99 pack of 12**

17. GLITTERED DOVES 2 x 1½ in. Coated
with non-edible glitter.
1006-W-166   **$1.69 pack of 12**

18. SERENE SWANS
A graceful and stately pair. 2½ in. high.
1002-W-11   **$1.99 pack of 2**

Beautiful Trims

1. NEW! PEARL BEADING
One of the most innovative creations to happen to cake decorating in years. With just one continuous row of pearls you can transform a beautiful cake into a glorious work of art. Stunning and easy to work with, these pearls will be a must for all serious decorators. Innovative new look for cakes and crafts. Have the beautiful lustre of pearls on one continuous 5 yard strand. Can be trimmed to size.
6 mm pearl   211-W-1990
$2.99 each
4 mm pearl   211-W-1989
$2.49 each

2. LOVE BIRD DOILY PANELS
Embossed white plastic frame, edged with lace, stands on pedestal base. 5¼ in. diam.
LAVENDER   205-W-3011
BLUE   205-W-3012
$4.99 each

3. CRYSTAL-LOOK HEARTS
5½ IN.   205-W-1674 $1.99 each
4¼ IN.   205-W-1672 $1.79 each

4. CURVED GOTHIC WINDOW
5 X 9 in. 2 pcs.
205-W-3059 $3.99 each

5. PICKET ARCHWAY
Gate swings. 5½ x 5¼ in.
205-W-344 $2.99 each

6. PETITE GARDEN HOUSE
5 X 9 in. Easy to assemble.
205-W-8298 $4.69 each

7. 6-PC. GOTHIC ARCH SET
Plastic pieces simply lock together for easy assembly. 10½ in. high.
205-W-3109 $4.99 set

8. OLD FASHIONED FENCE
2½ in. posts, 1 in. pegs, 144 snap-together links.
1107-W-8326 $2.49 set

9. LARGE DOUBLE WEDDING RINGS
3⅜ in. diameter
WHITE   201-W-1008 $1.99 each

Lacy Filigree

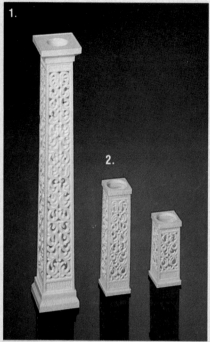

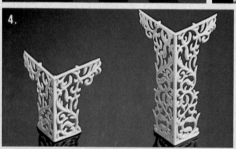

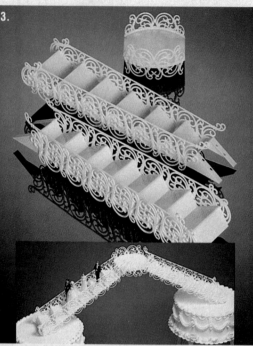

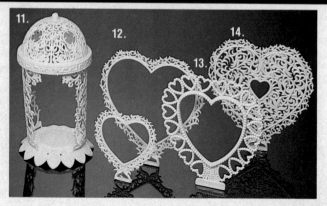

1. LACY-LOOK PILLAR
Just add ribbons or fabric to coordinate with bride's color scheme. 12-in. high.
303-W-8976 $2.99 each

2. SQUARE FILIGREE PILLARS
Airy, open design.
5 IN.   303-W-7717
$2.99 pack of 4
3 IN.   303-W-8071
$1.99 pack of 4

3. FILIGREE PLATFORM AND STAIRWAY SET
Bridge the gap between lavish tiers. Includes two stairways (16¾ in. long) and one platform (4¾ in. X 5. in.). White plastic.
205-W-2109 $11.99 Set
ONE STAIRWAY ONLY
205-W-1218 $4.99 each

4. SNAP-ON FILIGREE
Stoic Grecian pillars with a romantic touch.
FITS 3 IN. PILLARS
305-W-390 $1.59 pack of 4
FITS 5 IN. PILLARS
305-W-398 $1.99 pack of 4

5. FILIGREE FOUNTAIN FRAME
Perfect around the Kolor-Flo Fountain. Eight white plastic scallops snap together. 9 in. diameter. 3½ in. high.
205-W-1285 $2.99 each

6. SWIRLS
Variations on a delicate theme. Leaf-framed scrollwork. 1 X 2½ in.
1004-W-2100 $2.49 pack of 12

7. SCROLLS
Graceful flowing decorations. 2¾ X 1¼ in.
1004-W-2801 $2.29 pack of 24

8. LACY HEARTS
What delicate beauty. 3¾ X 3½ in.
1004-W-2306 $2.49 pack of 12

9. CURVED TRIANGLE
Dramatic addition. 3 X 3½ in.
1004-W-3001 $2.49 pack of 12

10. CONTOUR
Lattice and leaves. 3¾ X 2 ⅔ in.
1004-W-2003 $2.49 pack of 12

11. GARDEN GAZEBO
4 pcs. 4¼ X 8½ in.
205-W-4100 $4.69 each

12. FILIGREE HEARTS
7 IN. 205-W-1501 $2.69 pack of 3
4 IN. 205-W-1527 $1.69 pack of 3

13. 7 X 6½ IN. SEED PEARL HEART
205-W-1006 $3.69 pack of 3

14. LARGE FILIGREE HEART
7 x 6¾ IN.
1004-W-2208 $3.79 each

Angelic Bliss

1. ARCHED TIER SET*
Quite dramatic when used with Kolor-Flo Fountain. Includes: Six 13 in. arched columns and now with two super strong 18 in. round Decorator Preferred Separator Plates and six angelic cherubs to attach to columns with royal icing or glue.
301-W-1982 $44.99 set
18 IN. DECORATOR PREFERRED PLATE
302-W-18 $10.99 each
13 IN. PILLARS
303-W-9719 $3.99 each
13 IN. PILLARS
Save $4.95 on pack of six.
301-W-9809 $18.99 pack

2. HARVEST CHERUB SEPARATOR SET
Includes four 7 in. Harvest Cherub pillars, two 9 in. separator plates (lower plate has 12 in. overall diameter).
301-W-3517 $11.99 set

3. DANCING CUPID PILLARS
5½ in. high.
303-W-1210 $7.99 pack of 4

4. SNAP-ON CHERUBS
Accent Corinthian and Grecian pillars. (Pillars not included.) 3½ in. high.
305-W-4104 $1.29 pack of 4

5. FROLICKING CHERUB
Animated character. 5 in. high.
1001-W-244 $2.79 each

6. WINGED ANGELS
Fluttering fancies. A pair per package. 2½ X 2 in.
1001-W-457 $1.80 per package

7. MUSICAL TRIO
Setting just the right mood. Each 3 in. high.
1001-W-368 $2.29 pack of 3

8. KNEELING CHERUB FOUNTAIN
Beautiful when accented with tinted piping gel and flowers. 4 in. high.
1001-W-9380 $1.99 each

9. ANGELINOS
Heavenly addition to wedding, birthday and holiday cakes. 2 X 3 in.
1001-W-504 $3.29 pack of 6

10. CHERUB CARD HOLDER
What unique place makers, too. (Cards not included.) 1⅝ X 3⅜ in.
1001-W-9374 $3.49 pack of 4

11. ANGEL WITH HARP
Striking the perfect chord. 3½ in. high.
1001-W-7029 $4.49 pack of 4

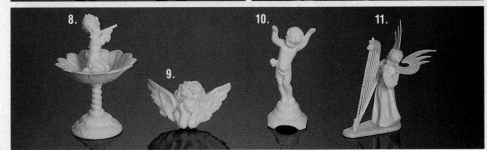

161

Majestic Enhancers

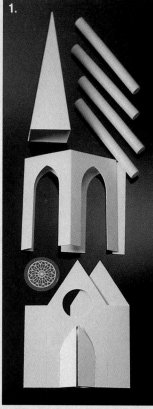

1. CATHEDRAL CAKE KIT
Transform basic wedding cakes into dramatic masterpieces. Kit includes: 5 easy-to-assemble white church pieces, 4 white plastic cake supports and a church window that can be illuminated from within.
2104-W-2940 $12.99 Kit

2. CRYSTAL-CLEAR CAKE DIVIDER SET
White plastic separator plates; ½ in. diameter 7½ in. high; clear plastic twist legs penetrate cake and rest on plate (dowel rods not needed). Includes 6 in., 8 in., 10 in. 12 in. 14 in., 16 in plates plus 24 legs. Save 25% on set.
301-W-9450 $45.99 set

Plates	Number	Price
6 IN.	302-W-9730	$ 2.99 each
8 IN.	302-W-9749	$ 3.99 each
10 IN.	302-W-9757	$ 4.99 each
12 IN.	302-W-9765	$ 6.99 each
14 IN.	302-W-9773	$ 8.99 each
16 IN.	302-W-9780	$10.99 each

7½ IN. TWIST LEGS
303-W-9794 $3.99 pack of 4
9 IN. TWIST LEGS   Add more height.
303-W-977 $3.99 pack of 4

3. TALL TIER STAND SET
Five twist-apart columns 6½ in. high with 1 bottom and 1 top bolt; 18 in. footed base plate; 16 in., 14 in., 12 in., 10 in., 8 in separator plates (interchangeable, except footed base plate). White plastic. Save 25% on set.
304-W-7915 $45.99 set

Plates	Number	Price
8 IN.	302-W-7894	$ 3.99 each
10 IN.	302-W-7908	$ 4.99 each
12 IN.	302-W-7924	$ 5.99 each
14 IN.	302-W-7940	$ 8.99 each
16 IN.	302-W-7967	$11.99 each
18 IN.	302-W-7983	$14.99 each

COLUMNS
6½ IN.	303-W-7910	$1.59 each
7¾ IN.	304-W-5009	$2.59 each
13½ IN.	303-W-703	$4.29 each

TOP COLUMN CAP NUT
304-W-7923   79¢ each
GLUE-ON PLATE LEGS
304-W-7930   59¢ each
BOTTOM COLUMN BOLT
304-W-7941   99¢ each

4. FLOATING TIERS CAKE STAND SET
Display three tiers on this graceful metal cake stand. Fast and easy to use! Set includes stand and 8 in., 12 in., 16 in. smooth-edged separator plates.
307-W-825 $59.99 set
Additional plates available (same plates as Crystal-Clear Cake Divider Set).

Plates	Number	Price
8 IN.	302-W-9749	$ 3.99 each
12 IN.	302-W-9765	$ 6.99 each
16 IN.	302-W-9780	$10.99 each

5. TALL TIER 4-ARM BASE STAND
Replace Tall Tier Base Plate (See No. 3) with this heavy-duty white plastic support; add separator plates up to 12 in. For proper balance, add up to 3 graduated tiers to center column. Includes base bolt.
304-W-8245 $11.99 each
BASE BOLT ONLY
304-W-8253   59¢ each

6. CAKE CORER TUBE
Prepare tiers quickly and neatly for the Tall Tier Stand column. Serrated edge removes cake centers with one push. Ice cake before using. 7 in. long solid center fits into 6½ in. long hollow corer to eject cake bits. Cleans easily.
304-W-8172 $1.99 each

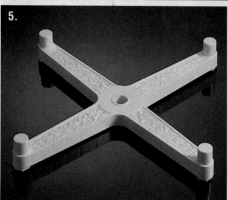

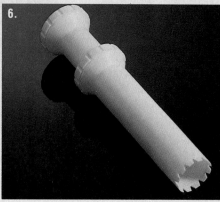

1. CRYSTAL BRIDGE AND GRACEFUL STAIRWAY SET

Create a dramatic masterpiece. Includes two stairways (16¾ in. long) and one platform (4¾ in. X 5 in). Plastic.

205-W-2311 $14.99 set
ONE STAIRWAY ONLY
205-W-2315 $7.99 each

2. THE KOLOR-FLO FOUNTAIN

Cascading waterfall with shimmering lights is the most dramatic way to underscore elegant formal tiers. Water pours from three levels. Top levels can be removed for smaller fountain arrangement. Intricate lighting system with two bulbs for extra brilliance. Plastic fountain bowl is 9¾ in. diameter. 110-124v. A.C. motor with 65 in. cord. Pumps water electrically. Directions and replacement part information included.

306-W-2599 $89.99 each
Replacement Parts

Pump	306-W-1002	$34.99
Piston	306-W-1029	$ 2.99
Pump/Bulb Bracket	306-W-1037	$ 2.79
Lamp Socket	306-W-1045	$ 4.49
Light Bulb	306-W-1053	$ 2.49
Cascade/Pump Connector	306-W-1088	$ 2.29
Floater Switch	306-W-1096	$11.99
Upper Cascade	306-W-1118	$ 6.99
Middle Cascade	306-W-1126	$ 7.99
Lower Cascade	306-W-1134	$ 8.99
Bowl	306-W-1142	$12.99
Bottom Base	306-W-1169	$ 6.99

3. FOUNTAIN CASCADE SET

Dome shapes redirect water over their surface in nonstop streams. Set includes 4 pieces; 2½, 4½, 8 and 11½ in. diameter. (Kolor-Flo Fountain sold separately.)

306-W-1172 $14.99 set

4. FLOWER HOLDER RING

White plastic. 12½ in. dia. X 2 in. high. Put at base of Kolor-Flo Fountain.

305-W-435 $4.99 each

5. CRYSTAL-LOOK TIER SET

Teams with the Kolor-Flo Fountain. Plastic. Two 17" plates; four 13¾" pillars.

301-W-1387 $39.99 set
17 IN. CRYSTAL-LOOK PLATE
(Use only with 13¾ in. crystal pillars.)
302-W-1810 $13.99 each
13¾ IN. CRYSTAL-LOOK PILLAR
(Use only with 17 in. crystal plate.)
303-W-2242 $3.99 each

6. CRYSTAL-LOOK PLATES

Use with crystal-look pillars.

7 IN.	302-W-2013	$2.99 each
9 IN.	302-W-2035	$3.99 each
11 IN.	302-W-2051	$4.99 each
13 IN.	302-W-2078	$6.99 each

7. CRYSTAL-LOOK BOWL

Perfect for blooms. 4½ X 1½ in. deep.

205-W-1404 $2.69 each

8. CRYSTAL-LOOK SPIKED PILLARS

Double cake circles for support.

7 IN.	303-W-2322	$3.99 pack of 4
9 IN.	303-W-2324	$4.99 pack of 4

9. CRYSTAL-LOOK PILLARS

Combine with crystal-look plates and Crystal Bridge and Stairway Set.

7 IN.	303-W-2197	$3.99 pack of 4
5 IN.	303-W-2196	$3.99 pack of 4
3 IN.	303-W-2171	$2.99 pack of 4

Note: The cut crystal design and slender railings of this set are fragile. Please take special care when using and storing them to prevent damage.

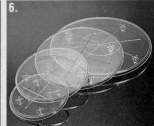

10. IRIDESCENT GRAPES 2" high
1099-W-200 $3.79 pack of 4

11. IRIDESCENT DOVES 2" wide
1002-W-509 $3.49 pack of 6

All plastic products made in Hong Kong. Kolor-Flo Fountain made in Germany.

Pillars

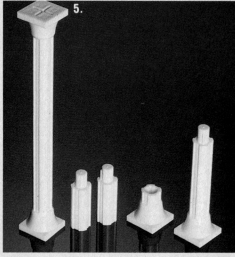

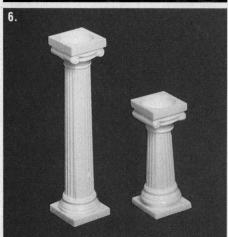

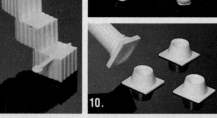

1. ARCHED PILLARS
Grecian-inspired with arched support.
4½ IN. 303-W-452 $2.99 pack of 4
6½ IN. 303-W-657 $4.99 pack of 4

2. CORINTHIAN PILLARS
Resemble authentic Greek columns.
5 IN. 303-W-819 $3.59 pack of 4
7 IN. 303-W-800 $4.59 pack of 4

3. ROMAN COLUMNS
Handsome pillars may be used with Kolor-Flo Fountain (remove one fountain tier if using 10¼ in.).
13¾ IN. 303-W-2129 $2.99 each
10¼ IN. 303-W-8135 $2.59 each

4. SIX-COLUMN TIER SET
NOW! Includes six 13¾-in. Roman columns and two super strong 18-in. round Decorator Preferred™ Separator Plates. A lovely set to use with the Kolor-Flo Fountain. White plastic.
301-W-1981 $34.99 set
13¾ IN. ROMAN PILLARS
303-W-2129 $2.99 each
DECORATOR PREFERRED PLATE
18 IN. 302-W-18 $10.99 each

5. EXPANDABLE PILLARS
Column is made up of six individual sections, adjustable from 3 ins. to 10 ins. high!
303-W-1777 $8.99 pack of 4

6. GRECIAN PILLARS
Elegantly scrolled and ribbed.
5 IN. 303-W-3703 $2.99 pack of 4
3 IN. 303-W-3606 $1.99 pack of 4

7. PLASTIC PEGS
Insure that cake layers and separator plates atop cakes stay in place. These pegs do not add support, so dowel rod cake properly before using (see page 106). 4 in. long.
399-W-762 $1.44 set of 12

8. STAIRSTEPS
24 1 in. high stairs with 3 in. candleholders.
1107-W-8180 $5.49 set

9. SEPARATOR PLATE FEET
Queen Anne-inspired feet fit all separator plates.
301-W-1247 $1.59 pack of 4

10. PLASTIC STUD PLATES
Just glue on to sturdy cardboard cake circles to create separator plate. Real money-savers, especially when cake is to be given away. Fit all white (not crystal) pillars, except 13 in. Arched Pillars.
301-W-119 $1.79 pack of 8

11. GRECIAN SPIKED PILLARS
Eliminate the need for separator plates on tier tops. Push into cake to rest on separator plate or cake circle beneath. Now, wider diameter bottom for increased stability. To prevent pillars from going through, double cake boards, or use separator plate when cakes are stacked.
9 IN. 303-W-3712 $3.99 pack
7 IN. 303-W-3710 $2.99 pack
5 IN. 303-W-3708 $1.99 pack

12. SUPER STRONG CAKE STAND
Holds up to 185 pounds of cake! High impact polystyrene and underweb of ribbing make stand super strong. 2¾ in. high. 18 in. diameter for larger cakes.
307-W-1200 $12.99 each

Classic Tiers

NEW!
DISPOSABLE
SINGLE PLATE SYSTEM
The Baker's Best Disposable Separator System features sturdy plates, pillars and adjustable pillar rings. Made of recyclable plastic.

1. DISPOSABLE PLATES
6 IN. PLATE
302-W-4000 $1.49 each
8 IN. PLATE
302-W-4002 $1.99 each
10 IN. PLATE
302-W-4004 $2.89 each
12 IN. PLATE
302-W-4006 $3.79 each

DISPOSABLE PILLARS WITH RINGS
7 IN. PILLARS WITH RINGS (4 each)
303-W-4000 $2.59 pack of 4
9 IN. PILLARS WITH RINGS (4 each)
303-W-4001 $2.69 pack of 4

2. 54-PC. GRECIAN PILLAR AND PLATE SET
Deluxe collection provides you with Decorator Preferred™ scalloped-edged separator plates and 5 inch pillars. Includes: 2 each 6, 8, 10, 12 and 14 inch plates; 20 Grecian pillars; and 24 pegs.
301-W-8380 $45.99 set

3. CLASSIC SEPARATOR PLATE SETS
Grecian pillars and scalloped-edged plates in 4 plate diameters and 2 pillar heights. Set includes 2 Decorator Preferred™ Plates. 4 pillars and 4 pegs.
6 IN. PLATE SET WITH 3 IN. PILLARS
2103-W-639 $5.99 set
8 IN. PLATE SET WITH 5-IN. PILLARS
2103-W-256 $6.99 set
10 IN. PLATE SET WITH 5-IN. PILLARS
2103-W-108 $8.99 set
12 IN. PLATE SET WITH 5-IN. PILLARS
2103-W-124 $10.99 set

4. SWAN PILLARS
Grecian pillars with romantic swan base add flowering grace to your masterpiece. 4 in. high.
303-W-7725 $2.99 pack of 4

5. PLASTIC DOWEL RODS
Heavy-duty hollow plastic; strong sanitary support for all tiered cakes. Can be cut with serrated knife to desired length. 12¾ in. long x ¾ in. diameter.
399-W-801 $1.99 pack of 4

6. WOODEN DOWEL RODS
Essential for supporting stacked cakes and tiers. Complete assembling instructions, on page 106. Cut and sharpen with strong sheers and knife. 12 in. long, ¼ in. wide.
399-W-1009 $1.99 pack of 12

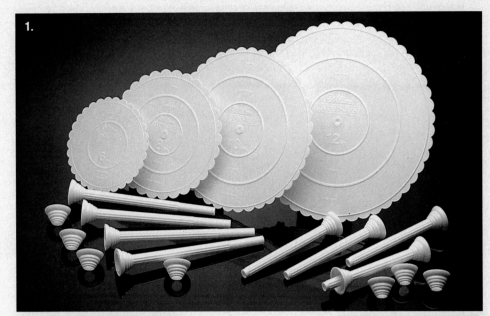
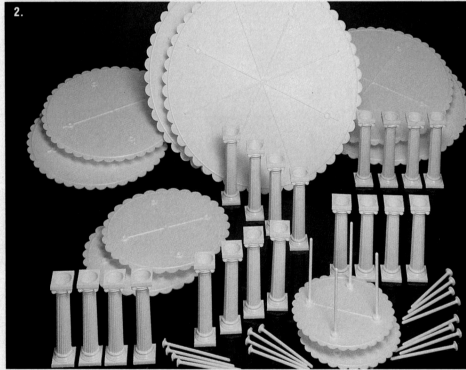

Separator Plates

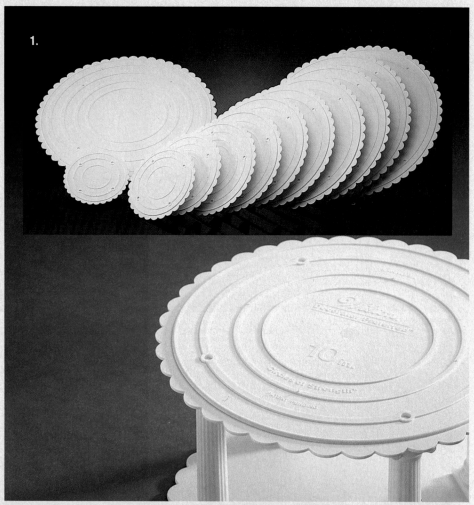

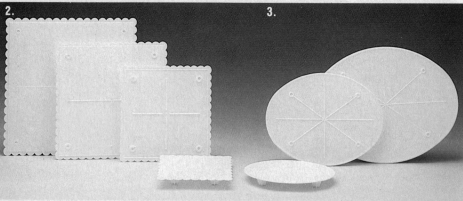

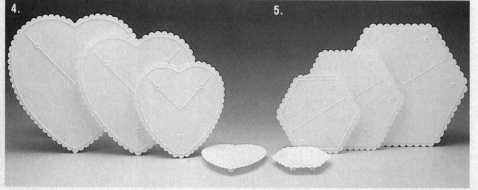

1. DECORATOR PREFERRED™ ROUND SEPARATOR PLATES

Guaranteed non-breakable round plates. Exclusive, patented Wilton Circles of Strength™ construction distributes the cake weight evenly. Scalloped edge is interchangeable and compatible with other Wilton separator plates and pillars. Sizes are clearly marked on each plate for easy identification. Plain, smooth back.

6 IN.	302-W-6	$1.99 each
7 IN.	302-W-7	$2.19 each
8 IN.	302-W-8	$2.49 each
9 IN.	302-W-9	$2.99 each
10 IN.	302-W-10	$3.49 each
11 IN.	302-W-11	$3.99 each
12 IN.	302-W-12	$4.49 each
13 IN.	302-W-13	$5.19 each
14 IN.	302-W-14	$5.49 each
15 IN.	302-W-15	$6.69 each
16 IN.	302-W-16	$7.49 each
18 IN.	302-W-18	$10.99 each

2. SQUARE SEPARATOR PLATES

Edges are gracefully scalloped.

7 IN.	302-W-1004	$2.99 each
9 IN.	302-W-1020	$3.99 each
11 IN.	302-W-1047	$4.99 each
13 IN.	302-W-1063	$5.99 each

3. OVAL SEPARATOR PLATES

Worry-free support for oval tiers.

8½ IN. x 6 IN.	302-W-2130	$3.99 each
11½ IN. x 8½ IN.	302-W-2131	$4.99 each
14½ IN. x 10¾ IN.	302-W-2132	$5.99 each

4. HEART SEPARATOR PLATES

Delicately edged with scallops. Perfect with our Heart Pan cakes.

8 IN.	302-W-2112	$2.99 each
11 IN.	302-W-2114	$3.99 each
14½ IN.	302-W-2116	$7.99 each
16½ IN.	302-W-2118	$8.99 each

5. HEXAGON SEPARATOR PLATES

Scalloped-edged; combine with hexagon, square or round pans.

7 IN.	302-W-1705	$2.99 each
10 IN.	302-W-1748	$3.99 each
13 IN.	302-W-1764	$5.99 each
16 IN.	302-W-1799	$7.99 each

PLEASE NOTE: All prices, certain products and services, reflect the U.S.A. domestic market and do not apply in Australia and Canada.

1. ROUND TIER SET
The perfect choice for engagement parties, anniversaries, religious occasions and more. Set includes 5 x 2½ in., 7⅛ x 2½ in. and 9 5/16 x 2⅝ in. aluminum rounds; eight 5 in. Grecian Spiked Pillars; 6 and 8 in. scallop-edged round white plastic separator plates; instructions. Takes 2 cake mixes.
2105-W-2531 $21.99 set

2. ROUND MINI-TIER SET
Takes one cake mix. Set includes 5, 6 and 8 in. round, 1 in. deep aluminum pans; 5, 7 in. separator plates; 8 clear plastic twist legs; decorating instructions.
2105-W-98042 $10.99 set
ROUND MINI-TIER PLATE SET ONLY
301-W-9817 $2.99 set

3. CLASSIC ROUND PAN SET
Set includes 6, 8, 10 and 12 in. aluminum pans. 2 in. deep.
2105-W-2101 $22.99 set

4. 2-PC. OVAL PAN SET
Set includes two 9 x 6¾ x 1¾ in. aluminum pans.
2105-W-1553 $9.99 set

5. 4-PC. OVAL PAN SET
Set includes four 2 in. deep aluminum pans. Sizes are 7¾ x 5⅝ in.; 10¾ x 7⅞ in.; 13 x 9⅞ in.; 16 x 12⅜ in.
2105-W-2130 $22.99 set

6. BEVEL PAN SET
Bakes beveled cake edges that can be positioned with layers. Set includes 8, 10, 12 in. tops and 14 and 16 in. base aluminum pans.
517-W-1200 $25.99 set

7. 3-IN. DEEP ROUND PAN SET
Set includes 8, 10, 12, 14 in. aluminum pans.
2105-W-2932 $31.99 set

8. 4-PC. HEXAGON PAN SET
Set includes 6, 9, 12, 15 in. aluminum pans, 2 in. deep.
2105-W-3572 $26.99 set
Individual pans available.
(not shown)
9 IN. x 2 IN.
2105-W-5125 $6.99 each
12 IN. x 2 IN.
2105-W-5133 $8.99 each

9. PETAL PANS
Also available
9 IN. x 2 IN.
2105-W-5109 $6.99
12 IN. x 2 IN.
2105-W-5117 $8.99

10. 4-PC. PETAL PAN SET
Set includes 6, 9, 12 and 15 in., 2 in. deep aluminum.
2105-W-2134 $26.99 set

Plastic products made in Hong Kong.

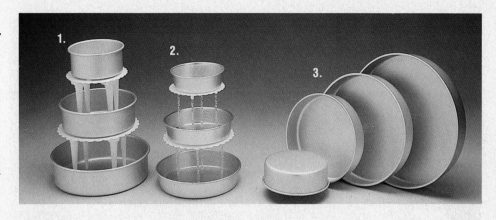

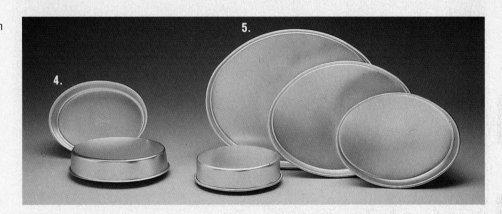

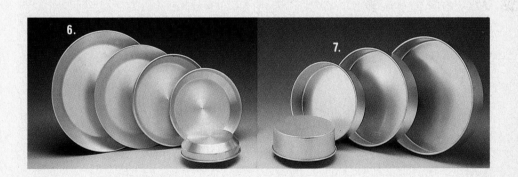

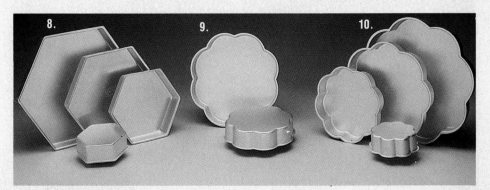

Performance Pans

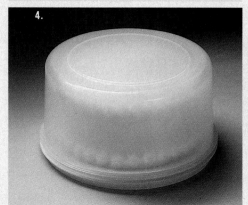

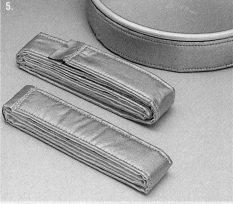

1. ROUND PANS...
A TIMELESS CLASSIC
With any number of pans, your decorating options will be never-ending.
2 IN. DEEP

16 IN. ROUND
2105-W-3963 $14.99 each
14 IN. ROUND
2105-W-3947 $11.99 each
12 IN. ROUND
2105-W-2215 $8.99 each
10 IN. ROUND
2105-W-2207 $6.49 each
8 IN. ROUND
2105-W-2193 $5.49 each
7 IN. ROUND
2105-W-2190 $5.29 each
6 IN. ROUND
2105-W-2185 $4.99 each

2. 9 IN. ROUND PAN SET
Bake two 9 in. layer cakes at one time. Great Value! Easy to store.
2105-W-7908 $9.99 set of 2

3. 3 IN. DEEP
Bake impressive high cakes. Perfect for tortes, fruit and pound cakes, and cakes to be covered with fondant icing.
8 IN. ROUND
2105-W-9104 $6.99 each
10 IN. ROUND
2105-W-9945 $8.99 each

4. CAKE SAVER
Designed to carry most elaborately decorated cakes. Generous size accommodates borders and top decorations easily. Use to carry or store all types of cakes, including bundt, angel food, cheese cakes, even pies, as well as layer cakes. Maintains freshness. Wide enough for a 10 in. cake with borders or a 12 in. cake without borders. Includes one 14 in. round base and one 6 in. high cover.
415-W-905 $9.99 each

5. BAKE-EVEN CAKE STRIPS
At last, an innovative way to bake perfectly level, moist cakes. Avoid high-rise centers, cracked tops or crusty edges. Just dampen strips and wrap around the pan before baking. Each band is 1½ in. wide x 30 in. long, with 1 in. overlap.

SMALL SET
Contains 2 bands, enough for two 8 or 9 in. round pans.
415-W-260 $5.49 set

LARGE SET
Contains 4 bands, enough for one of each of the following: 10, 12, 14 and 16 in. round pans.
415-W-262 $13.99 set

PERFORMANCE PANS

Depend on Wilton Performance Pans Premium Bakeware for baking your very best. You'll achieve repeated success with these professional-quality anodized aluminum pans. Not only are they durable, they're dishwasher safe. An unequaled variety of sizes and shapes gives you countless possibilities. Whether you're creating tall-tiered cakes or roasting prime rib, you can depend on Performance Pans for the finest results.

6. SQUARE PANS ... THE SHAPE OF SUCCESS

The most basic shape to bake plain or fancy cakes. A variety of sizes to create a first-class feast from bread to dessert. 2 in. deep.

16 IN. SQUARE
2105-W-8231 $15.99 **each**
14 IN. SQUARE
2105-W-8220 $13.99 **each**
12 IN. SQUARE
2105-W-8213 $10.99 **each**
10 IN SQUARE
2105-W-8205 $8.49 **each**
8 IN. SQUARE
2105-W-8191 $6.49 **each**
6 IN. SQUARE
507-W-2180 $4.99 **each**

7. 9 x 13 CAKE PAN COVER

Just the protection you need when transporting decorated cakes. Designed for use with the Wilton 9 x 13 in. Performance Pan*, this cover has raised dome lid which allows you to cover decorated cakes with ease. Keeps cakes and other foods fresh in the pan, even after slicing.

415-W-903 $3.99 each

*Cake pan not included

8. SHEET PANS ... BAKING ESSENTIALS

A must-have for the all-around cook and baker. The versatility coupled with dependability makes these pans the ones to always have on hand. 2 in. deep.

12 x 18 IN. SHEET
2105-W-182 $12.99 **each**
11 x 15 IN. SHEET
2105-W-158 $10.99 **each**
9 x 13 IN. SHEET**
2105-W-1308 $6.99 **each**
7 x 11 IN. SHEET
2105-W-2304 $5.99 **each**

**Cover cakes-to-go and leftovers with the Wilton Cake Pan Cover sold above. Made of natural polypropylene, this is a "must have" for anyone who takes cakes to picnics and get-togethers.

OVENCRAFT™
Professional Bakeware

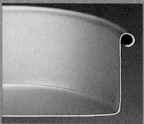

PROFESSIONAL DURABILITY
▽ Extra thick aluminum provides lifetime performance. Square sheet pans are .060-.065" thick. (Ordinary bakeware average is .015).
▽ Heavy weight never warps and withstands years of heavy use.
▽ High-quality aluminum evenly distributes heat for superior baking results.

PROFESSIONAL DESIGN
▽ Perfectly straight sides and precise 90° corners on squares and sheet pans bake beautiful straight-sided desserts and cakes.
▽ Welded corners provide lifetime durability.
▽ Designed with extra depth, versus ordinary bakeware, to reduce overflow of juices and desserts, insuring professional results.
▽ Four-sided lip on square and sheet pans makes lifting and handling much easier.

PROFESSIONAL FINISH
▽ Anodized aluminum finish will not rust, discolor, chip, crack, pit or peel.
▽ Smooth finish is very easy to clean.
▽ Smooth finish releases food quickly and evenly.

For the professional results you demand, begin with a professional pan – the Ovencraft Pan.

SHEET PANS
Discover endless options with this multi-use pan. 2³⁄₁₆ in. depth.
12 x 18 IN.
2105-W-5618   **$16.99 each**
11 x 15 IN.
2105-W-5617   **$14.99 each**
9 x 13 IN.
2105-W-5616   **$11.99 each**

3 IN. DEEP ROUND PANS
Bake beautiful, tall cakes.

18 x 3 IN. HALF-ROUND
Use to bake an 18 in. round cake in a conventional oven.
2105-W-5622   **$12.99 each**
14 x 3 IN.
2105-W-5610   **$12.99 each**
12 x 3 IN.
2105-W-5609   **$10.99 each**
10 x 3 IN.
2105-W-5608   **$8.99 each**
8 x 3 IN.
2105-W-5607   **$6.99 each**
6 x 3 IN.
2105-W-5620   **$4.99 each**

2 IN. DEEP ROUND PANS
Ideal for two-layer cakes and tier cakes.
16 x 2 IN.
2105-W-5606   **$14.99 each**
14 x 2 IN.
2105-W-5605   **$11.99 each**
12 x 2 IN.
2105-W-5604   **$8.99 each**
10 x 2 IN.
2105-W-5603   **$6.49 each**
9 x 2 IN.
2105-W-5619   **$5.99 each**
8 x 2 IN.
2105-W-5602   **$5.49 each**
6 x 2 IN.
2105-W-5601   **$4.99 each**

SQUARE PANS
Perfectly square corners and 2³⁄₁₆ in. depth produce professional quality cakes.
14 IN.
2105-W-5614   **$16.99 each**
12 IN.
2105-W-5613   **$13.99 each**
10 IN.
2105-W-5612   **$10.99 each**
8 IN.
2105-W-5611   **$7.99 each**

Dessert Molds

with lots of possibilities!

Delicious microwave cakes bake up in minutes. Gelatin salads, molded mousse and ice cream desserts take shape and come out great! Made in USA.

All are top-rack dishwasher-safe.

$3.49 each

TEDDY BEAR
2106-W-108

BIG BIRD*
2106-W-116

NEW! SPEEDY BUNNY
2106-W-138

CLOWN
2106-W-114

STAR
2106-W-110

FLAN
2106-W-112

RING
2106-W-118

FANCY RING
2106-W-124

ROUND
2106-W-100

CHRISTMAS TREE
2106-W-122

MINI HEART
2106-W-120

HEART
2106-W-106

SQUARE
2106-W-102

JUMBO MUFFIN
2106-W-130

SHORTCAKES 'N TREATS
2106-W-126

DOUBLE-MIX RECTANGLE
2106-W-104

Microwave Baking

Refrigerated Salad Molds

Molded Mousse

Microwave baking: Use your favorite microwave cake or dessert mix. Bake and decorate according to directions on our label.

Molding gelatin salads: Each holds a large package of gelatin and desired fruit. Follow recipe and molding instructions on gelatin box.

Molding mousse: Use your favorite recipe for molded mousse. Holds approximately 6 cups. Unmold per recipe instructions.

Molding ice cream: Place pan in freezer to chill. Soften a half-gallon of ice cream for 30 seconds on high in microwave. Place into a large bowl and stir until softened (not runny). Pack into pan and cover with plastic wrap or aluminum foil. Freeze overnight. Alternate method: Line chilled pan with plastic wrap and pour in ice cream. To unmold: Loosen sides with a straight-edge spatula. Wrap a warm, damp cloth around sides for a few seconds. Unmold onto serving plate; wrap well and return to freezer. Note: Basic shapes work best for molding ice cream.

Ice Cream Molding

Insulated Bakeware

INSULATED BAKEWARE
Now your cookies and delicate baked goods will brown, not burn, with Even-Bake™ Insulated Cookie Sheets. A layer of air insulates and separates two sheets of high quality aluminum. The bottom protects the top from direct, intense heat. Baked goods brown evenly on top and bottom.

1. EVEN-BAKE COOKIE SHEETS
Easy to clean. They are dishwasher-safe and fully immersible.
10½ x 15½ IN. COOKIE SHEET
2105-W-2646 $12.99 each
13 x 17 IN. COOKIE SHEET
2105-W-2644 $14.99 each

EVEN-BAKE JELLY ROLL PAN
It has an extra layer of air in the side walls to minimize crowning on cakes. 10½ x 15½ x 1⅛ in.
2105-W-2650 $17.99 each

Browns Evenly
An insulating layer of air protects baked goods from direct heat to promote even browning on top and bottom.

Dishwasher-Safe
Easy to clean. An exclusive patent pending system allows pans to be immersed in water or placed in dishwasher.

Durable Aluminum
High quality, durable aluminum will not warp or rust. The smooth finish aids in easy cookie release.

Basic Bakeware

2. JUMBO MUFFIN PAN
Bake super-size cupcakes and muffins. Aluminum, 13½ in. x 9¼ in.
2105-W-1820 $12.99 each

3. JUMBO BAKE CUPS
Paper liners for use with large size muffin pans. 50 per carton.
415-W-1113 $1.59 carton

4. SIX-CUP MUFFIN PAN
From muffins to cupcakes, desserts. Aluminum, 7⅜ x 10¾ x 1 in. deep.
2105-W-5338 $6.99 each

5. MUFFIN BAKE CUPS
Paper liners for use with standard size muffin pans. 75 per carton.
415-W-1115 $1.59 carton

6. MINI-MUFFIN PAN
Make mini mouthwatering delights. Muffins, fruit cakes, cupcakes, cheesecakes, more. Aluminum; 7¾ x 10 x ¾ in.
2105-W-2125 $6.99 each

7. MINI-MUFFIN CUPS
Paper liners for use with mini muffin pans. 100 per carton.
415-W-1117 $1.59 carton

8. SHORTCAKES 'N TREATS PAN
It's easy to make brownies, ice cream, gelatin and lots of other original treats. Aluminum; 12½ x 1 in. deep.
2105-W-5966 $6.99 each

Basic & Specialty Bakeware

1. 9 IN. SPRINGFORM PAN
Rich cheesecakes come out easily. Release springlock, remove sides and serve. The waffle- textured surface insures baking success. Aluminum, 3 in. deep.
2105-W-5354 $10.99 each

2. 6 IN. SPRINGFORM PAN
Unique smaller size with waffle-textured surface. Quality non-stick finish on heavy gauge steel. 3 in. deep.
2105-W-218 $6.99 each

9 IN. SPRINGFORM PAN
Quality non-stick finish on heavy gauge steel. Waffle-textured surface, 3 in. deep.
2105-W-219 $9.99 each

3. SHELL PAN
Include simple elegance in your collection of bakeware. With the recipe for delicate lemon cake printed on the label, create a delectable dessert topped with gorgeous yellow fondant. Here's a shaped pan that you'll turn to time and time again. Aluminum pan is 11 x 12 in.
2105-W-8250 $9.99 each

4. VIENNESE SWIRL PAN
Create elegant continental style desserts. Aluminum, 11½ in. diameter.
2105-W-8252 $9.99 each

5. FANCY RING MOLD/PAN
This unique pan offers a menu of cakes, gelatins, ice cream, mousse, more! Anodized aluminum, 10 in. diameter, 3 in. deep and takes 1 standard bundt-type cake mix.
2105-W-5008 $9.99 each

6. PETITE FANCY RING MOLD/PAN
Impressive desserts in dramatic individual servings. Aluminum is 14⅝ x 9¾ in.
2105-W-2097 $16.99 each

7. RING MOLDS/PANS
Two great sizes. Aluminum, each 3 in. deep.
8 IN. RING MOLD/PAN
2105-W-190 $6.49 each
10 IN. RING MOLD/PAN
2105-W-4013 $7.99 each

8. CONTINENTAL FLAN
So many international recipes are possible with this elegant pan. Aluminum, 11-in. diameter.
2105-W-2046 $7.99 each

9. ANGEL FOOD PAN
It even bakes pound or fruit cake. 2-piece, 10-in. diameter, 4½-in. deep. Aluminum. Lift inner core sleeve for easy cake removal. Takes 1 standard angel or chiffon cake mix.
2105-W-2525 $13.99 each

10. LONG LOAF PAN
Bake classic cakes or angel food. Takes 9 cups of batter or standard angel food mix. Aluminum; 16 in. x 4 in. x 4½ in.
2105-W-1588 $9.99 each

11. LOAF PAN
Perfect for sandwich loaf, cakes, bread, more. Aluminum, 8¾ in. x 4¼ in. x 2¾ in.
2105-W-3688 $5.99 each

12. MINI LOAF PAN SET
Great for individual-sized nut breads, cakes. Aluminum, 10¾ x 12¼ in.
2105-W-3844 $15.99 each

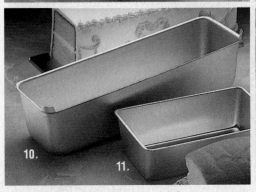

All Occasion Pans

SHOOTING STAR PAN
Write your warm wishes in the skies. Have a shooting star convey your thoughts. Whether it's the Pot of Gold at the rainbow's end or a meteor shower of happy greetings, our pan fits the bill. One mix aluminum pan is 15½ x 10 in.
2105-W-804 $9.99 each

STAR PAN
What better way to honor the celebrity in your life! Brighten birthdays, opening nights, even law enforcement occasions. New possibilities always emerging. One-mix aluminum pan is 12¾-in. across.
2105-W-2512 $9.99 each

WONDER MOLD KIT
In every season you'll find use for this shape at the greatest affairs—birthdays, graduations and bridal showers. Use the mold alone or as a part of another cake design. Aluminum pan (8-in. diam., 5-in. deep) takes 5-6 cups of firm-textured batter. Heat-conducting rod assures even baking. Kit contains pan, rod, stand, 7-in. doll pick and instructions.
2105-W-565 $11.99 kit

TEEN DOLL PICK
7-in. tall, same as in kit.
2815-W-101 $2.99 each

PETITE DOLL PAN
Couple this aluminum pan with Small Doll Picks for a quartet of party treats. Alone, it lends itself to all sorts of inventive cakes ideas. Great assembled with the Wonder Mold Kit as a color-coordinated bridal party centerpiece. One cake mix yields 4 to 6 cakes.
508-W-302 $9.99 each

SMALL DOLL PICKS
4½-in. on pick.
1511-W-1019 $4.99 pack of 4

NEW! LITTLE TRAIN PAN

The new little birthday and all-occasion train packs a cargo load of fun for party guests and the guest of honor. Lots of fun on board. One-mix aluminum pan is 8¾ x 15¾ x 2 in. Instructions included.

2105-W-6500 $9.99 each

CHOO CHOO TRAIN PAN

Here's the little 3-D engine that could-pulling through again with a trainload of uses. All aboard! Two-part aluminum pan snaps together. Pan is 10 x 6 x 4-in. Takes 6 cups of firm-textured batter. Instructions included.

2105-W-2861 $10.99 each

18-WHEELER TRUCK PAN

Why not go mobile with tons of warm wishes? It's easy to deliver a special greeting on Dad's Day, moving day and at life's major milestones. One-mix aluminum pan is 8¾ x 17 x 2-in.

2105-W-0018 $9.99 each

UP 'N AWAY BALLOON PAN

Get carried away in celebration for all your high-flying events. This cake also successfully transports greetings of ''congratulations'' and ''bon voyage'' Four ways to decorate included on label. One-mix aluminum pan is 14½ x 10½ x1⅞-in.

2105-W-1898 $9.99 each

GUMBALL MACHINE PAN

Children of all ages can't resist the lure of the gumball machine. In cake and colorful icing, it will be even more irresistible. The alternate decorating ideas are equally exciting. Takes one cake mix. 8 x 13½-in.

2105-W-2858 $9.99 each

All Occasion Pans

DOUBLE BELL PAN
Chime in the best of times. Future brides, anniversary couples and Christmas merry-makers will love having this cake made for them. One-mix aluminum pan is 13½ x 10½ x 2-in.
2105-W-1537 $9.99 each

MINI-BELL PAN
Six cakes baked at once that ring true with the festive spirit! A classic shape for birthdays, Christmas and wedding showers. The single-serving size can also be set on larger cakes with remarkable results. Aluminum pan is 9½ x 13 in.
2105-W-8254 $9.99 each

BOOK PAN
Special greetings in black and white, or whatever colors you choose. This open book details every one of life's important chapters—birthdays, baby showers, graduations and much more. Create a colorful greeting card cake, too. Five ways to decorate included. One-mix aluminum pan is 13 x 9½ x 2-in.
2105-W-972 $9.99 each

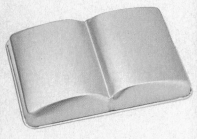

TWO-MIX BOOK PAN
Bake a cake of epic proportions. For larger parties, this great volume serves up to 30 guests. The story unfolds as the crowd gathers to celebrate most any major occasion. Aluminum pan is 11½ x 15 x 2¾ in.
2105-W-2521 $12.99 each

GUITAR PAN SET
From Country & Western to Heavy Metal, music fans will go wild over this cake. Just ice, place plastic trims and pipe simple borders. Strings (not included) can be added for even more musical effect. Includes plastic neck, bridge and pick guard. One-mix aluminum pan is 17¾ x 8½ x 2-in.
501-W-904 $9.99 set

GUITAR ACCESSORY KIT ONLY
503-W-938 $1.59 set

All pans made in Korea.

HAMBURGER PAN
Top off an all-American fast food party with this colorful cake with everything on it. Serve at birthdays, school parties, even picnics. One-mix aluminum pan is 11⅜ x 11 x 2-in.
2105-W-3306 $9.99 each

QUESTION MARK PAN
Pose the question. This quick and easy cake answers the who, what, when, where and why of every occasion. Think of how much fun it will be finding the answers. One-mix aluminum pan is 14⅞ x 11 x 2-in.
2105-W-1840 $9.99 each

DOUBLE-TIER ROUND PAN
Special effects are simple to achieve. Use just one 2-layer cake mix in one pan to create two classic tiers—6 and 10 in. Decorate this unique shape quite formally or with creative whimsy. A year round party pleaser. Aluminum pan is 9¾ x 3-in.
2105-W-1400 $9.99 each

T-SHIRT PAN
This universal casual standby will be the most welcome attire at many occasions—birthdays, baby showers and any other celebration you can imagine. One-mix aluminum pan is 13¼ x 12½ x 2-in.
2105-W-2347 $9.99 each

PLEASE NOTE: All prices, certain products and services reflect the U.S. domestic market and do not apply in Australia and Canada.

All Occasion Pans

CUDDLES THE COW PAN
Invite our barnyard beauty to your next party. This barnyard queen "moos" in the best of party circles. She'll even charm grown-ups with her fun. One mix aluminum pan is 12¾ x 12½ x 2 in.
2105-W-2875 $9.99 each

HUGGABLE TEDDY BEAR PAN
Now here's an old friend who's enjoying more popularity than ever. Maybe it's because he makes everyone feel so good. He'll bring his happy mood to any occasion. Ideas for birthdays and baby showers included. One mix aluminum pan is 13½ x 12¼ x 2-in.
2105-W-4943 $9.99 each

HAPPY CLOWN PAN
Color kids' parties happy. The circus funny man brings on smiles to kids of all ages. His alternate looks can entertain at many occasions. Aluminum pan is 12 x 12 x 2 in.
2105-W-802 $9.99 each

PARTYSAURUS PAN
Back from extinction and ready to party. This continued celebrity of dinosaurs makes our pre-historic party animal a must-have at all sorts of fun fests. One mix pan is 16 x 10 x 1⅞ in.
2105-W-1280 $9.99 each

All Occasion Pans

PRECIOUS PONY PAN
A little horseplay is always expected at a kid's party. Create a colt or a filly to prance about with happy birthday wishes. Captivating alternate ways to decorate are included. One-mix aluminum pan is 16 x 11 x 2-in.
2105-W-2914 $9.99 each

TEDDY BEAR STAND-UP PAN
You'll find this beloved buddy popping up at just about any occasion. Great for birthdays, baby showers, school parties and just warm wishes. Two-piece aluminum pan is 9½ x 8½ x 5-in. Core, stand and clips.
2105-W-2325 $15.99 set

BAKING CORE ONLY*
503-W-504 $3.59 each

*Although slightly smaller than the core included with the pan, this works as well.

ROCKING HORSE PAN
Indulge your hobby for decorating with this perennial favorite. The Wild West carnival or Christmas-time are just a few of the themes to give this lovable toy. It's a winner for birthdays and baby showers. One-mix aluminum pan is 13½ x 13½ x 2-in.
2105-W-2388 $9.99 each

PANDA PAN
Here's one of the cutest cakes in captivity! With so many great ways to decorate it, this 3-D Panda is a hit at all sorts of happy events. Two-piece aluminum pan takes 6½ cups of firm-textured batter. Includes 6 clips, heat conducting core and instructions. Pan is 9½ x 8⅝-in. tall.
2105-W-603 $15.99 each

BAKING CORE ONLY
503-W-504 $3.59 each

PANDA MOLD
Aluminum 2-pc. mold/pan is perfect for baking cakes and molding candy, ice cream, sugar. About 4¾ in. high.
518-W-489 $4.99 each

LITTLE MOUSE PAN
What trick does this little guy have up his sleeve? Nothing but the happiest of birthday wishes for every boy and girl. One-mix pan is 15¾ x 9½ x 2-in.
2105-W-2380 $8.99 each

Sports/Tribute Pans

BOWLING PAN SET
Strike up nothing but fun with this cake entirely in its own league. Even use this pan in other clever ways for birthdays and holidays. Set includes two 14-in. aluminum pans and two baking racks. Takes one cake mix for 2 halves.
502-W-4424 $9.99 each

SPORTS BALL PAN SET
Whether they're fans of sports or fans of fun, this ball will get the crowd to their feet. This multi-function ball can go from basketball to soccer and volleyball with ease. Many more uses in store. Set includes two 6-in. diameter half ball aluminum pans and two metal baking stands. Each pan half takes 2½ cups batter.
2105-W-6506 $9.99 each

BALL PAN BAKE STAND ONLY
503-W-881 $.99 each

MINI-BALL PAN
Make a grand slam entrance with a tray full of these cakes-for-one. These little treats are perfect in any championship season. Ice mini-balls and push together for 3-D effect. One cake mix will yield 12 to 15 balls. 11½ x 7½ x 1½ in. aluminum pan.
2105-W-1760 $9.99 each

GOLF BAG PAN
Here's a cake bound to be popular at the clubhouse. It links perfectly to birthdays, retirement parties and much more. One mix-mix aluminum pan is 15 x 8½ x 2½ in.
2105-W-1836 $9.99 each

NEW! FIRST AND TEN FOOTBALL PAN

Award them the game ball, just like the pros. From little guys to Monday morning quarterbacks, it's a cake sure to score. Perfect for Super Bowl parties, homecomings, award dinners and much more. One-mix aluminum pan is 00 x 00 x 00.
2105-W-6504 $9.99 each

FOOTBALL HERO PAN

Tackle every kind of sporting occasion with ease. Give this cake the colors and insignias of any team. Put any number on the jersey. There you have a customized cake any winning team would love. One-mix aluminum pan is 12 x 12½ x 2 in.
2105-W-4610 $9.99 each

BASEBALL GLOVE PAN

Have an entertaining victory in the palm of your hand. The home team will love this mitt that can be customized with names and team colors. Can also be used for many occasions. One-mix aluminum pan is 12 x 12¼ x 1¾ in.
2105-W-1234 $9.99 each

USA PAN

One nation, many cake ideas. Fourth of July, Memorial Day, Scouting events, even for winners of national awards. The ideas are endless and so is this pan's popularity. Aluminum pan is 14½ x 9¼ in.
2105-W-8251 $9.99 each

CONGRATULATIONS PAN

For joy that just can't be contained. Create our bouncing letter "congratulations" cake for that special winner of the day. Straight A's, job promotions, making an audition and much more. Our one-mix aluminum pan is 15 x 9½ x 1⅞-in. and includes alternate decorating ideas.
2105-W-3523 $9.99 each

All Occasion Pans

GOOSE PAN
This country charmer can grace many events. Mother Goose for kids' parties and baby showers, a welcome for new neighbors, even a warm yuletide greeting. Aluminum pan is 11½ x 12 in. and takes one cake mix.
2105-W-2499 $9.99 each

SHELL PAN
Add this sophisticated, streamlined pan to your collection. With the recipe for delicate lemon cake printed on the label, create a delicious dessert topped with gorgeous yellow fondant. A pan you'll use for so many happy times. Aluminum pan is 11 x 12 in.
2105-W-8250 $9.99 each

HORSESHOE PAN
A horseshoe by any other name still means "good luck" Whether it's a good omen for graduations, bon voyage or a Christmas stocking, it's a style you'll be glad to have. 12 x 1¾ in.
2105-W-3254 $9.99 each

KITTY CAT PAN
The reigning king is basking in the glow of being named the most popular house pet. Why not immortalize him in buttercream? Create sleek or long-haired breeds. 9 x 15 x 2 in. aluminum pan takes one cake mix.
2105-W-1009 $9.99 each

PUPPY DOG PAN
Finally, you can say "yes" when they ask for a puppy. Our frisky four-legged friend would just love a home for birthdays and kids' get togethers. Make him your party mascot. 17½ x 8⅞ x 1⅞-in. aluminum pan takes one cake mix.
2105-W-2430 $9.99 each

All pans made in Korea.

Halloween Pans

NEW! WICKED WITCH PAN
Invite this not-so-wicked witch to your Halloween bash. This fun-loving lady will bring hardy laughs to the party. Can also turn into other characters. One-mix aluminum pan is 11¾ x 13 x 1¾ in.
2105-W-4590 $7.99 each

SCARECROW PAN
Our timid little scarecrow will be happy to join all your autumn celebrations. From Halloween to Thanksgiving, you'll be keeping this little guy busy. Many alternate decorating schemes. One-mix aluminum pan is 15 x 11½ in.
2105-W-801 $7.99 each

BOO GHOST PAN
This giggling ghoul puts his message right up front for your celebration. It's a fun way to add all the extras to a party. Your goblins will love him. One-mix aluminum pan is 14¼ x 11¾ x 1⅞ in.
2105-W-1031 $7.99 each

MINI-PUMPKIN PAN
It's so easy to make little treats for all your favorite goblins. Or create kid-pleasing party cakes year 'round. Even try the fun alternate ideas shown. Each mold of this 12¼ x 8 x 1⅜ in. aluminum pan takes a ½ cup of cake batter.
2105-W-1499 $7.99 each

JACK-O-LANTERN PAN
Carve out this toothless grin for that next Halloween party. It's quick and easy to brighten up your celebration. One-mix aluminum pan is 12¼ x 11⅝ x 2 in.
2105-W-3068 $7.99 each

Valentine Pans

NEW!

NEW! HEART RING PAN
This delicate heart mold lets you put a little surprise in the center. Fill with fresh fruit, whipped cream, even shaved chocolate. A heart's delight. Two-mix aluminum. Size 11 x 2⅝ in. deep.
2105-W-3219 $12.99 each

HEART QUARTET PAN
A bounty of hearts expresses your love in four fold. The unusual shape provides many decorating ideas. Ideal for Valentine's Day, St. Pat's Day and birthdays. One-mix aluminum. 11 x 11 in.
2105-W-1414 $7.99 each

HEART MINI-CAKE PAN
Give away more than your heart for Valentine's Day. Why not give six or twelve! Sweet gestures of love for bridal showers and kids' parties. Each heart of this 8 x 11⅛ in. aluminum pan is 3½ x 1¼ in. deep. One cake mix makes 12 hearts.
2105-W-11044 $7.99 each

HAPPINESS HEART PAN SET
Let our lovely two-heart layer cake convey your sweet sentiments on any occasion. It takes just one mix to fill both pans; each 9 x 1½ in. deep, aluminum.
2105-W-956 $7.99 each

DOUBLE TIER HEART PAN
Romance is always on the menu with a cake of two pretty heart tiers. It's the perfect show of affection for birthdays, Mother's or Father's Day, wedding showers and much more. Instructions show 4 delightful ways to decorate. One-mix aluminum pan is 11½ x 11 x 2¼ in.
2105-W-1699 $9.99 each

HEART FLAN PAN
What a super idea – fill a flute-edged heart cake with surprises. Choose pudding, ice cream, fruit, even chocolates. It can also be trimmed with icing or whipped cream. Aluminum, 11 x 10½ in.
2105-W-3218 $7.99 each

HEART MINI-TIER SET
What a great special effect! Make a petite masterpiece using only one cake mix in three sweetheart tiers. Set includes 5, 7½ and 9 in. pans, two scallop-edged white separator plates and six crystal clear twist legs.
2105-W-409 $10.99 set

SEPARATOR PLATE SETS
Includes one 5½ in. and one 8 in. Heart Separator Plates with 6 crystal clear twist legs.
301-W-9728 $2.99 set of 2

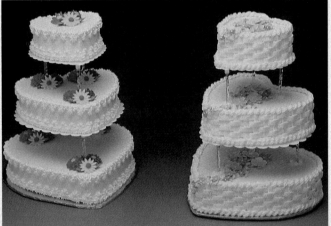

HEART DELIGHTS
Discover romance in full bloom with three lovely tiers. Just the perfect cake for the most romantic of occasions – anniversaries, bridal showers, birthdays and weddings. Our 2-in. deep aluminum pans are sold separately in three essential sizes, 6, 9, 12 in.
6 IN HEART
2105-W-4781 $3.99 each
9 IN HEART
2105-W-5176 $5.99 each
12 IN HEART
2105-W-5168 $8.99 each

HEART PAN SET
Love is at its grandest in four lovely tiers. Lavishly celebrate showers, weddings and more with the ultimate heart-shaped cake. Set includes 6, 9, 12 and 15½ in. diameter aluminum pans.
504-W-207 $24.99 set

Easter Pans

LITTLE DUCKY PAN
This little ducky is the one. He makes Easter so much fun. And that's not all. He's a cute addition to baby showers, kids' birthdays and more. One-mix aluminum, 13 x 10 in.
2105-W-2029 $7.99 each

EGG MINI-CAKE PAN
You CAN put all these "eggs" in one beautiful Easter basket. Or use them as colorful place markers at the holiday table. The label includes a variety of versatile decorating ideas. One cake mix yields about 24 cakes. Each oval well is 3½ x 2⅜ in.
2105-W-2118 $7.99 each

EGG PAN SET
Why not decorate the Easter egg to end all Easter eggs. This cake makes a great holiday centerpiece. Two-piece aluminum pan takes just one cake mix. Each half is 8¾ x 5⅜ in. and includes a ring base for level baking.
2105-W-700 $10.99 each
EGG PAN RING ONLY
503-W-954 $.99 each

COTTONTAIL BUNNY PAN
It wouldn't be Easter without him. This fluffy-tailed favorite is such an adorable addition to birthdays and baby showers, too. The label includes a bunny-quick way to decorate. One-mix aluminum pan is 14 x 12 in. x 2 in.
2105-W-2015 $7.99 each

LITTLE LAMB PAN
This precious little creature makes a beautiful centerpiece for your Easter table. Two-piece aluminum pan is 10 x 7-in. tall and takes 6 cups of pound cake batter. Baking and decorating instructions included.
2105-W-2010 $10.99 each

All pans made in Korea.

NEW! GENTLE LAMB
Invite this delicate little lamb to grace your Easter table. You can be assured where good times are this lamb is sure to follow. One-mix aluminum pan is 13⁵⁄₁₆ x 10½ x 1⅞ in.
2105-W-2515 $7.99 each

SUNNY BUNNY PAN
This little hare is just hopping to please. His big feet, big ears and big heart make him a most welcomed Easter guest and more. See label for ideas. One-mix aluminum pan is 12⅝ x 10¼ in.
2105-W-2435 $7.99 each

CROSS PAN
Celebrate a blessed day with a symbol of faith. Bake and decorate this meaningful cake for holidays, christenings and other religious occasions. Instructions include a birthday and family reunion cake. One-mix aluminum pan is 14½ x 11⅛ x 2 in.
2105-W-2509 $7.99 each

LOVABLE LAMB PAN
Wherever there's a springtime celebration, this lamb is sure to go. This easy-to-do cake is also a hit for birthdays and baby showers. Several designs included. One-mix aluminum pan is 13⅝ x 10¾ x 1⅞ in.
2105-W-2514 $7.99 each

GREAT EGGS!™ KIT
Create springtime magic! Ornate Easter basket sugar and candy confections. New designs have been added. Kit includes 2 egg molds, tips, coupler, brush, 2 candy mold sheets, recipes and instructions.
2104-W-3615 $9.99 each

Christmas Pans

MINI-CHRISTMAS TREE PAN
Trees, trees and more trees make the holiday merrier. Serve these little ones individually or use them to decorate each guest's place setting. Label includes alternate ideas for year 'round versatility. 13 x 10½ x 1¼ in., aluminum.
2105-W-1779 $7.99 each

TREELITEFUL PAN
Here's holiday decorating made quick and easy. Just cover with one-squeeze stars, add simple garlands and candy or cookie ornaments. Instructions include several ideas for throughout the year. One-mix aluminum pan is 15 x 11 x 1½ in.
2105-W-425 $7.99 each

SNOWMAN PAN
This jolly man packs lots of winter fun. Sprinkled with coconut and decorated with candies, this cake makes a tasty Christmas treat. Inventive ideas to adapt for all seasons included on the label. One-mix aluminum. 15¼ x 10¼ in.
2105-W-803 $7.99 each

HOLIDAY HOUSE KIT
Create this enchanted cozy cottage of cake and icing. Can be as simple or elaborate as you wish. One-mix pan is 8⅝ x 9 x 3 in.
2105-W-2282 $9.99 each

NEW! MINI GINGERBREAD BOY PAN
Populate your holiday fare with half a dozen of these fun-loving little fellows. The little ones will just love having their own individualized ginger boy at Christmas dinner. One mix makes approximately 12-15 cakes. Aluminum pan is 12½ x 11¼ x 1 in.
2105-W-6503 $7.99 each

GINGERBREAD BOY PAN
Find this happy-go-lucky guy popping up at all your yuletide get togethers. Simple decorating creates great effects with this easy pan. One-mix aluminum pan is 14 x 10½ x 2 in.
2105-W-2072 $7.99 each

JOLLY SANTA PAN
Send the sweetest season's greetings with the smiling face of old St. Nick. He's great fun for the whole family to decorate! One-mix aluminum pan is 13¼ x 11½ x 2 in.
2105-W-1225 $7.99 each

RUDY REINDEER PAN
It's Rudy, our irresistible reindeer. He'll soon be leading the fun at all holiday festivities. One-mix aluminum pan is 10¾ x 16¾ x 1¾ in.
2105-W-1224 $7.99 each

Favorite Characters

NEW!

NEW! BATMAN PAN
It's everyone's favorite crime-fighting caped crusader. Invite him to your next party for a POW! ZAP! BANG! BOOM! good time. One-mix aluminum pan is 13 x 13½ x 2 in.
2105-W-6501 $9.99 each

©DC Comics Inc. 1989

SUPER HEROES PAN
Double the crime-fighting power in one easy pan. Whomever you choose, he's perfect for many occasions. Set includes 13 x 13 x 2 in. pan, SUPERMAN and BATMAN plastic face masks and chest emblems.
2105-W-8507 $9.99 set
BATMAN MASK & EMBLEM
503-W-814 $1.99 set
SUPERMAN MASK & EMBLEM
503-W-857 $1.99 set

TRADEMARKS LICENSED BY
DC COMICS, INC. ©1978

SUPER MARIO BROTHERS®
This non-stop character will make sure everyone has a super celebration. Aluminum pan takes one cake mix. 14¼ x 9½ in.
2105-W-2989 $9.99 each

©1989 Nintendo of America, Inc.

GARFIELD® ONE-MIX PAN
Count on this mischievous cat to be on his best party behavior, birthdays, holidays and more. Five ways to decorate are included. The plastic face-maker is a super decorating timesaver. Pan is 11½ x 12½ x 2 in.
2105-W-2447 $9.99 each

GARFIELD® STAND-UP CAKE PAN SET
Nothing can keep this trouble-making cat down. He has to sit up and take notice at your party scene. Plastic facemaker included. Set also contains a 2-pc. aluminum pan, clips, baking stand and instructions. Finished cake will be 6 x 6 x 9 in. high.
2105-W-3147 $14.99 set

©1984 GARFIELD. United Feature Syndicate, Inc.

BUGS BUNNY PAN
Lots is up, Doc! This silly wabbit will hop his way into many fun-loving events. On the cartoon balloon, pipe in a special message to suit the situation. Aluminum pan takes one cake mix. 14 x 9 x 1⅞ in.
2105-W-8253 $9.99 each

Bugs Bunny
Trademark and
©1988 Warner Bros. Inc.

Favorite Characters

BIG BIRD PAN
This big playful bird has been synonomous with fun and learning for over two decades. From Sesame Street to your table, Big Bird is sure to be received with opened arms. One-mix aluminum pan. 13 x 11 in.
2105-W-0805 $9.99 each

ERNIE CAKE PAN
Bert's best friend comes carrying an armful of birthday wishes for any lucky pre-schooler. One-mix aluminum pan is 14½ x 10 x 1⅞ in.
2105-W-3173 $9.99 each

COOKIE MONSTER CAKE PAN
He loves cookies, and birthdays, too. This googly-eyed monster makes a great happy birthday surprise. Alternate designs turn his cake into other great ideas. One-mix aluminum pan is 14½ x 11½ x 1⅞ in.
2105-W-4927 $9.99 each

TEENAGE MUTANT NINJA TURTLES
Hey dude, it's those crazy crime-stopping amphibians. Michaelangelo, Leonardo, Donatello or Raphael. Create your favorite creature. Any kid would just love them. One mix aluminum pan. 15 x 9½ x 2 in.
2105-W-3075 $9.99 each

Many of your children's favorite characters are also available in Cookie Cutter Sets (p. 124) and Candy Molds (p. 120). Make the party complete with these easy-to-do kid pleasers!

Decorator's Index

Pan Index